"*Film School* is a result of life experiences, teaching, and ɑ̶ ̶ ̶ ̶ ̶ ̶ ̶ ̶ ̶ ̶ ̶ not an academic dissertation or a technical treatise. Raɪ ̶ ̶ ̶ ̶ ̶ ̶ ̶ man's gifted teaching style, he presents the art of filmmaking as journey. Pepperman shows that a film is the possibility of a true encounter, offering insights equally valuable to the movie buff, aspiring filmmaker, and professional in the field. Finally, filmmaking can be considered '*par coer*'!"
— Simonetta d'Italia-Wiener, Professor of Italian,
Crossroads, New York Cultural Center

"Pepperman reveals filmmaking gems for screenwriters, cinematographers, directors, and editors alike. He puts forward an easy-to-understand analysis of moviemaking details with passion and dedication. It has been an honor to study with him at the School of Visual Arts; *Film School* lets you learn from Pepperman's priceless insights."
— Nellie Dumont, Editing Major, School of Visual Arts

"Here is a one-of-a-kind tool that every filmmaker — and film lover — must have. Each scene is so beautifully examined, giving you an inside look at what it takes to craft a masterpiece. As a film student I long for knowledge on the art of film. *Film School* explains and examines it with such ease, I feel inspired with each turn of the page."
— Oliver Jevremov, Directing Major, School of Visual Arts

"Richard Pepperman's latest book on movies, and moviemaking, provides an abundance of insights. *Film School* is a great book for anyone interested in movies, most especially for those who can't study in a traditional film school program. Here is a wonderful reminder of the great films to be watched, and slowly re-watched, for all the grand little things. *Film School* is a great resource for students of cinema, and all those who love movies!"
— Robert Hyams, Post-Production Supervisor,
LaserPacific Media Corporation

"*Film School* reads like a conversation with a friend. Pepperman is clear and concise, so that whether you have formal training in film, or none at all, you'll enjoy the book's offerings. Pepperman puts you into the process of thinking like a real filmmaker."
— Katherine Brislin, Cinematography Major, School of Visual Arts

"Mr. Pepperman, using mostly classic films, breaks them apart in ways that teach the reader how films are put together on many different levels. I have always watched films and ended up analyzing them — Mr. Pepperman takes it to a whole other level. Amazing."
— Matthew Terry, *www.hollywoodlitsales.com*

"Pepperman dissects important scenes shot-by-shot to give the reader a more clear understanding of film language and grammar than I have seen in any other book."
— Paul Chitlik, Author, *Rewrite*, visiting Asst. Professor of Screenwriting,
UCLA, Genesis Award Winner, Writers Guild Award Nominee

"Richard Pepperman is well aware that everything relates to telling a story, and he presents an invaluable clarity in showing how every aspect of filmmaking (editing, cinematography, dialogue, subtext, juxtaposed images, movement, etc.) contributes to this unique art form. His examples, from many masterpieces of international cinema, are highly eloquent. *Film School* is extremely useful to everyone who wants to learn the craft of filmmaking, or understand more about the art. Pepperman's idea of cinema as a highly collaborative art is a real key to understanding the process of filmmaking."
— Armando Fumagalli, Ph.D., Director of the Masters Program in
Screenwriting, Università Cattolica del Sacro Cuore, Milan,
Script Consultant, Lux Vide

"Pepperman's new book, *Film School: How to Watch DVDs and Learn Everything About Filmmaking*, is an intelligently written study of cinema, from its birth with Edison's Kinetoscope and the Lumière brothers' Cinématographe, in a beautifully constructed melody of classic scene selections. Here is an easy-to-understand course of study worthy of a filmmaker's Ph.D. If you love movies you will love this book!"
— Abbas Ebrahimi, Filmmaker, Fashion Photographer,
Photojournalist (American International News Service)

"A wide-ranging and sharply focussed book on how to watch a movie, and a fascinating compendium of movies we have all seen and been affected by — seen in a new way. Anyone who cares deeply about movies and moviemaking, from the student to the casual viewer, will be captivated by Richard Pepperman's excellent book."
— Christopher Keane, Author, *Romancing the A-List: Writing the Movie the Big Stars Want to Make* and *How to Write a Selling Screenplay*

"No matter whether your focus is writing, directing, acting, editing or producing, *Film School: How to Watch DVDs and Learn Everything About Filmmaking* will help you in your chosen craft. Richard D. Pepperman gives us an analysis of sample scenes from a wide variety of motion pictures, including the blockbusters, the beloved classics, adaptations, foreign movies, and the often-overlooked independent films."
— Kathie Fong Yoneda, Script Consultant, Seminar Leader, Author, *The Script-Selling Game: A Hollywood Insider's Look at Getting Your Script Sold and Produced*

"Now you can go to film school in your bathrobe and bunny slippers — and still learn an awful lot. With Richard Pepperman's *Film School* book in hand and a stack of suggested DVDs, you can learn about how stories are put together for visual and emotional impact. The book is categorized according to concepts taught in traditional film schools and offers specific chapter and frame to access the examples; you also learn why and how the filmmakers applied the concepts. This is a book you should read through once to get the ideas, then go through again watching all the film excerpts, all the while learning about film-making theory and practice. Then keep this book on your desk or on the set as you construct your own stories."
— Pamela Jaye Smith, Author, *Inner Drives* and *The Power of the Dark Side*

FILM SCHOOL

How to Watch DVDs
and Learn Everything About Filmmaking

RICHARD D. PEPPERMAN

Published by Michael Wiese Productions
3940 Laurel Canyon Blvd., # 1111
Studio City, CA 91604
tel. 818.379.8799
fax 818.986.3408
mw@mwp.com
www.mwp.com

Cover Design: Michael Wiese Productions
Book Layout: Gina Mansfield Design
Editor: Paul Norlen

Printed by McNaughton & Gunn, Inc., Saline, Michigan
Manufactured in the United States of America
Printed on Recycled Stock

Library of Congress Cataloging-in-Publication Data

Pepperman, Richard D., 1942-
  Film school : how to watch DVDs and learn everything about filmmaking / Richard D. Pepperman.
    p. cm.
  Includes bibliographical references and index.
  ISBN 978-1-932907-41-4
  1. Motion pictures. 2. Cinematography. 3. Motion picture authorship. I. Title.
  PN1994.P383 2008
  791.4302--dc22
                              2007037648

for
my father
&
my son

table of contents

film selections & themes

Catch-22
light
motion

Central Station
character
motion

Colonel Redl
structure
light
setting
dialogue
performance

The Day of the Jackal
dramatic Irony
set-ups

Dr. Strangelove
structure
atmosphere

Dog Day Afternoon
contrasts
atmosphere
dialogue

8½
place
light
a conclusion

The Exorcist
contrasts
subplot
light

The 400 Blows
objects
dramatic irony
a conclusion

The French Connection
fragments
atmosphere
light
dialogue
reactions

The Godfather
fragments
setting

High Noon
telling
structure
contrasts
space

Hiroshima mon amour
contrasts
set-ups

Jean de Florette
irony
space
motion

Ju Dou
fragments
telling
structure
light

Kolya
character
objects

The Ladykillers
atmosphere
light

Little Big Man
telling
set-ups
character
performance

The Loneliness of
the Long Distance Runner
showing
atmosphere
light
dialogue

The Miracle Worker
telling
dialogue

Osama
showing
place
subtext

Plenty
place
light

Psycho
dramatic irony
showing
setting

Rosemary's Baby
showing
reactions

Rififi
atmosphere
space
obstacles

Serpico
structure
subplot
transitions
space
character
reactions
performance

The Shop on Main Street
irony
obstacles
performance

The Steamroller and the Violin
contrasts
space
objects

"Whether he likes it or not (and as a rule he does not like it much), the man who wants to express himself on celluloid is part of a group. If individual and personal self-expression is what he wants, he is in the wrong business."

— Alexander Mackendrick

acknowledgments

This book owes its shape, character and spirit to an impressive group of film professionals and educators/mentors — most often they are all — who generously provided their time to be interviewed, submitted syllabi, and imparted their work and teaching philosophies and experience.

Everett Aison: screenwriter, author of *Artrage*, co-founder of the School of Visual Arts Film School, colleague and valued friend; *Rebecca Alvin*: digital video artist, received an M.A. in Media Studies from New School University, where she teaches an on-line Cinema Studies class; *Zoran Amar*: production teacher and thesis advisor at the School of Visual Arts; *Mark Biggs*: Associate Professor, Missouri State University and Chair, Missouri Film Commission; *Lilly Boruszkowski*: friend and colleague, Associate Professor teaching film production at Southern Illinois University, Carbondale; *Diane Carson:* Ph.D., Professor of Film Studies, St. Louis Community College at Meramec; *Jacqueline B. Frost*: Associate Professor, Department of Radio-TV-Film, California State University, Fullerton; *Norman Hollyn*: Associate Professor and Editing Track Head, School of Cinematic Arts, University of Southern California, and author of *The Editing Room Handbook*; *Sheila A. Laffey*: Echo Mountain Productions, Ph.D., Adjunct Professor, Santa Monica College; *Terry Lindvall*: author, film professor and Distinguished Chair of Visual Communication, Regent University, Virginia; *Vincent LoBrutto*: author of *Selected Takes*, *By Design*, and *Kubrick: A Biography*, Thesis Committee member, instructor of production design at the School of Visual Arts; *Chris Newman*: Three-time Academy Award–winning Production Sound Recordist, colleague and early Monday morning tutor; *Robert G. Nulph*: Ph.D., Associate Professor, Communication Studies, Missouri Western State College; *Andrea Odezynska*: Filmmaker/Director, Film Faculty member, the School of Visual Arts; *Salvatore Petrosino*: Director of Operations and production instructor, the Film Department, School of Visual Arts and trusted friend; *Louis Phillips*: poet, playwright (*The Last of the Marx Brothers' Writers*), recipient of the Distinguished Scholar/Teacher Award, the School of Visual Arts and distinguished good friend; *David Porfiri*: Independent Filmmaker, Professor of Film and Media Arts at American University; *Ellen L. Shepard*: Director of the Film for Theatre & Film Program at St. Augustine's College in Raleigh, North Carolina; *Amresh Sinha*: teaches courses in cinema studies at the School of Visual Arts and New York University; *Igor Sunara*: Director of Photography, *The Keeper* (Official Entry: Sundance Festival), Advanced Cinematography teacher and thesis advisor at the School of Visual Arts; *Jon Waterman*: film reviewer/columnist at *www.filmbrats.com/dvdpaper.html*; *David Lewis Yewdall*, M.P.S.E.: Supervising Sound Editor/Sound Designer, faculty, Editing Discipline, School of Filmmaking, North Carolina School of the Arts.

Happy and grateful recognition must go to *Michael Wiese* and *Ken Lee* at Michael Wiese Productions for all their terrific and smart ideas that they entrust to me; *Jordan Winter* and *Sky Gewant* at WinterSky Productions for their reliable work in providing the DVD covers.

For the overall reading enjoyment and delightful appearance of this book I am once again indebted to the professional care and discriminating taste of editor *Paul Norlen* and designer *Gina Mansfield.*

preface

The acknowledgment record is scarcely suitable to account for the collaboration in this text. I think the worth of this book, and thus its application, requires a chronicling of its zigzagging journey.

Initially proposed, and discussed, was a series of essays on the many disciplines which come together to create a film, each essay to be written by a film department faculty member from a broad selection of college and university programs. Teachers, instructors, and professors would describe the specifics of their syllabi, the philosophy and strategy in presenting topics, and the DVDs they use to illustrate course material. As the publisher purported, "You'll be the task master and editor."

A group of colleagues, and friends, from various departments at the School of Visual Arts have been holding weekly get-togethers for the past several years, and I thought to bring up the book idea, and its individual essay structure. The consensus was that editing the essays would be the easy part; the *impossible* part would be task mastering! "Good luck getting a few dozen people to get you essays." Before I could pass along this flash of pragmatism, the publisher communicated an additional apprehension about an "essay structure": "I'm concerned about a book that would have so many, and perhaps conflicting, voices and styles… with clashing viewpoints."

We went on to talk about doing a series of interviews with previously contemplated academic spokespeople, which I would transcribe and edit. There!

I gathered a contact list and began sending e-mails seeking film faculty interviewees. Before the first interview was scheduled I began to have doubts about this new approach. My first misgiving had to do with the tedium — if not downright drabness — of audiences reading transcripts. I know that there have been several excellent books with transcribed interviews; but they were (most often) specific in topic or person. My second and central misgiving was that I could not see myself spending more than 34 seconds editing transcripts.

Curiously and in synchronicity, the publisher contacted me to tell of his sudden unease, which corresponded to my first misgiving; he had *no* qualms about my spending years editing transcripts.

Thus began my many interviews via telephone, and in person, with a new plan in mind: A book covering the multi-disciplined art and craft of filmmaking harvested from the ideas and strategies of film teachers from various faculties, focusing on the DVDs that serve to illustrate course topics.

With a yellow legal pad of scribbled questions — something akin to an attorney's preparation for a deposition — I arranged a first interview which was to be recorded over the telephone. Within minutes of a pleasant enough Q&A I suffered new misgivings: What am I failing to uncover?

It seemed to me that without some sort of collaboratively spontaneous discussion — in keeping with the lively back & forth, even interrupting, School of Visual Arts (SVA) get-togethers — there would be far less opportunity for serious disclosure to take place; and a greatly reduced chance to unearth the genuinely vital knowledge that comes from teaching experience. I, for one, had more than three decades experience teaching introductory courses in film and editing, so I felt foolish reciting from my list of questions, which I followed with frequent, "Uh-huhs" so as to signal to the cooperative and kind interviewee that I was still on the line listening to the response. This kind of long distance "press conference" could not possibly define, or lead to, instruction in the art of filmmaking!

I swiftly shifted from Q&A to chatting. Immediately — at least for me — there was a collegial feel to the interview, reminiscent of the wonderful weekly sessions with SVA colleagues; some interviewees even befriended me! Now, the "telephone meetings" cultivated a spirited back and forth; an examining of creativity — less about *what* and *how*, much more about *what* and *why*.

Teaching filmmaking falls into two models: training and educating. With the arrival of the efficient and automatic everything of digital technology, with portable devices permitting low-cost production, and in-school post-production refinements, *training* (technical instruction) began to emerge as dominant; risky especially in institutions of *higher education*.

Along with the technical swell came an inadvertent harm to, if not near disregard for, collaboration. I had been sensing this double shift — more technical instruction and a de-emphasis on group — since the mid-1990s, but was nevertheless surprised by how common the corroboration was. Many teachers expressed concern that "we are teaching film as a solo art!" I was elated to learn about new approaches to correct both. Tilting back to *educating* was beginning to occur with efforts to integrate Communication, Media, Performance, Theatre, and Film programs, and experiments in the hard work of co-teaching, and even team-teaching: A single course taught by a screenwriter, director, cinematographer, and editor (and others from the long list of needed craftspeople) so that students might recognize the collaborative nature of filmmaking, and how the labors of the team focus their good energies on the what and *why* requirements of a project.

One other, nearly unanimous apprehension was compellingly confirmed: Students seem to be losing storytelling savvy! I suspect this could be linked to the "solo art" alarm rung loudly in the interviews.

Good collaboration permits an ongoing evaluation of story: The art and craft of storytelling does not terminate in the script. There is a reason that movie house lights are not left bright while three hundred popcorn eating patrons *read* the featured screenplay. No! There is a *showing!* That *showing* is the grand outcome — or unfortunate consequence — of collaboration.

Some time ago I was asked to be an editing consultant on an independent, feature-length film. The picture had received an unfavorable response. I worked closely and candidly with the director to re-cut the film. Before I was satisfied with the storytelling structure — we were close — the director invited some half-dozen friends to watch and comment. The director provided a pad and clipboard for her "audience."

The director was caught somewhere between "Two heads are better than one" and "Too many cooks spoil the broth." A more accurate characterization would be "Too many friends...." The director's friends were neither cooks (as far as I know) nor filmmakers. Genuine cooks don't spoil broth. Even genuine friends can spoil a film!

A careful reading suggests the possibility of a significant link between the clashing adages and the art of filmmaking.

The "two heads" expression implies a focus on a particular problem, even if the heads are more than two, while "too many cooks" reminds us that lousy soup is the likely result when cooks are "self-serving." Yet, when cooks come together, however many — even only two — a tasty treat can be expected *if* the cooks' service is in the dedicated interest of the broth. Good broth can be the product of teamwork and cooperation.

I have listened to (and believe I've heard) all the fine ideas and misgivings. I trust that I've been fair and true to the insights, and perspectives, articulated during the interviews.

Thesis students in the film department at SVA — and I'd bet in every other film program — show their appreciation to staff and faculty by listing their names in the end roll credits under the heading *Thank you*. One of my students followed his *Thank you* list with a *Special Thank You* list, and my name appeared. I felt proud and contented. Then the *Special Thank You* list rolled up and off the screen. It was followed by a *Very Special Thank You* list. Of course I was not on it. "Ooohhh"! Vanity can be hazardous! It is also enticing....

My chats with exceedingly dedicated teachers have turned up more than a few teaching — and learning — innovations. And so... to all those already, though merely, acknowledged, I tender a *Very, Very, Very Special Thank You!*

introduction

Attending a Continuing Education Career Night forum, I presented an overview of my "Art of Editing" course. I explained *why* I thought editing was a good initial course of study no matter in which filmmaking discipline a student might select to specialize. I mentioned director Edward Dmytryk's reflection in *On Film Editing* that if one wants to fully understand an art form, then it is crucial to begin with the process unique to that art. Dmytryk emphasized that while film derives much from painting, photography, theatre, and literature, the post-production process of editing is what makes cinema unique, or, as director V. I. Pudovkin put it, "Editing is the creative force of filmic reality."

There was a time during the height of Hollywood's studio system when it was mandatory for all nascent directors to gain editing experience. Some studios required no less than eight years in the editing room.

My Career Night presentation led to a debate about just which craft was the most essential and significant to filmmaking. I stay, and stayed, clear of such arguments because I believe the answer is: none! Although the correct answer is likely: *all!*

I don't want my suggestion to study film editing to lead to any misunderstanding or animosity. I did not, and do not, mean that editing is the most important of all the filmmaking crafts. It most certainly is not, comments about movies being saved in the editing room notwithstanding. I agree with (one-time editor) Dmytryk's humbly accurate observation: The editor did not write the script, select cast, crew and locations, shoot, or direct. The material that was turned into a good film was made available by the contributions and collaboration of many others.

If the editor's work brings about an artistically satisfying film in post-production from the material provided by pre-production and production, well… that's what the editor is supposed to do; it's the editor's job.

Editing does teach us about the complexities of collaboration, as well as afford an overview of the measured obligations the individual disciplines *should* deliver. An actor's performance may need more than a little "stage-managing" because camera set-ups were too few or guarded; not decisively diverse; an inflection transition was clearly inscribed on the script page, but difficult to act; a location somehow hindered the actor and the scene, and therefore its place in the story.

In other words, as I point out in *Setting Up Your Scenes: The Inner Workings of Great Films*: "Filmmaking is a *backward* art form. Not as in 'its place in history,' but in the lessons it provides the artist. There's no better way to grasp — and appreciate — the required creative skills of the screenwriter, cinematographer, actor, editor, producer, director, and all the many others in film's collaborative process than to view a *completed work*."

Let me get to the significant point and spirit of this introduction, and the entire book. You will notice that Screenwriting, Cinematography, Sound Recording & Design, Composing, Make-Up, Costume, Production Design, Acting, Directing, and Editing are not to be found in the *Table of Contents*. *Why* is that?

There are currently dozens upon dozens of terrific books on filmmaking. Most are dedicated to a single craft and offer an array of technical, philosophical, historic, and creative information. I was downright dubious and unhappy about writing a book that in the end would represent an addendum to the very fine texts currently available. I did not want *Film School* to become a large sheath into which simulations of already accessible writings on the subject might fit.

My chats led to a happy scrapping of the more probable inventory to be found in a film book.

The totality of interviews and personal experience has brought me to consider a new and, I think, more far-reaching method in film education. It is based on *collaboration* in *storytelling*, and presents what you need to know in three sections: Story, Place, and Character, each containing numerous themes.

I have selected fifty films from around the world in seventy years. You will find the films in alphabetical order with their corresponding themes in a cross-reference to the Sections and Themes. This should make it easier to select a film (or two), and locate all their entries.

I won't claim masterpiece status for my selections, but they do demonstrate storytelling collaboration, a dedication to excellence, and an ample film history in time and genre.

I have not divided the films by genre. No matter if Adventure, Comedy, Drama, Horror, Intrigue, or Western, I've sprinkled the films under a variety of themes, because no matter the genre, all films necessitate *comparable* stratagems in the art of storytelling. You will more than likely find that they fit into *identical* stratagems, but framed within an adjusted milieu.

I have attempted to describe the images and sounds of the scenes and sequences in such a way as to have the text alone make the themes comprehensible, but the full worth of the writing requires that you screen the DVDs. I urge you to watch the films!

I know that you'll value the extraordinary work of the many artists who labored as a team and fashioned these fifty films. I believe that this book can be an engaging contribution to your film studies and professional career.

I wish you satisfying benefit from the reading and the screenings!

film school: purpose & context

Recent newspaper articles have pointed out that the ubiquitous, and portable, DVD has inspired a remarkable boost in homegrown film careers. Thousands of DVD screeners go directly from Eject/Open to Final Draft®, Sony®/Canon® and/or Final Cut Pro®. The principal difference between the DVD and VHS generations is that the *Digital Revolution* makes it possible to produce movies at practical prices: Aspiration and a few reliable friends can provide cast, crew, and picture.

Self-teaching via DVD screenings sets several factors at risk. Beginners unavoidably miss many of the most vital particulars. They often confuse what they think they've uncovered and noted with what is actually before them — bigger than life on the silver screen, or far smaller on a laptop — simply because movies are not, as expected and accepted, a duplication of space and time authenticity! Far more worrisome is the amateur production that imitates without judicious thinking and feeling: a derivative of movies that are poor facsimiles of other movies.

Ignoring film's history and the fundamentals that make cinematic art achievable can't help but promote indiscriminant preferences and unsophisticated taste.

The ambitions of the DVD generation are not limited by age, education, or profession. Continuing Ed courses are packed full with budding directors, cinematographers, editors, and screenwriters: Many are (long ago) graduates in other disciplines who suddenly feel film's calling. There are high schoolers (and younger) impatient to break into the business with a first film, or wanting a heads-up in experience before the hoped-for acceptance from an accredited film school.

This text is neither a substitute, nor a competitor, to the many fine film programs. It is a heads-up for college-bound film students; a very good guide for homegrown production people; a valuable template for film buffs who can't argue enough about movies; and, I do believe, it offers a constructive overture for film faculties: an interconnected method to teach cinema studies and filmmaking.

Film School: How to Watch DVDs and Learn Everything About Filmmaking is all about teaching, and learning, via a guided tour through movie-story context; and context is everything! It should spotlight each and every chosen component within the creative process.

With a commitment to collaborative storytelling — and a modest secret — I offer a couple of brief tales about cinematography and context. The examples easily extend across all the filmmaking crafts. I was told these stories second hand; and since circumstances are such that anecdotal accuracy matters less than significance, I am more comfortable not identifying the tellers, or the DPs. The accounts give noteworthy — and ideal — expression to the hurdles inherent in cinema's collaborative procedures; and the intricacies in teaching (and learning) filmmaking.

Some half-dozen years ago a noted cinematographer began teaching master classes. The students included working professionals, and, on at least one occasion, an Academy Award nominee. I mention the Oscar nomination to emphasize the recognition and respect the teacher deserved and received from the students. It was beyond an honor to study with this cinematographer.

The cinematographer/teacher gave notice to the film school that he would no longer be available for the master classes. He was disappointed and frustrated that screening and discussing DVD (and VHS) selections of his work — and the work of others — seemed to elicit more "How?" inquiries from the students than "Why?" "How" was directed toward imitation and, in large part, about training. "Why" is about the uniqueness of the project, and the collaborative context. "Why" is about educating the film artist!

Some fifty years ago another highly regarded cinematographer was a film student in Eastern Europe, at a school with limited resources. A thesis project that he DPed earned him admiration, and an abundance of praise. His ingenious rigging and equipment adaptation made it possible for him to replicate the beauty of Hollywood's master craftsmen. The student, his head far along into swelling, received a note to meet with the film school's chairman.

Of course he expected still more approval. Instead he was scolded: "The images are beautiful, but they are worthless. You did not serve the story!"

Though upset, the student promptly recognized the truth in the chairman's reproach. Throughout a prestigious career of nearly half a century this cinematographer has never forgotten the admonition.

Film art requires a cohesive collaboration in multi-disciplined interpretations. This may seem an impossible task, if not a supreme contradiction. At its best it is not only doable, but when the cast and crew bring a single-minded focus to the context(s) of a project — the story — the film tallies up to the brilliance of concentrated teamwork!

rdp
Mount Holly Vermont, March 2007

STORY

The March 21, 1994 issue of the *New Yorker* magazine was devoted to filmmaking: *The New Yorker Goes to the Movies*. Throughout, under the heading "Collaborations," were articles by writers about their working relationships with directors, and especially about the initiation of story. With *collaboration* in mind, here's a very good *story*.

On July 28, 1979 director Louis Malle telephoned playwright/screen-writer John Guare to ask if he had any ideas for a script. A group of Canadian producers was eager to invest in a film during that particular calendar year, as Canadian tax law would allow — until midnight of December 31 — the full investment to be deductible.

Along with the 1979 proviso, the producers insisted that the film star Susan Sarandon and a "bankable male star."

John Guare had become captivated by the goings on in Atlantic City, which had only recently legalized gambling, promising that an economic recovery, initiated by new casinos, would bring about better lives for the city's destitute. On July 29 Malle and Guare drove into town.

Brainstorming began at Resorts International's casino: Aspiring blackjack dealers often began their careers staffing oyster bars. Sally (Susan Sarandon) would be, and do, just that!

Malle and Guare assumed grand ambitions for Sally: Her dream is to become the first woman dealer in Monaco, requiring tutorials to learn French and acquire sophistication. She'll have a cassette player for lessons in language and culture.

Guare remembered reading in "Hints from Heloise" that rubbing yourself with lemons was the best way to "clean away" the smell of fish.

In a picture book about Atlantic City, Malle and Guare came across a photo taken during a 1920s gangster convention; they both took note of a "young thug" standing in the back row: He would now — some fifty years later — be the age of the necessary "bankable male star." Actor Burt Lancaster suited Lou Pascal.

Chapter 1, "Lemon Ritual" @ 00:00:24

The title is the place, but the opening image is not a panorama of the old resort town. Instead we see an Extreme Close-Up (ECU) of lemons. They are cut with a small knife.

Here is an illustration of lovely, simple and commanding cinematic storytelling. The *story* has already begun; time is neither spent — nor withered — with introduction. Each proceeding shot moves out and reveals ever newer information about *place* and *character* and so, the story. Moving back (or out) from a Close-Up (CU) imparts new information because an ever-increasing "landscape" naturally offers more and more visual facts.

The second image is a CU of a portable cassette/radio. A bare arm presses the play button. Immediately and abruptly, Maria Callas sings from Bellini's opera, *Norma*.

The third shot is a Medium Shot (MS) — still moving back — revealing Sally at her window. She "bathes" in the juice of the cut lemons. The camera zooms out slowly from the window, across an air shaft of the building, and into the adjoining apartment where we "meet" the now very much "older thug." Lou Pascal stands in his dark room taking voyeuristic pleasure in the topless, bathing Sally. Maria Callas sings!

I assign a semester paper which asks the editing students to do their own review of a movie review. The movie is one of their choosing, and does not have to be current. Film libraries and Netflix make nearly any film accessible, and the Internet allows for locating (even very old) film reviews from newspapers, magazines, and periodicals.

We discuss how infrequent the review is that gives credit beyond the work of screenwriter, director, and actor. The students' papers are to address those aspects of their selected movie which owe recognition to post-production efforts.

In nearly all writings about *Atlantic City*, the city itself is cited: "[A] city living with its faded past, and a fragile optimism for the future." "[T]he background is the city of dreams...".

There are references linking the *place* to the *characters*: "a gone-to-seed resort town supported, like the principal characters, by memories of a glorious past"; "[Malle] mercilessly reveals... his wounded characters'... dreams, for [their] hopeless illusions."

In the end, the link between *place* and *character* provides conflicts in age, era, memory — usually inexact, if not farfetched — and buoyant dreams that offset anxiety of insignificance. We are on the way to *story*.

The concentration of the class movie review discussion is not a grumble over the indifference to the editor — or any other film crew member — but is rather a highlighting of the inherent, and irresistible, allure of story: Chronicle; Account; Narrative; Legend, or Tale (as in Fairy or Folk).

What passes for a film review is literary paraphrasing, a summation of story, not that much different than a book or theatre review. The telling of a *story* is what matters most!

fragments

In 1895, with improvements to Thomas Alva Edison's (1847-1931) Kinetoscope, Auguste (1862-1954) and Louis (1864-1948) Lumière patented a combination movie camera and projector: the Cinématographe. *La Sortie des ouvriers de l'usine Lumière* ("Workers Leaving the Lumière Factory") was shown to a paying audience in Paris that same year. It is considered the first motion picture.

In 1896 the brothers made some forty films depicting everyday French life. It wasn't long after early showings of their amazing invention that they came to believe that motion pictures would have a short existence.

The Lumières' forecast held that once audience's paid for an initial viewing (or two) of their magical light beam, projecting panoramas of the commonplace, they would soon grow weary: Why continue to pay for comparable shows?

Movies began as all preceding art forms, as a method of documenting reality, depicting, as accurately as possible, the natural world of people and events.

The Lumières' movies ran for less than a minute. Their work went beyond painting and still photography in that it provided moments in motion. "A Boat Leaving Harbour" did that, but was little less than a still, the title declaring the action to be seen, and setting the boat's direction as well.

A photograph provides depictions that fascinate in that what it captures can never be glimpsed: a moment sheltered forever, an instant that concurrently takes place and comes to an end.

It would take the collaboration of others to find the unique "poetic license" of moving pictures for the invention to survive.

Georges Méliès (1861-1938), a professional magician and manager-director of the Théâtre Robert-Houdin in Paris, enlarged the reach of the Lumière brothers: He was the first to film fiction narratives. His film experiments (such as *A Trip to the Moon*, 1902) exploited camera tricks of slow motion, dissolve, and fade-out. Méliès made more than four hundred films which combined illusion, comic burlesque, and pantomime in fantasy productions.

His 1899 film *Cinderella* was approximately 410 feet, and displayed its story in staged tableaux which ran for twenty episodes. Méliès' films advanced storytelling beyond a single shot, but while they presented a primitive continuity, they secured their presentation to a theatrical paradigm.

It is worth noting that with all the illuminating innovations that proceeded from Méliès, cinema seems easily and eternally at risk to theatrical temptation.

In their August 1928 Statement, Sergei Eisenstein (1898-1948) and his colleagues V. I. Pudovkin (1893-1953) and G. V. Alexandrov (1903-1984), innovators to the language, theory, and structure of cinema, expressed their misgivings about the invention that permitted Talking Pictures. Sound used "for highly cultured dramas and other photographed performances of a *theatrical sort*... will destroy the culture of montage." That clash (or should I say mêlée) continues.

Edwin Porter (1870-1941), an assistant to Thomas Alva Edison — and one of his first cameramen — recognized the potential vitality of motion pictures. Porter discovered that *fragments* of partial actions in individual shots could be joined to show a story, and constructed the principles of editing, which, in all likelihood, saved the Lumière brothers' invention!

There is irony in the realization that the very quintessence of film form — its harmony, unity, and completeness — is derived from the "invention" of fabricating fragments!

Legend has it that Porter filmed a horse-drawn fire truck as it arrived at the scene of a burning apartment building. In continuous long shot, he filmed a woman at a window frantically calling for help. Here was an event less commonplace; an event of life-threatening danger. When Porter screened the material he was bewildered and disheartened that much of the excitement, anxiety, and intensity of the life-and-death drama had somehow vanished from the film footage: A second-hand watching seemed to diminish any emotional connection.

A more accurate (perhaps), but nonetheless legendary and similar tale, holds that Edison's film footage collection held a majority of fire truck material, and Porter, sensing the emotional indifference to the viewing, took it from there!

Porter went on to make *The Life of an American Fireman* (1902), which took into account film's unique structural conditions. Porter staged the scene of the woman inside her apartment, combining that narrative with the documented material of the fire trucks — from Edison's collection — "on their way"; in the end the woman is rescued from the burning house. The integration of separately gathered images returned the urgency to the event.

Stefan Sharff, an apprentice to Sergei Eisenstein and a professor of film at Columbia University's School of the Arts, presents the fragments theme in his *The Elements of Cinema: Toward a Theory of Cinesthetic Impact.*

Mr. Sharff views *fragments* (he uses the term "separation") as "an arrangement of shots showing subjects one at a time on the screen… [It] can accommodate any given thematic situation, but cinematically, its specialty lies in the ability to create intimate relationships between parts seen separately on screen. This element of structure is a singular and superb vehicle of cinematic expression. Unparalleled in any other medium, it contains the ingredients of cinema 'language' in the purest sense."

This "unparalleled" ingredient foretells a viewer relationship of Observer/Participant to events on screen.

The term *fragments* implies far greater flexibility than separation; it promises structural benefit in conjunction with structural jeopardy. Collaborative choices in process can do wonders or see the film's form fall to pieces.

Here are examples that illustrate just how fragmented the fragments can be.

THE TREASURE OF THE SIERRA MADRE

Chapter 1, "Credits" @ 0:00:58

Take special note of the early shots that integrate images of a stand-in for actor Humphrey Bogart (Fred C. Dobbs) with shots of the real Bogart. The opening scene is a combining of sound stage set filming, with rear screen projections, and actual location filming: fragments in production techniques.

Watch the low-angle shot @ **0:01:44 – 0:01:50** as Bogart (but it's not Bogart) follows the man in the white suit (the film's director, John Huston). There are but a couple of frames, just before and after the balloons block our view, that reveal for certain that Dobbs is (temporarily) played by a stand-in.

Pay attention to the earlier two-shots @ **0:01:29-0:01:36**: Here we are made aware that the initial shot, from the stand-in Fred C. Dobbs, followed by the cut to the Bogart Dobbs, demonstrates the chimera potential inherent in fragments, and makes use of them in image and audio.

Dobbs' dialogue — and certainly Bogart's voice — "Say, buddy, will you stake a fellow Am…" cannot possibly be the voice of the stand-in, and so it was not necessary to have it recorded at the time of filming.

This fragment of Bogart's recorded dialogue was synchronized sometime later in post-production, and the cut to the genuine Bogart gives credibility to an invented make-believe moment.

Why are such "schemes" devised? The availability of actors; availability of locations; the need and number of crew members; to simplify shooting; changes in production plans; budget considerations, and/or work strategies and preferences: Multiple crews and actors can be working simultaneously. In this case the *why* is less relevant than the fact — and the knowledge — that film successfully tolerates such astonishments.

Let me give you another example from the same film. Here's an illustration of how superbly compliant are the *fragments*:

Chapter 15, "Seeing Monsters" @ 0:45:56

This is a four-scene sequence. In the first — a single set-up — Dobbs banters belligerently to himself, as he ties knots in a burro's rope. The camera sits near the ground with the kneeling Dobbs in Medium-Shot. Curtin comes toward the camera, framed between Dobbs and the burro's torso on screen left. Curtin leads another burro passing behind Dobbs and, as he exits the frame, the camera moves in to a Close-Up on Dobbs, "Anymore lip out of you and I'll haul off and let you have it," and "If you know what's good for you, you won't monkey around with Fred C. Dobbs."

The second scene @ **0:46:32** — also a single set-up — is a low-angle Long-Shot looking upward to Curtin and Howard. Curtin advises, "You ought to get a load of Dobbs. He's talking to himself a mile a minute." Howard starts downhill, saying "Something's eatin' him alright; he's just spoiling for trouble."

The third scene @ **0:46:48** consists of five set-ups and "explains" Dobbs' quarrel with his partners, as he continues talking to himself: "We're running short of provisions Dobbsie. How about you going to the village?" Dobbs expects that Curtin and Howard have planned to locate and steal his portion of the prospected gold while he's gone.

Two of the set-ups are Close-Ups: one of Dobbs, the other Howard. Keep Howard's CU in mind.

The fourth scene @ **0:47:59**, consisting of fourteen set-ups, assembled into twenty cuts, heightens the quarrel and brings temporary resolution.

Dobbs believes his suspicions are confirmed when he stops Curtin, who is about to use a dead tree limb to lift a rock. We (the audience) know that Curtin is hunting a Gila monster that he (and we) spotted crawling under the rock.

Let me mention that it would have been possible for the filmmakers to keep "secret" (from the audience) that Curtin did see a Gila monster. Neither Dobbs nor the audience would know for certain.

Curtin realizes that he has inadvertently come across Dobbs' hiding place for his share of the gold, but he can't seem to convince Dobbs: "Okay, I'm a liar. There isn't a Gila monster under there. Let's see you stick your hand in and get your goods out. Go ahead."

The fifth set-up in the scene @ **0:48:58** is a Close-Up of Howard, the "keep Howard's CU in mind" shot. It is a portion of the set-up from the previous scene @ **0:46:48**! This shot maneuvers the cut before it — the Medium-Shot of Dobbs on screen left and Curtin on the right — to the cut after it: The Long-Shot (a reverse Master-Shot) shows Curtin on the left and Dobbs on the right. Without the assist of Howard's CU, Dobbs and Curtin would, in an instant, appear to flip screen sides, causing a spatial confusion — or break — in what is known as the *180-Degree Rule*.

Take special note of the care that went into the selected portion of Howard's CU: Facial signals (observe his eyes) incorporate expressions to "find" an expected reaction to Curtin's words and action. And! Take into account how astonishingly accommodating *fragments* are.

Pudovkin proposed a magical, yet pragmatic, view of cinema: "[The] material from which [the] final work is composed consists not of living men or real landscapes... but only of their images, recorded on separate strips that can be shortened, altered, and assembled according to [the filmmaker's] will.

"[By] combining [the material] in [a] selected sequence, the [filmmaker] builds... his own "filmic" time and "filmic" space. [Filmmakers do] not adapt reality, but [use] it for the creation of a new reality, and the most characteristic and important aspect of this process is that… laws of space and time [that are] invariable… become tractable and obedient."

A modern illustration of Porter's separate shot construction, and the visual persuasiveness of Eisenstein's (and his colleague's) theory of (European) montage — a juxtaposition of images which, together, construct, foster, encourage, and shape a new, and more significant, tension — can be seen in:

JU DOU

Chapter 3, "Attractions" @ 0:27:10

A dissolve as transition from the previous night brings us to an Extreme Long-Shot of this day in a 1920s dye factory in China. We can see Tianging and Ju Dou — they sit apart eating with chop sticks — amid the heavy beams, driven on giant wooden gears, stirring the soaking ribbons of silk in vats of freshly made dyes.

Ju Dou is the new young wife taken by the factory owner who is Tianging's uncle. Uncle has gone off to see to the care of his ailing pack horse.

The clock-like pounding of the moving timbers pervades the mill: The sound increases the sensually charged scene.

Ju Dou's licking and lip cleaning of her chopsticks is provocative to the viewer, but Tianging avoids all eye contact — yet we know that he is tempted by her presence. Ju Dou seductively approaches and embraces him. Her words, spoken from behind Tianging: "It's virgin and for you" cues a haunting human-like wind instrument. Tianging takes Ju Dou's dye-stained hands into his, and turns pushing Ju Dou backward onto the wooden planking.

Here we have the full impact of montage:

In Extreme Close-Up Ju Dou's slippered foot kicks away a wooden Y-shaped brake, releasing the mill's fly wheel. Ju Dou's pleasure squeals join the sounds of pounding timber and music. The spinning wheel pulls red-dyed silk upward out of a large woven basket, as it sprays rain-like droplets. The hoisting whipping cloth adds additional sounds. The silk falls back into the vat filled with red dye. Extreme Close-Ups of Ju Dou's face are intercut with the wheel and falling silk.

Ju Dou's mouth is open to her pleasure; silk caresses her face, until violently piling upon itself in the blood-like bath of red dye.

All sound fades slowly, until only the wind instrument lingers, as the camera tilts upward in Long-Shot displaying yellow and red draping silks. Take note of the respite from the sexual passions. It allows needed beats for the "conceivability" of the next scene: Ju Dou is pregnant.

Watch and experience the scene. While it is not an example of pure montage — it is not a silent film, after all — the images, colors, and "modern" aural stimulation do give proof to the theories of nearly a century ago.

If I may indulge in another legend:

CASABLANCA

Chapter 27, "The Mighty Marseillaise" @ 1:12:06

We are in Rick's Café in World War II occupied Morocco. German officers, accompanied on a piano, begin one of their patriotic songs. Rick, the American owner, watches from a balcony. The camera pans left across a Medium-Shot of the Germans, past bar customers, finally resting on Captain Renault. Renault looks to the left and upward, initiating a cut to a low-angle Medium-Shot of Rick and, behind him, Victor Lazlo, an anti-Fascist resistance leader. Lazlo exits to frame right. Rick reacts with a head turn to his left and then returns his focus to the Germans.

A Long-Shot shows the singing officers with champagne glasses held in a toasting gesture. Lazlo enters the crowded floor and determinedly stops in front of the café's orchestra: "Play the Marseillaise. Play it!"

Two of the horn musicians look to screen right. A cut reveals a Close-Up of Rick; he nods his approval. The orchestra begins to play, and a "battle" arises between the German officers, and the French customers' increasingly louder rendition of their national anthem.

Legend has it that the Close-Up of Rick @ **1:12:44**, was filmed much later — an added *fragment* — during a "break" in Bogart's next project. The filmmakers wanted Rick's reaction, suspecting that only *he* could plausibly sanction the playing, and the risk.

The above examples are all indications of an attempted adherence to life-like continuity. That is, they represent an effort to find a technique that holds the *fragments* in such a way as to present a "faithful" rendition of humankind on earth, but film is far more supple and poetic than authentic.

Lajos Egri, playwright, director, screenwriter, and founder, in the 1930s, of the Egri School of Writing in New York City, points out in his book, *The Art of Dramatic Writing: Its Basis in the Creative Interpretation of Human Motives*, that "art is not the mirror of life, but the essence of life."

The boldly simplified opening moments of *The French Connection* provides a good illustration of *fragments* as the life essence of film:

THE FRENCH CONNECTION

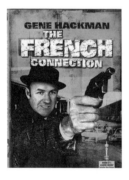

Chapter 2, "A Death in Marseilles" @ 0:01:00
Bells toll to a Fade-In of a serene Marseilles waterfront street. The text identification of place zooms back into the sky, diminishing in size and disappearing as a segue from the last "stinging" musical note plays continuing church bells

At **0:01:14** a man exits a shop and walks toward the camera, taking a passing route to screen left. There is now a gentle wind indicated by sounds of fishing nets and slightly billowing canvas.

The man is busy with a pizza slice, and keeping an eye out! We see his point of view (POV). A Long-Shot of two cars: A small, white (very European) vehicle, and a large dark town car — very American. The cut back to the man with a pizza brings us to his Close-Up.

I want to mention here the effective ordering of shots. There is a visual strategy and logic to the joining of the different scales of composition. The next cut is a Medium-Shot over the large car as two men exit a local restaurant. A cut takes us back to a Close-Up of the pizza-eating man. He takes another bite as he watches. Next, a cut continues the previous camera set-up as the two men come around the front of the car, and their screen direction shifts from right to left.

At **0:01:46** a cut brings us back to the CU (yet again) of the pizza-eating man. His body moves to the left, initiating the sound of an engine start-up and a car door slam. At **0:01:47** (barely more than a second later), a cut takes us to a Long-Shot as the large dark car drives off. Our pizza-eating man is no longer watching from the sunshine of the street, but rather, as the car passes him, he exits the shade of an alleyway. The camera stays with him as he keeps an eye on the vehicle.

The central, and remarkable, significance of this scene can be found in its bold deletions: an extraordinary, yet believable, compression in time and action. Reminiscent of the New Wave cinema of Truffaut and Godard, this is perhaps the more essential *French connection*. The eyes of the pizza-eating man and our engaged interest keep us from the inconsequential "realities" of a driver behind the wheel for the first time; the never-shown action of the two men getting into the car, nor how suddenly a group of red-clad youngsters can be seen sitting in one of the wooden boats on screen left.

Sound, most especially in the form of music, is an indispensable ally in film's effort to unite its fragments. Karel Reiscz, in the first printing of his classic, *Technique of Film Editing*, used Alfred Hitchcock's thriller, *The Man Who Knew Too Much* (1956), to illustrate the director's discovery of a way to unite the cross-cutting fragments of the climactic Albert Hall concert scene. The filmmakers' cutting, between Jo McKenna at the concert, and husband Dr. Ben McKenna hurrying to get there in a taxi to prevent an assassination, looked and sounded disruptively chaotic: The symphony played only when we were witness to the concert hall shots, cutting out to the assumed reality of taxi and traffic sounds when we accompanied the doctor. In the end, the symphony was the solution! The music continued throughout the two locations.

Sixteen years later Francis Ford Coppola faced a similar cross-cutting pattern which went well beyond delineation of scene to scene separation, and might well have crossed into the conspicuousness of fragments.

THE GODFATHER

Chapter 21, "Baptism and Murder" @ 2:36:18

The baptismal invocation in Latin — and the music of a pipe organ — conveys not only the cathedral location, but is maintained across the multiple scenes of the preparation rituals and brutal killings conducted by the Corleone family in a purge of their adversaries. As Hitchcock before him, Coppola unified cinema's intrinsic structure of separation/*fragments* into a dream-like compelling dance.

telling

Director and screenwriter D. W. Griffith (1875-1948; *The Birth of a Nation*, 1915; *Intolerance*, 1916) contributed to Porter's editing innovations by splitting (separating) the action — no longer necessary due to the physical limit of film — for dramatic reasons, thus expanding the narrative power of cinema as a storytelling medium.

The Academy of Motion Picture Arts & Sciences sees fit to present an Oscar for Best Screenplay Adaptation as well as for Best Original Screenplay. The fact is that in both categories, the screenplay needs adapting, because the *telling* needs adjustments, modifications — often a transformation!

The distinction between the needs of a film and the needs of the screenplay rests within their storytelling prerequisites. The principal divergence is to be found in their methods of *exposition*: explanation and discourse designed to convey information.

There is a profound difference between how information is distributed via words on paper — description and explanation in text and written forms of dialogue — and how that same information gets distributed via sound and image on screen. It is indispensable to submit a screenplay that is lucid, one capable of being read. To produce an exact duplicate on celluloid is neither required nor ideal, if even possible!

I am reminded of writer Raymond Chandler. His detective fiction, which featured Philip Marlowe, a case-hardened private eye working in Los Angeles, led him to Hollywood and screenwriting: *Double Indemnity* (1944), *The Blue Dahlia* (1946), and *Strangers on a Train* (1951). After some twenty years of on and off anguish — clashes with director Billy Wilder conveyed collaborative struggles — he expressed a yearning that life in the movies would have been less painful if someone had advised early on that, "[S]creenwriting isn't even a second cousin to real writing." Could Chandler's (unnecessary) suffering have been a result of his "real writing" being a solo art?

Sometimes discourse is presented literally: in the form of titles, sometimes in voice over (VO) narration, sometimes in dialogue, and sometimes in all three; better is the communication that includes principles of the juxtaposition of moving pictures.

Griffith used the camera to take in a new and extensive view of *place* and *character*, presenting a more "modern" *adaptation* in set-ups and coverage. He is credited, through his collaboration with cinematographer Billy Bitzer — both hired by the Biograph Company, founded by (another) former Edison employee, William Dickson (1860-1935) — with the creation of the fade-out and fade-in. *And* their collaboration introduced the Close-Up, Scenic Long-Shot, and Parallel Action, granting a (recognizable) contemporary look to the silent era.

Let's begin with a film "doubly" adapted: A screenplay, from Henry Fielding's classic eighteenth-century novel, written by playwright John Osborne, presented on celluloid by Tony Richardson and cast and crew. We might consider the work "triply" adapted. This 1963 movie makes the most of early era techniques; employing — if not consuming — D. W. Griffith's storytelling innovations.

TOM JONES

Chapter 1, "Sudden Baby/Title" @ 0:00:24

Osborne indicates *Title* for early exposition which appears on screen as in a silent film–era adventure: "In the West of England there was once a Squire Allworthy. After several months in London he returns home."

Dialogue too is conveyed by way of titles: "*Mrs. Wilkins*," shouts Squire Allworthy, and "*aaah!*" Mrs. Wilkins says, seeing Allworthy's night-shirted bottom (almost) and "*a baby*" when she sees what Allworthy has discovered in his bed.

The score by John Addison joyfully impersonates the silent era, and influences the opening photography, creating a feel of sped-up staccato motion as if produced by cameras and projectors of the "olden days" — though in full color.

To be sure, the screenplay and film possess dialogue, and the finished work contains a full and grand musical score and all the sound design that any great work is expected to encompass. The storytelling, its asides in sarcasm, wit and wisdom are soon heard in the exuberant narration of Micheál Mac Liammóir.

This sequence illustrates needless, as well as redundantly peculiar, discourse. The exposition is undeniably shaped by "Griffith's camera" of some seven decades earlier, but it demonstrates fuzzy links to silent picture days.

I think this is a good selection because "the advent of sound" is *not* the source of the overlooked opportunities from script to screen.

Chapter 1, "Funeral Rites" @ 0:01:03

The head credits continue from their black background to superimposed titles over live-action: A Close-Up of wind-stirred high grass brings a first image; the frame, horizontally halved, holds a bright blue sky over the grass. Adjoining this visual dance is the (previously begun) passage of protracted notes in strings and flute.

Moving into this frame (from right to left) are folks of a nineteenth-century community. They are all in black. The camera follows, panning left. A cut to another Long-Shot picks up a horse-drawn carriage moving from left to right. The camera pans with the carriage, till it all but vanishes into the fuller frame of grass. Another cut, across a nearly complete frame of green, "watches" as a line of the black-clad folks emerge from the high grass. They walk toward the camera. A low-angle shot follows; a long line of carriages rolls past; the camera zooms in with an upward tilt to a blur of horse and carriage. A Medium-Shot catches the walking folks; they cross the frame from right to left, against a background of sky alone.

Finally, an Extreme Long-Shot, from behind this group, shows them to be following the horse-drawn carriages down a dirt path to a distant farm house. Over this shot is superimposed: Pennsylvania 1984.

The location and *year* (if not century), in literal exposition, are *not* needed! Here is specificity in time and place best suited to screenplay form alone.

A tranquil nineteenth-century America, (not always) co-existing with the threatening, urban twentieth century will soon be more skillfully expressed. Isn't it remarkable that expository *title cards* are still hanging around?

Chapter 2, "The Journey" @ 0:07:06

A Long-Shot of farmland shows Grandfather's horse-drawn carriage reach center frame when, entering screen left, an eighteen-wheel "menace" comes air-braking behind it, followed some nine seconds later by a shot of the carriage "holding up" a long line of traffic: the tranquility transformed by a noisy suburban setting. We are visually "told" the *time*.

The *place* is more effectively identified a few minutes later:

Chapter 3, "Material Witness" @ 0:09:50

In an Extreme Long-Shot we see the mezzanine of Philadelphia's Pennsylvania Station. I'd bet most audience members have already deduced Amish, Lancaster County, and Pennsylvania. Would the storytelling falter if the time was 1982 or 1986?

Because plays and screenplays are paper arrangements — blueprints of a sort — for presentation via other forms, we ought to scrutinize, and I am most particularly intrigued by, the *telling* adjustments from stage to screen:

Director Arthur Penn generously gave his time to students at the School of Visual Arts to discuss his experience as a novice film director after successful years in theatre.

When he was asked to direct the feature film version of *The Miracle Worker* in 1962 he was secure in his abilities. "After all," he said, "I'd directed the *Playhouse 90* television presentation (1956), and the Broadway production." He had received the Tony Award as Best Director (Drama) for the play in 1960. "Who better to direct the film version?"

THE MIRACLE WORKER

Chapter 15, "W-A-T-E-R" @ 1:39:12

Annie Sullivan, teacher to the blind, deaf, and mute girl Helen Keller, takes her by the wrist, leading her with determination, out the kitchen's screen door to the water well. At the dinner table, Helen, in a fit of frustration and rage, has emptied the water pitcher over her teacher, and Annie intends "to make her fill this pitcher again."

This scene on stage left not a dry eye in the theatre. "You could hear full and uninhibited sobbing coming from the audience," Mr. Penn told the students.

The *Playhouse 90* version (more than likely) elicited the same response from the TV audience watching in their living rooms.

Penn decided to make that scene the first day's shooting. It was completed in Master-Shot. The director took note, after calling "Cut," that the production crew was in tears.

The next evening the dailies were screened. Arthur Penn experienced a disappointment similar to the legendary fire rescue footage of Edwin Porter. The scene did not inspire the expected response from those in attendance, including Penn himself. "This is not cinema!" he realized.

The next day critical *fragments* were "gathered": A Close-Up of Helen's palm feeling a drip from the pump's spigot; Medium and Close-Up shots of Annie and Helen framed together at the pump; Medium-Shots of Annie's and Helen's signing hands, and confirmation from Annie's nodding gestures, in angles and axis that clearly demonstrate the actions and reactions!

Playwright Peter Shaffer's *Amadeus* is particularly useful in the study of the resemblances and distinctions of the two *telling* forms; especially because Shaffer was screenwriter for the adaptation to film.

THE PLAY:
Act I. Scene 2. Salieri's Apartment. November 1823. The small hours.

Court composer Antonio Salieri confesses to the audience — "I can see you" — his sin of gluttony, "Sticky gluttony... I have never been able to conquer a lust for the sweetmeats of Northern Italy." He then introduces another of his sins: "And now, gracious ladies! Obliging gentlemen! I present to you — for one performance only — my last composition, entitled *The Death of Mozart*; or *Did I Do It?*"

Salieri then bows deeply. When he straightens we are jolted, as in a bolt from the blue, to the court of Emperor Joseph II.

Here, on the spot, and in *live theatre*, Shaffer incorporates a cinematic stratagem: a *flashback*.

Theatre structure most definitely allows for events out of chronology, but this employment is startling in its instantaneous replication of a movie cut!

The bowing Salieri unfastens his tattered old cloak so that upon rising he drops it to the stage, uncovering a "sky-blue coat" of the young man in "the prime of his life"; throwing his head back, his cap and gray musty hair fall, disclosing beautifully groomed brown hair.

Simultaneously, and in precise union, a glowing light fills the stage. We are in the Viennese court. It is 1781.

In the film *Amadeus*, the (imaginary) fourth wall is not broken by an acknowledgment of the audience. The exposition is instead directed to a father confessor — a substitute for the audience.

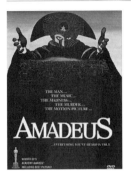

Chapter 2, "Can't Name Tune" @ 0:4:48

The chapter's title reflects Salieri's ongoing resentment of Mozart's genius. The priest cannot recall a single "tune" of Salieri's, but he immediately recognizes *Eine kleine Nachtmusik*, easily humming the melody of Mozart's composition.

During the conversation with the Father Confessor — "For God's sake, my son, if you have something to confess, do it now" — Salieri takes the priest *and* the audience to 1780s Vienna, his work as court composer, and his meeting and rivalry with Wolfgang Amadeus Mozart.

The flashbacks to the youthful Salieri are integrated within the current (present-time) setting of a hospital, and his *telling* as confession.

I've taken time to talk about theatre, and its *telling* forms, because there is currently a strong inclination to incorporate theatre arts into film production courses and cinema studies programs. It provides analysis and dissection of scene beats, and it especially attempts to make students competent in their collaboration with actors.

Students need to be made aware of this obvious, though often ignored, fact: When shooting a scene, the director — and the entire crew — experience it live. This fact needs emphasizing because film production can easily develop into a "rehearsal" for the stage! This is particularly true when coverage is limited to Master-Shots and/or Set-Ups that do little else but duplicate the camera angles and axis, restraining the images to nothing more than enlarged views of the Master.

One solution to this has been the advent of a video-tap on the film camera, permitting the director to "have a look" at film-like images during the course of production. Director Sidney Lumet — who began his *telling* days in theatre and television — recommends that the director (always) sit alongside the camera's lens.

An all too common form of exposition (*telling*), which holds a long theatrical tradition, and is best left on the editing room floor — if it makes it that far — is back-story information by way of dialogue. It sounds heavy-handed and scheming, is usually unnecessary and far too obvious for cinema, and worst of all, it eliminates later curiosities.

Chapter 1, "Uncle's New Wife" @ 0:03:17

When Tianging, the nephew who works in the dyeing mill, returns after a long journey delivering fabric finished at the mill, Erlaiza (a young man who has worked for "Uncle" in his nephew's absence) tells Tianging (and of course the audience as well), "Your Uncle has bought himself a woman. Her name is Ju Dou, and she's quite pretty. Your Uncle is a bastard! How do you think your other two aunts died? He tortured them to death because they didn't give him a child. Listen carefully at night, you can hear your new aunt screaming."

The proceeding scene @ **0:04:24** shows, in an above shot, village rooftops in a deep monochromatic blue of night. At **0:04:30** in a single set-up, we see Tianging asleep, and as expected, he (and we) hear a woman's cry. Tianging is awakened. The audience knows too much too soon. There is no mystery, nor tension, nor curiosity!

Imagine that none of Erlaiza's exposition has occurred: @ **0:04:24** we know *nothing* about a new aunt, so that following a woman's cry which wakens Tianging @ **0:04:52** a dissolve takes us to morning. The hue, though still blue, is somewhat lighter, and a rooster calls out. A lone female figure, in Extreme Long-Shot, exits a doorway and moves along the side of the house. Then, @ **0:05:12**, we see Tianging — also up early — feeding his Uncle's horse and donkey. He furtively watches the woman as she prepares to bathe, only to be frighteningly disrupted by the sudden raucous hee-hawing donkey. I think this better without the earlier *telling*.

An unusual *telling* can be found in the opening of:

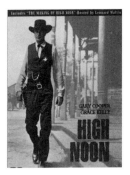

Chapter 1, "Main Credits with Song" @ 0:00:10

Tom-tom beats barely precede the opening Extreme Long-Shot. A lone figure, framed by two trees, sits on a rock. A saddled horse to screen left. A Medium Long-Shot reveals the smoking "cowboy" as he looks off to the distance, and approaches the foreground. Another Extreme Long-Shot reveals his point of view (POV) across a plain of grass. A figure rides at a quick gallop. It is over this shot that the head credits begin.

The story's central premise and plot are expressed in the lyrics of a ballad written by Dimitri Tiomkin and Ned Washington, and sung by Tex Ritter.

The "cowboys" who meet at the trees do speak to each other, but in lip movements only; their dialogue is not heard. A third rides up, and the first two mount their horses to join him. No words, location ambiance, sound effects or even hooves hitting the earth are heard. The ballad and plot-describing lyrics carry past the last of the head credits.

Griffith's contributions to cinematic telling also extend to a break from the theatrical convention of beginning a scene with an entrance, and often ending with an exit. In this you'll find an abundance of needed modifications from the screenplay's *telling* and production's *dailies*. The accomplished and influential editor Dede Allen, another émigré from theatre, has cautioned, "Watch out for entrances and exits."

Here's an illustration in *telling* from one of the many collaborations between director Arthur Penn and Ms. Allen.

LITTLE BIG MAN

Chapter 1, "Turn That Thing On" @ 0:00:10

Jack Crabb asserts that he is "the sole white survivor of the Battle of Little Big Horn, popularly known as Custer's Last Stand." He also claims he's 121 years old!

Perhaps this, and a good deal more of Jack's story, is so terrifically curious that, though presented as a film, it touches all of the appeal we embrace in the traditions of oral folklore. The filmmakers succeed in the frequent difficulties of voiceover (VO) tales constructed in evident flashback. There can easily be a vital loss of urgency, and a resulting audience disengagement, because, as Alexander Mackendrick points out in *On Film-Making: An Introduction to the Craft of the Director*, there is a diminishing of dramatic tension in a presentation of *former* events; especially when they are clearly offered as the past. But! There are flashbacks, and there are *flashbacks*: Excessive and gratuitous breaks in the structure of the *telling* can become mannered artifice — a storytelling showing-off!

Jack's craggily squeaky and faltering voice begins on a black screen, "I am beyond a doubt the last of the old-timers." A fade-in finds a Close-Up of the abundantly crinkly Jack — and his long-ash cigarette. The camera moves outward and left, as a younger voice is heard, "I'm more interested in the primitive lifestyle of the Plains Indian than I am in tall tales about Custer."

Jack takes offense ("are you calling me a liar?") and drops his cigarette into his lap.

A Master-Shot displays a hospital ward with Jack, in a wheelchair, and the younger man seated at a small table, upon which sits an upright tape recorder. The "researcher" retrieves the still-lighted cigarette and places it between Jack's fingers.

After putting up with a few more unintentional insults, Jack points to the tape recorder. "Turn that thing on... I said turn that thing on and shut up. Now you just set there and you'll learn something." A Close-Up of Jack brings his intense stare. "I knowed General George Armstrong Custer for what he was. And I also knowed the Indians for what they was."

A tender pause results in Jack's head-quivering attempt to keep from crying. With eyes beginning to show the redness of fought-back tears, Jack Crabb begins his long and altogether true and tall tale; his wrinkled face dissolves to a panorama of the Great Plains.

Another illustration of folklore's *telling* tradition can be heard in *Ballad of a Soldier*. Its content, however, stumbles into sentimentality with voiceover (VO) narration of a non-participating "stranger."

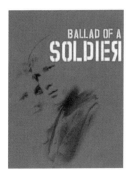

Chapter 1, "A Son and a Hero" @ 0:00:28

The film opens in an old-world village. It is peaceful and picturesque. White ducks and chickens peck in the dry roadway. A woman slowly approaches. The trees sway in the steady breezes. A laughing line of young women dance onto the road and meet more friends. Together they skip off into the background, kicking up dust. The older woman in a black dress and shawl continues toward the camera. A young couple with a wrapped infant enters frame right. They draw nearer the woman. The woman acknowledges the infant with a brief smiling glance. The young couple turns to watch as the older woman passes across and out of the frame.

At **0:01:29** a point of view (POV) rests on a Long-Shot of the older woman as the young couple sees her. A somber score begins. It is both funereal and military, the rhythm somewhat in synchronization to the older woman's walk. She is, after all, dressed for mourning.

She continues into the distance, along what is now a more distinct road-way which moves away from the village. It is narrow and meanders along fields of flourishing grain.

A male voice *tells* about the comings and goings on this road "in and out" of the village. Over a beautifully composed Close-Up of the woman, the *telling* goes on: "She is not waiting for anyone. The one she used to wait for, her son Alyosha, did not return from the war. He is buried far from his birthplace…."

I think you'll agree that as each line of narration — in reverse order — is deleted, the storytelling becomes more and more intriguing and captivating.

The opening scene is very much a prologue. It separates itself as an overture to a structure, and as the requirement for the film's head credits. The obligation to list (tell) the cast and crew is a burden, but it must somehow fit, and not be an imposition on the storytelling.

The start of the story does not require narration as an introduction to *flashback*. The images, and the suitable sounds derived from the location, are all that is needed. The village road as past, as *sorrow*, and as *lonely yearning* is commanding enough.

Sometimes an abundance of *telling* modes require discrimination and simplification.

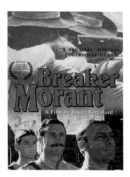

Index 1, Chapter 1 - 3, "Ambush" @ 0:00:01

The film opens on a title card, giving (telling) in brief the history which preceded the events of the story: *The Boer War (1899-1902) was fought between countries of the British Empire and the Boer (mostly Dutch) population of South Africa... [fighting] for independence from England.*

A desolate wind can be heard.

Pietersburg. Transvaal. South Africa. November 1901

is superimposed over a Long-Shot of a multi-racial gathering around a gazebo, accommodating an army band.

The head credits are already underway, with a variety of fonts across new scenes, which contribute to a "feel" of add on, start-and-stop beginnings. This is made all the more complicated because the military music is discontinued, and soon after resumed.

At **0:01:18** an Exterior Medium-Shot shows two men of color scrubbing clothes from a stack of British khaki. A pan left brings into view the outer wall of a small fort; soldiers of the British force march past. A cut takes us into a sparsely furnished hall. In Long-Shot, soldiers sit at two facing tables which are situated in frame right and left.

A dolly left and a pan right introduces Harry Morant as he stands to offer testimony at a preliminary inquiry. Harry's standing cuts from the Long-Shot to a Close-Up. The cut across the action allows his face to enter the bottom of the frame.

An interesting series of formal and military Close-Ups — a profile facing right, another facing left, before a return to the original full face — play out Harry's testimony, which covers some personal history in Australia and South Africa.

His final declarations — well "disguised" expository dialogue — do boost the audience's inquisitiveness: "I take full and entire responsibility for the... the events at Fort Edward. I was however acting under orders. I was also deeply disturbed by what happened to Captain Hunt."

A conflict arises in the *telling*, which is vital in setting-up and initiating the pivotal event in the story, because the head credits — though carefully positioned on screen in the colors (black and red) of the Australian military kilts — contend with our listening to Morant. The credits create a conflict between inclinations to read, while at the same time listening to Morant, and looking him in the eye.

Breaker Morant is among my favorite films. It does approach masterpiece standing, so it is ironic that (likely) contract requirements — an ego-consoling matter — are allowed to meddle with inspired storytelling.

Editor Zach Staenberg says it as clearly as anyone, "At the end of the day all this stuff has to work to tell a story. And if you're not *telling* a story it doesn't matter how much razzle-dazzle there is; it's not about the tools it's about the story."

structure

At its most pragmatic, film structure has everything to do with finding the best arrangement in the distribution of information. While at the outset, words such as "pragmatic" and "structure" may seem to suggest a cold calculation of scene to sequence assembly, they should not, primarily because calculation — even the most brilliantly conceived calculation — does not guarantee the indispensable emotional well-being of storytelling.

Whatever the best arrangement of information might be, storytelling in cinema requires developing a "feel" for visual inflection, a juxtaposition in pacing and rhythm: the fundamental reason that the most important aspect of "finding" structure is ongoing adaptation.

I would discourage the premise — believed by many filmmakers, and more than ever, by film students — that a story can be squeezed, stretched, or dragged into a shape reminiscent of, or inspired by another, often favorite, film.

I am not proposing an absolute adherence to traditional or classic forms. Ignoring creative influences that contribute to broadened structural parameters is foolish and detrimental, not just to the rich art of cinema, but to an individual movie as well.

I agree with Jean-Luc Godard: "Every film should have a beginning, a middle, and an end. But not necessarily in that order."

Legend — you'll excuse me, but the film business is overloaded with legends — has it that when Frank Capra's classic *Lost Horizon* was previewed, it was laughed off the screen, not intended for distribution. It was some while later that Capra — on his way to the airport — unexpectedly recognized the movie's quandary in storytelling structure.

He turned his car around and drove instead to the Columbia Pictures film vault, and "turned" his picture around. He took the head credits off of reel one — discarding the balance of the reel — and spliced the credits to the beginning of reel two.

The original, and now discarded, opening sequences introduced the featured characters in such tedious cliché that the spirit of the story sagged into inane disinterest. Without the balance of the first reel, the film opened on the terrifying chaos at the Shanghai Airport. Travelers desperately sought escape from the invading Japanese army.

The eyes and emotions of the audience were affixed to the screen. Here was a solution supported by an expanded version of "Watch out for entrances!"

The excitement in discovering a flourishing new structure is expressed by director Andrei Tarkovsky in his memoir *Sculpting in Time*: "We somehow managed to devise one last, desperate rearrangement — there was the film."

Let's begin with a good illustration of such an effort in "enlightened" rearrangement.

SERPICO

Chapter 1, "Courage and Integrity" @ 0:00:09
The frame depicted in the DVD's Scene Selection of Chapter I, shows several rows of police officers at the commencement address during graduation from the police academy. It is probably just coincidence, but I mention this because the film, as scripted and originally completed, opened with this scene.

The structure was in the chronology of Frank Serpico's experience as a New York City policeman beginning with his academy graduation.

A (near) last screening before "locking" picture and dialogue set off a pressing exploration for a fresh assembly. The film seemed to have squandered so much of the energetic spirit of an exhilarating screenplay, though many of the scenes and sequences still retained a poignant and disturbing vigor that the overall structure now lacked.

The story of Officer Frank Serpico and the subsequent Knapp Commission investigation into police corruption was public knowledge. The story had been extensively covered in the press and on television. Somehow an assumption had taken hold: Everyone knows about Frank Serpico. A chronology of events made the most sense.

A structure founded on these assumptions was, it turned out, not in the best observance of storytelling. In the end, it was decided — and satisfyingly discovered — that structure should unreservedly emerge from good and sturdy storytelling.

That is, an arrangement that grasps and holds the audience. Remember your high school English teacher's admonition about essay writing? You have but a few sentences to take hold of, or lose, your reader.

The opening credits were no longer displayed against the hum-drum of a commencement speaker. Instead, an ever-increasing scream of a siren, and the sound of wiper blades clackity-smears across a windshield.

The first image brings the protagonist with evocative disclosures and emphasizes audience distress and inquisitiveness: A dark Close-Up of a bloodied, bearded man in the back of a car.

By combining parallel editing, cross-cutting, and intercutting, the structure demands our attention and questions: This scraggly and bloody guy is a cop? A cop might have shot him? This disheveled cop is known to the New York Times?

The above three editing techniques are often interchangeably defined in film glossaries. I have offered a distinction to my editing class, and recently one of the students brought in a Barnes & Noble glossary of film terms which matched my definitions:

Parallel Editing is the joining of two or more fully completed scenes. In *Serpico*, the INTERIOR. EIGHTH PRECINCT. NIGHT scene is joined in sequence with the INTERIOR. CHIEF SIDNEY GREEN BEDROOM. NIGHT and INTERIOR. NEWS ROOM. NEW YORK TIMES. NIGHT scenes. The cross-cutting is demonstrated with *revisiting* the INTERIOR. POLICE CAR. NIGHT scene.

Cross-Cutting is the joining together of two or more scenes without a conclusion to one or any.

Intercutting is the joining together of two or more shots that make up a *single scene*: INTERIOR. POLICE CAR. NIGHT. The cutting *between* (and at times back again) the Close-Up of Frank Serpico; the Close-Up of another officer inside the car and the over-the-shoulder Medium Shot which shows Frank and the other officer.

The totality of the new structure presents urgency beyond the horror of siren and bleeding face. It creates a frame that permits the audience a glimpse into the future. You'll also note that when the "actual time" is delivered in the story, a recollected tension is felt, but there is no reappearance of the opening moments.

Movie structures reside in duration: the "feel" of time, its psychological impact, regardless of whether precise or imprecise in measurement. But if story-telling brings into play specific reference to time, in word or image, an arranged bond between story time and running time may be necessary and desired!

HIGH NOON

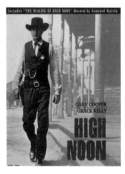

This American classic — the first "adult western" — attempts to be specific in measured time. Its reference to time is made all the more obsessive with frequent shots of clocks, yet the dedication to story drama averts the otherwise expected cliché!

Chapter 2, "Trouble at the Depot" @ 0:02:53

Three bad guys ride into town, and we get every hint that they are recognized and up to no good. Church bells call townsfolk to Sunday prayer, and a man watches the riders pass and turns to his wife; an elderly woman genuflects as the three ride into town. And let's not forget Tex Ritter's opening exposition in ballad form, "High Noon (Do Not Forsake Me, Oh My Darlin')".

We get a first look at a clock @ **0:04:25**. The bad guys ride past the impending wedding ceremony for our protagonist Marshall Will Kane and his bride Amy. The wall clock behind the gathering sets the time at 10:35. At **0:05:23** the three riders reach the Hadleyville depot, and the station clock, behind the agent, is very near 10:36!

Chapter 17, "Waiting For…"

The train carrying Frank Miller arrives precisely as a pendulum clock hits noon. A fierce train whistle echoes through the pounding instrumental of the ballad. The film's running time is now just shy of **1:10:00**.

The structure's success results from "ticking" anticipation; unstoppable clocks convey Will Kane's approaching peril. An unusually "truthful" rendition in time, and certainly worth the viewing for its absolute achievement in chronology!

What is essential to good storytelling structure is an ability to evaluate the relationship between the "feel" in story time, and its strengths — the audience's emotional engagement, sequential order, choices in deletions, and plausibility of events — within the measured running time of the film.

DR. STRANGELOVE

Dr. Strangelove is also structured in chronology, with near accuracy in story and running time, but — at the same time — dissimilar to *High Noon* in its time purpose. Here the structure is less *personal*; an ensemble of characters contributes to the film's catastrophic sarcasm. In the Nuclear Age, total calamity hangs over *all* no matter the strict protocol in order and security. How much time do *we* have?

Chapter 2, "Condition Red" @ 0:04:54
General Ripper has ordered Group Captain Mandrake "to transmit Plan R; Plan R, for Robert, to the Wing."

Chapter 3, "Wing Attack Plan R" @ 0:07:23
On board a B-52 bomber, a console panel rapidly beep-toots a code: F G D I 3 5. A crew member opens his *Top Secret: Aircraft Communications Codes* book. While snacking on chocolate éclairs, he (Goldie) reports to his commander on board, Major Kong that, "I know you'll think this is crazy... but I just got a message from the base over the C.R.M. 114. It decodes as Wing attack Plan R. R for Romeo."

At **0:10:10**, after reconfirming Plan R, Kong puts away his U.S. Air Force headgear, replacing it with his — held in an onboard safe — cowboy hat: "Well, boys, I reckon this is it. Nuclear combat toe-to-toe with the Ruskies."

Chapter 7, "Captain Mandrake" @ 0:19:17
Mandrake brings a small transistor radio, turned on, to Ripper's office, "Listen

to that. Music; Civilian Broadcasting." There can't have been a Soviet nuclear attack. What is going on is clearly a test. "Personally I think it's taking things too far." At **0:19:44**, Mandrake advises, "Our fellows will be inside Russian radar cover in about twenty minutes."

General Ripper refuses to withdraw the attack orders: "The planes are not going to be recalled."

While there are no images of clocks or watches to depict time, there are frequent and precise time references, and animated lights.

Chapter 8, "In the War Room" @ 0:24:34
General "Buck" Turgidson briefs the President, aides, undersecretaries, Pentagon officials and the Joint Chiefs of Staff. "About 35 minutes ago, General Jack Ripper, the commanding general of Burpelson Air Force Base issued an order for the 34 B-52s of his Wing… it appears that the order calls for the planes to attack their targets inside Russia." A large map high on the war room wall displays Russia, the B-52s' current position, and their targets.

At **0:28:24** Turgidson estimates eighteen minutes till the planes penetrate Russian radar.

Chapter 13, "Merkin & Dimitri" @ 0:43:01
The President, with the Russian ambassador seated alongside, briefs the Russian Premier. "They will not reach their targets for at least another hour."

Chapter 25, "Final Checks" @ 1:23:56
The bomb doors will not open; all attempts at over-ride mechanisms and manual efforts fail. Major Kong goes "below" to "get them doors open if it harelips everybody on Bear Creek." The sequence plays against a drum and bugle rendition of "When Johnny Comes Marching Home."

Even here, the navigator's countdown in miles to the target is "accurate" to an air speed approximating 600 miles per hour. At **1:26:28** Major Kong sits atop a hydrogen bomb, working to rewire the damaged circuits. At **1:26:50**, with the target in sight, Kong reattaches wires, and the bomb doors open.

Chapter 26, "Yahoo!!!" @ 1:27:01
The bomb drops from the B-52. Major "King" Kong rides it with enthusiastic rodeo shrieks of hoots, hollers, and yahoos! The bomb explodes @ **1:27:19**!

With the B-52's fuel leak, and in-flight change to a "closer" target (the

ICBM complex at Kotloss), the film's running time corresponds well to the story's time references.

An altogether peculiar and feeble moment in story time, event and dramatic need occurs between:

Chapter 21, "Deviated Pervert" @ 1:10:50

Mandrake is in a telephone booth, short on change to reach the president. He demands that Colonel "Bat" Guano open fire on a hallway Coca-Cola machine to retrieve more change. And...

Chapter 22, "One Plane Left" @ 1:13:12

A dissolve joins the two scenes — an indication in storytelling trouble? The animated lights on the War Room wall map "back away" from the Russian targets as a P.A. announcement explains the success of the code to recall the bombers, and the destruction of all but *one plane* that did not respond. Major Kong's crew is the one still in the air. The information distributed is rushed and heavy-handed; not of the *time* and care of earlier pacing.

It is much more common for film to take on large to vast episodes — if not epics — in time.

JU DOU

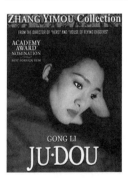

Chapter 3, "Attractions" @ 0:29:36

In the next scene following Tianging and (his new aunt) Ju Dou's illicit intercourse, a dissolve brings us to the Uncle and "doctor" conferring about the reclining, blanketed Ju Dou: "My charm has worked. She is pregnant."

At **0:29:59**, Uncle hurries to a shrine of candles and incense: "Dear ancestors, bless me with a son."

Chapter 4, "Ju Dou Had a Boy" @ 0:30:45

Little more than a minute after the pregnancy is pronounced, a baby's cry is heard. An Extreme Long-Shot looks up to a second floor walkway. A midwife exits a room, and peers down from the railing transom: "Ju Dou hasn't disappointed you."

With the pregnancy comes time specificity: nine months. But the many months are presented in a minute!

Here is cinema's remarkable, convincing, efficient, and dominant structural distribution in time!

Let's view some examples of sequence and scene structural flexibilities in time.

Sergei Eisenstein's "The Battle on Ice" scene is an excellent example of *extending* time for dramatic effect.

ALEXANDER NEVSKY

Chapter 8, "Lake Chudskoye" @ 0:55:28 & Chapter 9, "Assembled for Battle" @ 0:57:47
This thirteenth-century heroic tale recounts Prince Nevsky's defense of Mother Russia against the invading German (Teuton Ritter) knights. On April 5, 1242, the Prince and his Russian peasant army await the Germans on the far side of frozen Lake Chudskoye.

I'll use Eisenstein's work to examine the fragments/separation as they form a personal as well as structural relationship to storytelling. This sequence provides a good illustration of the integration of multiple elements in storytelling's collaboration.

Eisenstein's images inspired the majestic score by Sergei Prokofiev, and Prokofiev motivated the director to additions and adjustments in the sequence. Their partnership developed dramatic tension by magnifying the duration and excitation in visual and aural beats.

Eisenstein begins the sequence with images that announce a new day. The increasing first light benefits from an "optical" transition: Fade-In. The simple slow pulse of Prokofiev's score — music in time-keeping instrumentation — accentuates the Russian army's surveillance of the frozen horizon, and, so too, it initiates an apprehension in waiting.

Film does, for the most part, compress time and events, finding the essence alone. Securing the essence of a scene, sequence, and the entirety of a film from screenplay through editing is an intricate and arduous collaborative challenge.

At **0:57:47**, the start of Chapter 9, watch how the production *fragments* are assembled — at times redundant, and even delayed beyond what "real world" experience teaches — to take advantage of the dramatic impact by prolonging the time it takes for the armies to collide.

At **0:59:32**, approaching the two-minute mark since the Teutonic knights began their gallop across the frozen lake, we finally see several spike-bearing Russians react. At **0:59:39**, a Russian in the foreground announces, "*The Germans!*" At **0:59:52** (now past two minutes), Prince Nevsky's gesture indicates that he has spotted something. Then @ **1:00:06** the Prince lowers the face guard of his helmet, a move that intensifies, while continuing to extend, the anticipation.

The use of repetitive overlapping of the wooden spikes, initiated in the shot of Bulsai's drawing his sword @ **1:01:30** is a common "localized" extension of an action that Eisenstein was fond of using. Its decisive gestures are especially effective as a final expectation of the fight.

Let's take a look at several examples of what might be described as mini-structures in extended time. Whether "invisible" or "visible" — as in the overlapping assembly of the wooden spikes — they are influenced by the films of the Russian director and montage theorist.

COLONEL REDL

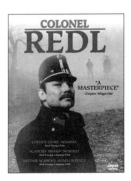

Chapter 21, "Waltzing with Danger" @ 1:46:04 Redl attends a masked ball in a Habsburg Palace. At midnight the orchestra's horns announce a call for the hundreds of formally attired guests to remove their black and white masks.

Over the course of sixteen seconds across six shots, a lovely and inconspicuous structure — in a mini-essay — of "masks coming off" is displayed: More than quadruple the time needed for the masks to come down, yet a convincing and delightful duration.

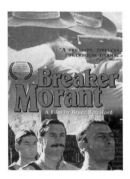

Index 2, Chapter 10, "The Trial Begins" @ 0:17:04
Witton, Handcock, and Morant, and their army appointed lawyer, Major Thomas, enter the court-martial chamber. There are several tables: On the right is the table for the defendants; for the prosecution, there's one on the left; a small desk sits along this same side, occupied by an African court stenographer, in black suit and hat, and in the background stands the long table for the court-martial officers. In the center foreground is a single chair reserved for witnesses.

The defendants and their lawyer enter in formal parade steps, salute, and take seats at their table. In five shots — beginning with this initial Master-Shot — a mini-essay captures the removal of helmets and hats over an approximate time of eight seconds. Again, an improbable, but beautifully satisfying extension of time!

Lastly, here is a wonderful illustration of complexities in structure that nevertheless are understandable, and most vital of all, support and complement the story. The film provides a rich lesson in non-chronological and non-continuous time.

THE SWEET HEREAFTER

Chapter 1, "Head Credits" @ 0:00:35
The musical theme plays in its simplest instrumentation. The camera dollies right, along wooden siding; shadows sway across the boards, casting a rough-hewn look. The color shifts from blue to yellow-brown, shedding light on the initial illusion: We were not moving along wooden siding, but "over" floor boards. The camera begins to lift upward, and a mother, young child and father are revealed in a high-angle shot. They are asleep on all-white bedding, the mother's breasts exposed and available to the child.

This family portrait will turn out to be the earliest *flashback* in the story's time.

At **0:02:11** the music pauses and the gentle flute is replaced by a more powerful drumming and deeper instrumentation of the theme as the sleepy image ends. A cut takes us inside a car. The audience's view is from the backseat. Attorney Mitchell Stephens is about to enter a car wash!

There is a continuum in time to **Chapter 2, "Fathers and Daughters"** **@ 0: 03:35**. In an Extreme Long-Shot we see an older model car approach. The setting and its sounds designate a warehouse-factory area — tough and in disrepair — on the outskirts of town. A young woman defiantly struts from the passenger side of the car. The camera pans right following her into a telephone booth.

A cut returns us to Mitchell Stephens in his car inside the car wash. He answers his cell phone: The woman in the booth — his daughter Zoe — is calling collect.

The "now-time," the most up-to-date scene, or the ultimate moment of *present tense* is not recognized until **Chapter 5, "Mitchell and Allison" @ 0:18:06.**

Mitchell Stephens is onboard an airplane. He is having difficulty with his head set, and learns that the woman to his right — who offers her head set to him — is an old family friend.

The central events of the story continue in the time setting begun with the car wash.

In **Chapter 12, "The Spider Story" @ 0:56:21** we are returned to the (opening) high-angle shot of the sleeping family. The image rotates as Mitchell Stephens in voice over (VO) begins to tell about, "The summer we almost lost her... it happened one morning at this cottage we used to rent."

A Close-Up of Mitchell and Allison still aboard the airplane brings the story back to the "now-time," and Mitchell Stephens' story of the earliest time.

The structure is a confident crafting of events, arranged in parallel structures — in time and place — which are visually delineated. Flashbacks describe and expand the details of a terrible school bus accident.

The distribution of events is never confusing. The structure grips the audience in an expectation that more and more information will be forthcoming and comprehensible. This is a crucial point: Not yet having all the necessary story information is *not* the same as being confused and befuddled!

contrasts

The masterful time protraction in "The Battle on Ice" scene from the last chapter provides an opening to this one: Some thirty-eight years later *Dog Day Afternoon* "re-created" anticipation and tension with similar measures.

DOG DAY AFTERNOON

The robbery should have taken 10 minutes. 4 hours later, the bank was like a circus sideshow. 8 hours later, it was the hottest thing on live T.V. 12 hours later, it was all history. And it's all true.

AL PACINO in DOG DAY AFTERNOON

Chapter 26, "Bus Brigade Leaves" @ 1:51:01.

The bank robbers and their hostages take a good deal more than "real time" to get to the curb, and into the "get-away bus" waiting to take them to Kennedy Airport. But! *Here* and *now*, we'll focus on the success of such maneuverings by the *contrasts* in image and sound.

A quiet "hum," and soon a more "choppity-whirl" of an overhead helicopter greets a series of intercut shots: A high-angle Long-Shot looking past the bus, all its doors opened and waiting; an over-the-shoulder shot of a police marksman, the focus on the background view of the street and front of the bus; another angle in Long-Shot, over the top of the bus, this time a view further to the rear of the vehicle, and showing the first stirrings of people moving toward the bank's glass doors; a Medium-Long-Shot of a prone police marksman atop a vehicle of floodlights; FBI agent Sheldon and an undercover N.Y.C. officer in Close-Up watch the bank entranceway, and a Long-Shot from street level with a view along the wall of the bank: It is in this shot the exterior doors to the bank open and the group exits to the street. All becomes silent — the helicopter "flies off" — but for the footsteps of the circle of robbers and hostages.

Just as the stillness of the Russian peasants presented a contrast to the galloping Teutonic knights, the stillness of the police, FBI agents, and gathered crowd contrasts the moving robbers and hostages as they exit the bank, and their dash to get into the bus. Here, too, an extension in time "sees" the group (nearly) fill the bus two full times!

The contrast is then reversed. At **1:53:41** FBI agent Sheldon announces over his car radio, "We'll be starting up right now." Police cars start up, engines roar, and tires squeal as the patrol cars turn completely around, even bouncing up onto the sidewalk; helicopters gather in the air, their noise grows to overwhelming!

Meanwhile: Inside the closed bus, the hostages and robbers — in individual Close-Up portraits — sit hushed and still. The scene is a perfect display of European montage theory applied in conflicting juxtapositions; along with a little *contrasting* irony, as the scene's *motion* pictures are fortified in stillness.

Let's get to examples of *whole* story contrasts!

HIGH NOON

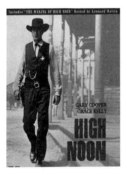

High Noon is a classic illustration of perhaps the most common of storytelling contrasts: Good vs. Evil.

Chapter 3, "Hanging Up His Star" @ 0:08:00

Will and Amy are married, and he has promised to end his career as a lawman. The Justice of the Peace, who performed the wedding ceremony says, "Marshall, turn in your badge." Good Will Kane responds, "To tell you the truth I hate to do this without your new marshall being here."

Seconds later Will learns that Frank Miller has been pardoned, that his brother Bob Miller and two other bad guys are at the train depot waiting for Frank's arrival, and that they plan to settle an old score with the Marshall. Will argues, "I think I ought to stay."

High Noon would not be considered the first "adult western" for this contrast alone. Amy is a Quaker, and a key reason that Will is retiring as marshall; they plan to open a store and settle down. Amy's peaceful spirituality initiates another key contrast during the climactic gun battle between Will and the Miller gang: Vengeance vs. Nonviolence.

Chapter 20, "Showdown" @ 1:21:12

Amy has vowed to leave Will when he decides to be in Hadleyville for the noon train's arrival. Upon hearing the first shot, Amy hurries back to town. She watches from upstairs at the Marshall's office as the Miller brothers — the two remaining bad guys — pin down the now wounded Will, in the Saddlery Shop.

At **1:22:09**, Bob Miller realizes that both guns are out of ammunition. He begins to reload, and is shot in the back at close range. As he falls forward we see Amy through a side window in the Marshall's office. She holds a revolver!

I think that while the genre contrast of Romance and Western certainly assists the work to adult viewing appeal, an additional contrast adjoins to the significance of the movie: Public (Community) Obligations vs. Private (Personal) Loyalties.

Andrei Tarkovsky's diploma film, *The Steamroller and the Violin*, presents an immediate contrast — and attractive allure — within its title. The film offers distinctions between the lovely sounds of Sasha's violin strings and the rattling rumbles of the heavy-duty construction "instruments"; the elegance of the music lesson studio and crumbling tough streets; the gentle creative arts and the more physical of labor.

THE STEAMROLLER AND THE VIOLIN

Chapter 8, "Sasha and Sergey Go Back To Work" @ 0:35:26

Sasha has learned that his new friend Sergey will be finishing work in the neighborhood this day. He hints with appreciated obviousness that he'd like to go with Sergey to a movie: "Did you see *Chapayev?*"

The story's contrasts are addressed — and "enforced" by Sasha's mother upon her return home.

Chapter 9, "Sergey Waits" @ 0:37:39

Sasha (the violin) and Sergey (the steamroller) have planned to meet at "7:00 sharp" to see a movie. Sasha is dressing when his mother arrives. From **0:37:39** through **0:38:54** (with a return to this set-up for some twenty-five additional seconds after cross-cutting to the waiting Sergey) is a beautifully choreographed shot of Sasha, Mother and camera coming together to a dressing table with mirror.

In *In The Blink of an Eye: A Persepctive on Film Editing*, Emotion and Story top editor Walter Murch's list of the six most vital considerations in determining a cut. Don't underestimate *contrasts'* link to both.

A most beautiful illustration of how *contrasts* stir an audience's emotional connection to story, educing tears of hope and smiles of charming joy — a simultaneous contrast in responses — can be found in *Born into Brothels*.

This Academy Award–winning documentary displays contrasts in culture, gender, social class and age.

BORN INTO BROTHELS

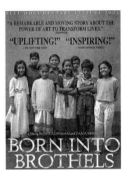

Chapter 10, "Photos by Avijit" @ **0:36:45**, adds contrasts in *Place*: A journey from infectious city alleyways to a new path and an enchanting ocean beach.

"Escaping" the red-light district of Calcutta, the children's bus trip to India's coast presents additional contrasts: Rest and Play; Dry and Wet; Motion and Still; Sullied and Clean.

THE EXORCIST

Chapter 1, "Iraq: Interesting Find" @ **0:00:43**. The new DVD release contains chapters which present material not in the original version. An unnecessary prologue introduces the dark street in Georgetown, and a Madonna.

I mention this as a brief caution: New versions of films — as in a Director's Cut — leave me skeptical; as does the routinely included Commentary. Additions are easily self-serving and, in all probability, have more to do with business, rather than with aesthetics, craft, improvements or educating.

Music of Middle Eastern instruments fades-in during the head credits. An Imam's call to Morning Prayer against a shimmering sun above a desert, setting a sequence of *immediate* contrast — Islam and Catholicism — and prophesy. A foreboding is prompted by Father Mirrin's archeological find in Iraq, and so the more obvious conflict in the story: Innocence and Evil.

This is however a contrast furnishing limited distinctions between a horror film and one of suspense.

Chapter 17, "You're Gonna Die Up There" @ 0:42:31

We are nearly one-third of the way into the film, and this is where the fundamentals of the Georgetown portion of the story begin. The essential plotting that puts forward contrasts generating ambivalence, intrigue and (at times) out-and-out fear.

A small group of friends remain at Chris' party; they sing-along at the piano. The camera moves from right to left, and "backs away" to an increasingly wide Master-Shot. One of the guests, a middle-aged NASA astronaut, stands to screen left, gesturing in rhythm to the singing, with a drink in his hand. The gathered group turns with a smile to see Regan who has entered the frame, her back to the camera. A Close-Up of Regan shows a spell-like stare; her lips, but a bit apart, hardly move as she softly "promises" the astronaut, "You're gonna die up there."

In Close-Up, the astronaut's eyes react quickly and just as suddenly shift downward. In Close-Up we see Regan's bare feet on the living room rug. Her pee begins to pour steadily and loudly across a cut to a Medium-Shot of startled guests; and a Medium Close-Up of a concerned and upset Chris, "Oh my God honey."

Chapter 18, "Make It Stop" @ 0:44:00

Chris has tucked Regan in for the night. She exits the bedroom still in her party evening dress. She begins to descend the stairs, the camera panning and tilting to follow. At the bottom of the stairs a housekeeper scrubs at the stain in the rug.

There is the quietest of ambiance, broken with pointless dialogue:

> CHRIS
> Is it coming out Willie?

> WILLIE
> Yes, I think so.

CHRIS
Good.

Chris seems about to return upstairs — accenting the ineffectual dialogue with the housekeeper — just before Regan's awful scream and call, "Mother!" has her hurry back to the bedroom. Bulbs on wall sconces flicker, and inside the room Chris is horror struck. Regan's bed bounces wildly. Chris throws herself onto the bed, embracing her daughter.

Chapter 20, "Temporal Lobe Diagnosis" @ 0:47:45

The title expresses the doctor's explanation of the events in Chapter 18: "a type of disturbance in the chemical-electrical activity of the brain... it causes bizarre hallucinations... and usually just before a convulsion." Chris tries to convince the doctor that what happened was neither an hallucination nor a convulsion, "The whole bed was thumping and rising off the floor... and shaking... with me on it."

At 0:50:38 procedures are underway to acquire brain scans for further diagnosis. Both the macabre and high-tech side of modern medicine — a *contrast* of dramatic value — are displayed.

Chapter 21, "This Sow Is Mine!" @ 0:52:08

Finally, the film embraces its predominant plot contrasts! Reverberating hums hoist a rack of skull X-rays on an illuminated wall. Reflections in the radiologist's eyeglasses depict another set of skull pictures sliding into his view. The doctors can find nothing!

A mostly exasperated Vincent Canby referred to the *The Exorcist* as "elegant occultist claptrap." He wrote in the December 27, 1973 issue of the *New York Times* that "[The film] is not... unintelligently put together... [T]he physical production and... the rhythm of the narrative, which achieves a certain momentum... is obviously intended to persuade us to suspend disbelief."

I'd venture to guess that the source of Canby's dislike of *The Exorcist* is, in large part, a result of the many literary-like subplots that hang about in the movie for far too long.

The "certain momentum" to which Vincent Canby ultimately reacts is in evidence when the story arrives (finally) at contrasts between Theology and Science; Mysticism and Knowledge; the Demonic and the Divine.

There are times within a story when a scene furnishes an immediate contrast from the larger settings of plot and genre, that is, the contrast is not (so) directly linked to the essentials of the story and its premise.

The overall structure of *The Bridge on the River Kwai* delivers one of the finest war films ever made, yet here is a good example of *contrast* that affords a respite — in this case as metaphor and in fact — which inescapably must, and does, bring the story and the audience back to "reality."

THE BRIDGE ON THE RIVER KWAI

Chapter 28, "Bathing with the Enemy" @ 1:50:25
A "cawing" sound, which turns out to be not a bird but a giant bat flying above the lush Burma jungle, opens the scene with a Fade-In. The call is as if a plea of "Help... help... help... help." A low-angle Long-Shot reveals leafless tree tops swathed in a score of more bats.

The camera tilts downward. A lightly audible babbling of water across and over rocks is increased, nearly "drowning" the songs of exotic birds. A bathing paradise rests below the bats — an immediate contrast certainly, and a hint: How long can this Eden-like garden last?

The commando team and their aides and guides bathe, and cleanse each other, in pools of perfect water held by the soft, smooth ancient rock formations.

Major Warden patrols past the camera with his automatic weapon, and a cut to an Extreme Long-Shot brings the major to the top of an easy waterfall. Laughter and chatter of the female aides can be heard as another downward tilt of the camera brings the eye to them in other pools of bathing delight.

The sublimely corporeal ecstasy unexpectedly, but unavoidably, ends with a piercing cry — a near-mimicking of the wildlife calls — when one of the lovely aides runs into the clutches of a Japanese soldier!

Hiroshima mon amour incorporates daring and unusual contrasts. The story begins within a compelling structure that blends the literary arts, film genres, forms, and styles:

Chapter 2, "Everything and Nothing" @ 0:02:12

The music is at once Western and Eastern; Modern and Primitive; Sensual and Dangerous. Are we viewing the Surreal or the Real? Is the form Narrative or Documentary? Are the voices a Dialogue or Narration; in Poetry or Prose?

The bodies move in love — or is it agony? What falls in spreading cover? It's sand! No, it's snow! Ice; beads of perspiration; droplets of glistening metallic particles?

The prevailing story contrast in *Hiroshima mon amour* is evident from the outset in the sexual encounter of the Japanese architect and the French actress. This contrast also plays out through the history each brings to the fleeting relationship:

Chapter 5, "Morning In Hiroshima" @ 0:18:30

A glorious morning and the French actress views bicyclists on the street below. In kimono and with her morning coffee — it does turn out *not* to be tea, and a subtle addition in contrast — she returns to the hotel room; an easy smile — in her eyes — of last night's reminiscence, as she takes notice of the still asleep architect. Listen to the change in the mood of the (music) score, *prior* to a Close-Up of the actress, from one of "sun and air" to an expression more menacing. The sleeping hand brings a memory of another lover's hand.

The story advances inquiries which contrast the circumstances created by the atomic bombing of Hiroshima, and the end of World War II: Conqueror and Vanquished; Joy and Despair. The character of the Japanese architect conveys an ironic contrast to the story's place: Build and Demolish.

This chapter brings to mind — my mind at least — the adage, "Opposites attract." Let's add, "Opposites confer immediate contrasts; and contrasts are a vital key to story attraction."

irony

Contrasts initiate opposites, and they in turn take a (good) turn to this chapter, and the value of its theme to story premise, subject matter, and a transfixing meaning, as in: Significance; Worth; Implication; Consequence.

Contrasts in degree and frequency in Pedro Almodóvar's *Talk to Her* are nothing less than astonishing: What might well be considered a film of the romantic vies with the platonic; probable characteristics of male and female contrast with the far less likely; opposing notions of gender, devotion, the idealization of desire, and the peculiar entanglement of characters provoke unforeseen *ironies*.

TALK TO HER

Chapter 2, "Benigno Martin, Nurse" @ 0:03:33

A Close-Up of the gently amusing Benigno begins the scene. We recognize him from Chapter 1. He was in the audience at a dance recital of *Café Muller*, choreographed by Pina Bausch, the music continuing into this chapter. He speaks to someone off screen: "The stage is full of wooden chairs and tables." Benigno is describing the performance as the camera tilts downward — the music fades-out — and soon pans right; and we come to realize, in the ease of the camera's motion and the male nurse's soothing temperament, that Benigno is grooming the tips of the sleeping Alicia's fingers. "You can't imagine how moving it was. There was a man sitting beside me, in his forties, good-looking. He cried several times from emotion." Benigno presents an autographed photo of Bausch as "a surprise" to his patient. He holds the photo to Alicia's closed eyes and reads the inscription: "I hope you overcome all your obstacles and dance again very soon."

A Close-Up of Alicia's face, and a cut to moving Close-Ups of Alicia's motionless body being bathed, reveals a receptacle at the front of her throat for a breathing attachment. Alicia is comatose.

Benigno and a female nurse tenderly wash Alicia's middle when they see that this month's menstruation has started.

Chapter 3, "Marco Zuloaga, Journalist" @ 0:07:37

Marco is in vigorous motion on a cross-country ski-like workout machine. We recognize him! He is the "good-looking" man who was sitting beside Benigno at the recital. The television "speaks" to him and he becomes curious, and soon fascinated, by an interview with bullfighter Lydia Gonzalez. He plans to do a story "in depth" about her.

The film thus establishes the four central characters.

Chapter 5, "Lydia & Marco" @ 0:12:50

Marco asks Lydia if they can speak, and she agrees if he'll drive her to Madrid. Marco proposes an article about her. It is a short ride and a quick rejection. Lydia suspects that Marco is only interested in the romantic gossip of her recent break-up with bullfighter Nino de Valencia. A relationship does take hold soon after Marco "rescues" her. A snake — Lydia's single phobia — has been left in her kitchen, and Marco bravely kills it and takes Lydia to a hotel.

Chapter 7, "Gored" @ 0:24:05

A masterful traveling shot holds Lydia in Close-Up as she marches across the arena. She stops mere yards from a heavy wooden door. A bull waits on the other side. The bull rushes into the courageously kneeling Lydia!

Chapter 8, "Nino de Valencia" @ 0:26:58

The opening shot — it is several weeks later — looks slightly upward to a Medium Close-Up of Lydia. The left side of her face and neck still show serious scratches; the lobe of her left ear is sutured, and a breathing tube attaches to her throat.

Chapter 9, "Cucurrucucu Paloma" @ 0:35:07

Marco has spent the night in Lydia's room. He exits to the hall to meet with her doctor. En route he peeks into a room with a partially opened door. Marco opens it a bit more. A beautiful naked Alicia awaits her bath. Marco notices a nurse at the far side of the bed, and, embarrassed, he moves away. Marco no sooner exits when we hear: "Rosa, close the door, there's a draft." It is Benigno, and we can be certain of that when he approaches the camera and closes the door. Alicia and Lydia, both comatose, are in the same hospital on the same floor! Here we have irony as mythological: Coincidence so profound it must surely result from providence commanded by the Gods.

The most common definition of irony links it to literary or theatrical forms: *The use of words to express the opposite of what one really means*; although the etymology from the Greek *eiron* reveals *dissembler*: Hypocrite, imposter, fraud, faker, bigot, cheat. These define far greater intrigue and value for storytellers and filmmakers.

The *dissembler* meanings are volatile in their absoluteness, and cantankerous in their evaluation. Let's start with a film that ironically grants sympathy to a faker.

THE SHOP ON MAIN STREET

Chapter 16, "Closed for Inventory" @ 0:44:25
Tono has been appointed Aryan Controller, by his Fascist brother-in-law, of a button shop owned by Mrs. Lautmann, an elderly Jewish widow. Tono arrives at work to find the shop closed, and Mrs. Lautmann unwilling to open on the Sabbath.

On the day of the button shop's transfer by decree, Tono was told that, but for the generous alms of other Jews, Mrs. Lautmann is destitute. There are very few, if any, buttons in the stacked boxes!

An arrangement has been made with the Jewish community of the Czech village for Tono to be "like a son" to the old woman, and in return the community will pay him a wage.

The DVD's chapter title gives away this day's ingenious solution: An Aryan is now the official manager, and the shop should be open on Saturdays. At **0:47:22**, Tono hurries off and finds Kuchar, the "arranger" for Tono and Lautmann. Tono returns @ **0:48:26** with a notice which he pins to the shuttered doors: Closed For Inventory.

Yes! Tono is a faker-fraud (far worse if we consider the Holocaust) to Mrs. Lautmann; to his wife — who is ecstatic that she and her handyman peasant husband have been guaranteed (another irony) the riches of the merchant class — and to his charitable (isn't that *ironic?*) brother-in-law.

Sympathy for Tono is derived by contrasts in his complicity within the context of the story's *opposing* forces.

The prevailing use of irony in modern cinema (and even more commonly in television) is "synonymous" with the meaning of the word at its most mean-spirited: sarcasm, ridicule, taunt and derision. This version of irony may hold an irresistible appeal in adolescence and explains a common fondness in students. This is explored in Jedediah Purdy's book, *For Common Things: Trust and Irony in America*.

Ballad of a Soldier provides an illustration of an earlier (1959), unsullied (maybe naïve) and poetic application of *irony*.

BALLAD OF A SOLDIER

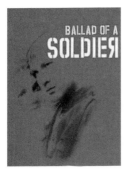

Chapter 18, "Sosnovka" & Chapter 19, "Mother & Son" @ 1:20:32

Alyosha, a Russian soldier in the Second World War, has finally made it home to his small village — Sosnovka — and his mother. He has been granted a six day leave to honor his battlefield heroism; turning down a medal, he asked instead to be allowed to return to his village to fix the leaking roof of his mother's house. Alyosha's encounters en route have caused delays, many self-imposed by his compassion.

As he enters Sosnovka aboard a small truck he is recognized by village women: "That is Alyosha; Katarina's son!" A woman hurries to get the news to his mother: "Katarina is in the fields. Go get her quickly."

Alyosha leaps from the truck, bounds up the wooden steps and joyfully knocks at the old door. There is no answer. He hurries next door; his cousin Zoika greets him and confirms that his mother is at work in the fields.

The old truck driver hurries Alyosha and Zoika toward the farm fields; their ride in the back of the open truck is joined to shots of Katarina running to see her son.

Alyosha's decency — many selfless deeds for strangers — has *ironically* sacrificed all the time awarded him. He embraces his mother in one long hug. In the distance the truck driver honks and honks a raspy horn: Alyosha must start back to the front.

A contemporary presentation of the story might instill a sardonic theme, "No good deed goes unpunished," rather than a noble expression of the story's more "innocent" irony. Alyosha's heroism on the battlefield is surpassed by his heroic benevolence.

I don't deny the effective uses within more selfishly ridiculing definitions. There is nothing intrinsically wrong with wittiness, or a dramatically functional repartee of sarcasm or cynicism. The difference is in an ongoing, ridiculing tone which signifies an *overall* subtext, rather than in distinctions which are to be expected within a scene's context.

Let's begin with a couple of first-rate and scene-relevant examples of irony as sarcasm and mockery.

BREAKER MORANT

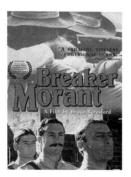

Index 1, Chapter 8, "Ambush" @ 0:11:26.
Major Thomas enters the confinement quarters of Morant, Witton, and Handcock. He has been assigned to represent the three at their court martial. The opening dialogue is jousting sarcasm:

HANDCOCK
New South Wales Mounted....
what sort of a lawyer are you?

THOMAS
They haven't locked me up yet...what sort of a soldier are you?
Are they looking after you here? It looks a bit Spartan....

MORANT
Well, it's not exactly the Hotel Australia....

HANDCOCK
More like a coffee palace... no grog!

With that, Major Thomas tosses Handcock a flask of whiskey to share, and the men get down to a discussion of the seriousness of the charges.

Through effectively "disguised" exposition — dialogue with lots of questions and answers — the balance of the scene provides the audience with the principal outline of the plot.

BURNT BY THE SUN

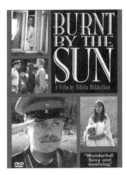

Chapter 26, "Taking the Colonel for a Ride" @ 1:56:49

Colonel Kotov is seated between two Cheka (Stalin's secret police, and predecessor to the KGB) men in the back seat of a car. To his right is Mitya — *ironically* known to Kotov's young daughter Nadya as "Uncle" Mitya — the ranking officer of the four Cheka agents. The audience recognizes that Kotov is a target of the Stalinist purges, and Kotov, a hero of the Russian Revolution, imagines the same. In a coincidence — another form of irony — Colonel Kotov begins his little jousting by pulling a *flask* from his tunic pocket.

> KOTOV
> Mitya. I have what you need.

The agent to Kotov's left attempts to take the flask.

> KOTOV
> Calm down. You think I'll poison myself?
> Not at all.

Kotov offers his flask to two of the agents; they refuse.

> KOTOV
> (offering the flask)
> Mitya?

> MITYA
> No, thank you.

Here is a lovely and restrained bit of *irony*: Mitya's rebuff — you'll note he looks away and out the car window — is unexpectedly well-mannered given the context of the car ride. This "refined" *irony* is soon surpassed by exaggeratedly *ironic* self-righteousness.

> KOTOV
> (again offers his flask)
> A drop of cognac old man?

> AGENT
> (in the front passenger seat)
> I don't drink and I don't smoke!

Isn't it *ironic* that Kotov is not carrying a flask of vodka? Or is he? Perhaps he is, and can't resist the enticing sarcasm. Kotov interjects a few more teasing gems:

> KOTOV
> Of course I won't offer any to the driver.

When he is asked to turn over his pistol:

> KOTOV
> Careful. It's loaded. Do you know how to use it?

Later:

> KOTOV
> Perhaps we could go to a restaurant. It's my treat. No?

The irony supplies a harassing contrast to the scene's incisive turn: menacing and lethal. The scene illustrates irony that reaches for something more vital and sustaining than ridicule alone. There is gripping psychological veracity that rouses purpose — and meaning.

Here are a few more precious aspects to "irony":

1. A combination of circumstances that are the opposite of what is, or might be, expected.

2. An attitude of mind, characterized by recognition of the incongruities of experience. Or, as Woody Allen once observed, "No matter how cynical you get, you can't keep up!"

3. A numinous twist in an outcome.

This last holds — as in *Talk to Her* — the primitively potent appeal of mythology: The sway of the Gods on our fortunes and fate.

A good illustration of the first — and also the third in the larger context which includes *Manon of the Spring*, the second film in the epic, "which follows (all) the characters to their fate" — can be found in the "doings" and purpose of Cesar Soubeyran (Le Papet) and his nephew Ugolin (Galinette) in *Jean de Florette*.

JEAN DE FLORETTE

Chapter 1, @ 0:04:38

Ugolin has returned from military service. After a welcoming by Uncle Cesar, he climbs the rugged Provence hillside of the family's farm land. Entering a long closed stone outbuilding — note the sandy dust roused into the air, and crumbs of dry earth and pebbles on the small table — Ugolin opens his suitcase, and devotedly sets about unwrapping roll upon roll of newspaper that safeguards an undisclosed plot — *plot* as in Ugolin's scheme; a parcel of land, and as narrative scenario. Irony is well underway!

Ugolin adoringly removes fresh green seedlings! The gentle piano notes assist in the emotional subtext of Ugolin's "child-like" anticipated venture.

Let me call your attention to a somewhat conspicuous cut @ **0:05:46**. Ugolin exits the frame to the left, and a cut takes us to an Extreme Close-Up of hands planting a row of the seedlings. When Ugolin exits, we are left with a background — the center of the screen — that is in soft focus; our eyes are suddenly jolted left again when a shadow hits the wooden door.

Remember to "watch out for exits" (or entrances) across a cut. This should be of particular concern with exits, as in this example: the shot, and so our eyes, no longer has a focal point; our eyes — and minds — will likely, if for only an instant, be disengaged from occupied viewing.

At dinner in Cesar's house Chapter 1, @ **0:08:28**, Ugolin, asked if he has "any plans," answers "Maybe." Cesar expresses a heartfelt wish to restore the family's orchard, "to the way it was in my father's prime" by planting a thousand trees of figs, plums, and almonds. "It'll be like a cathedral — and every farmer will make the sign of the cross." Ugolin interrupts his uncle's dream, and declares, "I have another idea." But, when his uncle asks about his idea, Ugolin pours red wine into his soup and bringing the bowl to his mouth, answers, "It's a secret."

There is a hideous overriding irony in *Jean de Florette*: Uncle and nephew perpetrate merciless deeds so as to implement Ugolin's plan. His "secret" is to grow beautiful carnations!

Breaker Morant also supplies a very good example of the second form of irony:

BREAKER MORANT

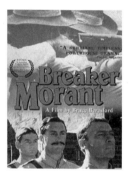

Index 9, Chapter 37, "The Verdict" @ 1:28:40
A champagne bottle cork is popped in celebration of an official acquittal on one of the court martial charges. The cheers and toasts conclude on Morant's soft prophetic phrase, "Live every day as if it were going to be your last; for one day you're sure to be right."

Captain Alfred Taylor — himself facing proceedings — asks to speak privately to Morant.

TAYLOR
I wouldn't be too certain of this verdict, Harry....

Taylor gives good reasons why (at the least) "a simple fellow like Handcock, and a black sheep" (Morant) are more than likely to be found guilty on the remaining charge.

Listen and you'll hear the rejoicing in the other room become chatter which disappears in the "wake" of a slowly increasing bagpipe chant: An ironic foreboding!

MORANT
We won't be missed....

> TAYLOR
> I could have a horse standing by for you... some of the guards
> are sympathetic.
>
> MORANT
> Where would I go?
>
> TAYLOR
> Lorenzo Marques; Portuguese territory. You could take a boat
> and... see the world.
>
> MORANT
> I've seen it.

Take note of the many beats before Morant's response to "see the world." Without them, "I've seen it" would be irony deficient. Instead it would hold a benign point of fact: Morant would be advising Taylor as one might a travel agent.

Breaker Morant also holds an overriding irony: Harry Morant, fighting in South Africa to help keep the British Empire together, is an officer charged with murdering enemy prisoners and a German missionary... and he is a poet!

THE VIRGIN SPRING

Chapter 12, "Hospitality" @ 0:45:26
A Fade-In brings a view of a darkening spring sky above the Tore family farm. Wild calls add to the chill as night advances.

Herr Tore stands as a sentinel, his large hands clasp his belt; he is clothed as a king. His eyes adjust right. In a point of view (POV) shot — no matter the contrast extremes in light and dark — we are unnerved by the alarming irony: Three goat-herd brothers stand behind the livestock gate at the Tore farm. The audience was witness to the elder brothers' brutal rape and murder of Karin, the daughter and only child of Herr Tore.

The chapter's title, "Hospitality," offers irony: Herr Tore will provide warmth and sustenance to his daughter's killers! Whereas the *audience* knows of the goat-herd brothers' shocking deed, this illustration from *The Virgin Spring* guides us to:

dramatic irony

Alexander Mackendrick, director of such classics as *The Ladykillers*, *The Man in the White Suit*, and *Sweet Smell of Success*, and former dean and teacher of the California Institute of the Arts' Film School, compiled thousands of pages of notes during his twenty years as a teacher. Paul Cronin, editor, author, and film-maker, has made Mackendrick's teaching techniques and filmmaking philosophy accessible in *On Film-Making: An Introduction to the Craft of the Director*. The book contains an entire chapter on Dramatic Irony: "It occurs to me," MacKendrick writes, "that the device of dramatic irony is so standard a formula of dramatic construction that, in truth, it is quite rare to find any really well-structured story that does not make use of it."

Dramatic Irony: The effect achieved by leading an audience to understand an incongruity between a situation and the accompanying speeches, while a character remains unaware. More simply and directly: When the audience has information that a character — or characters — does not have, or misunderstands.

Playwright Tom Stoppard, in a lecture some years ago, provided a perfect illustration of dramatic irony's various influences and how the stratagem in structure is essential to the storyteller's establishment of conflict, tension, and humor. Dramatic Irony might even identify genre. Stoppard's examples build Drama, Suspense, and Comedy:

A man and woman stand in a living room before a small bar. The man asks, "Would you like a drink?" "That would be nice," the woman responds. The man fills two glasses from a whiskey bottle, and hands a glass to the woman. So far, so trivial!

But, what if the audience knows that the woman recently signed on to Alcoholics Anonymous? What if the audience knows that the man is a suspected poisoner? What if the audience knows that, earlier in the day, the man's room-mate used the whiskey bottle for a urine sample?

Chapter 2, "A Murder in Mexico" @ 0:00:58

An Extreme Close-Up displays a science fiction–like contraption of batteries, wires and kitchen timer in someone's hands. The stranger's right hand sets the timer to less than five minutes. The laughter of a woman spins the bomber to screen left, and the camera sweeps left with the turn and finds a couple far in the background, walking along a street under an archway. The man and woman — arm in arm — turn to screen right, disappearing behind a wall of an open shop. The bomber runs right as well, his shadow cast along a parallel wall at the other end of the shop. The camera follows the bomber, catching up with him as he opens the trunk of a sleek Cadillac convertible, leaves the device inside, closes the trunk, and hurries away as the man and woman approach the Cadillac. The camera rises to a high-angle Long-Shot as the couple gets into the car — jazz from the car radio supplants the Latin rhythms of the sound track. The high-angle view follows the car down the main street, into the busy-ness of the border town's night life.

A single continuous shot (running 3:18) lasts until the bomb and car explode at **0:04:16**.

Orson Welles' opening scene gives perfect expression to Alfred Hitchcock's words: "There is no terror in the gunshot; only in the anticipation of it!"

Here's a beautifully easy, and more delicate, rendering of dramatic irony from Mr. Hitchcock:

PSYCHO

Chapter 5, "A Woman on the Run" @ 0:13:37

Marion Crane has impulsively stolen $40,000 in cash from her realtor boss Mr. Lowry. She flees her home in Phoenix, Arizona. Suffering the effects of a headache, she drives into the night, hardly able to keep awake; headlights from on coming traffic indicate her eyes' straining fatigue.

A fade-in brings us to a Master-Shot which opens this chapter. Marion's car sits at the base of a power pole in a rural landscape. A California Highway Patrol car drives past, pauses and backs up to a position behind her car. The officer exits his vehicle and walks toward Marion's car. She is asleep on the front seat, but is awakened by the officer's knocks at her window.

Marion's efforts to portray herself as a sleepy innocent motorist are naïvely amateurish and raise the officer's suspicions. He asks to see her driver's license; and a Medium-Shot @ **0:15:44** heightens the tension: Marion, with her back to the officer, removes the envelope containing the stolen cash from her handbag, slipping it between her bag and the seat, before fetching her wallet and license.

Dramatic Irony cultivates a compound tension; it fosters ambivalence in the audience. The audience knows that Marion is "on the run" with stolen money — she is committing a crime — and presumes the officer does not; but has word gone out to law enforcement?

During Marion's encounter with the officer we feel an urge to call out to her with guidance in feigning innocence. Dramatic Irony so fully engages the audience in psychological projection/identification that we become desperate to see Marion escape capture. We experience a near-exhausting relief when, after following Marion, the Highway Patrol car exits the road to screen left as we watch out the back window, and Marion watches in her rear-view mirror.

This scene points to one of the vast and wondrous characteristics of movie storytelling: The instantaneous — and continuous — audience transformation from observer to participant; and how Dramatic Irony contributes a most important function: Consider the "participatory" Close-Up of the Highway Patrolman @ **0:14:22**, his face filling the frame of Marion's driver side window as Marion (we) in her (our) close to flustered conscience looks into the oversized dark lenses of the officer's glasses, and Marion's (our) point of view (POV) out the windshield @ **0:15:58**, as the officer checks her (our) Arizona license plate.

Dramatic Irony holds so much staying (engaged) power, an entire story can benefit.

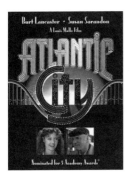

Chapter 2, "Family" @ 0:02:12

Dave watches a drug drop in a telephone booth in what turns out to be Philadelphia. He collects the dope (cocaine) before the dealers get to it.

Dave and his pregnant girlfriend Chrissie make their way to Atlantic City, New Jersey, and a "reunion" with Sally, Dave's ex-wife and Chrissie's sister.

Chapter 3, "Grace" @ 0:13:31

Dave steals Sally's wallet.

Chapter 7, "Abracadabra" @ 0:27:37

Dave obtains the help of Lou Pascal, Sally's elderly neighbor and voyeuristic admirer, to help weigh and "cut" — with powdered Italian baby laxative — the "stolen" cocaine.

Chapter 9, "Caught" @ 0:36:24

Dave promises, "there's another hundred in it" if Lou delivers the dope to a customer in a hotel: "I can't, not the way I'm dressed. You look sharp."

At **0:38:20** the drug dealers arrive to catch Dave on the street. They kill him!

Chapter 11, "Born Again" @ 0:43:21

The police arrive at the oyster bar where Sally works. They have her wallet. They take her to the Atlantic City Medical Center's Frank Sinatra Wing to identify Dave. Lou is there to offer his assistance.

Chapter 13, "Back on the Map" @ 0:53:28

Lou, following Dave's technique, "cuts" some more cocaine; makes funeral arrangements for Dave; purchases a dapper all-white outfit, and makes another delivery to Dave's hotel customer.

Chapter 16, "Numbnuts" @ 1:08:25

The drug dealers are waiting outside the apartment building for Sally. Lou is with her; they've spent an afternoon of lunch and flirting. The dealers shove the "old man" aside; Sally is hit, her clothes and pocketbook torn apart, and her cassette player smashed. But Sally does not have the dope; remember Sally doesn't even know about the dope! At **1:11:56** Sally finds everything in her apartment turned upside down and shredded! In the bathroom, crouched behind the toilet is Chrissie, chanting Krishna prayers.

At **1:14:30** Sally learns that Dave and her sister came to Atlantic City to sell the dope Dave got his hands on in Philadelphia. Chrissie tells Sally that "Dave went out with (Lou) that old man." Sally finds cocaine residue on the Weight Watchers scale in Lou's kitchen.

More than 90% of the movie is complete before Sally catches up with all the information the audience has been gathering; and now she looks to catch up with Lou.

It is of value to consider a kind of opposite in Dramatic Irony: When a character knows something the audience does not. We can assume that a character has lots of information — a good deal of it personal history — that is of little interest, and unrelated to the needs of the story. What is relevant, and, in this opposite scenario, essential is that the audience is somehow "signaled" that a character has realized some meaningful information.

Let's begin with a wonderful cliché. It is wonderful because it so perfectly says a character has figured something out:

THE DAY OF THE JACKAL

Chapter 13, "A Ticket to Paris" @ 1:57:58

The French government has been tracking an international assassin who is targeting President Charles de Gaulle. The killer (code name Jackal) is in the country, but the likely *time* of his planned attempt is unknown, until:

Attending a meeting of high government officials, Deputy Commissioner Claude Lebel — a detective personally assigned the task of finding the Jackal — suddenly realizes the time threat: "Excuse me. It's just occurred to me that we have *two days* to catch the Jackal." Here is a very direct indicator by way of dialogue that Lebel knows something we don't. The government officials overlap each others' inquiry with murmurs of, "What…

why... how do you know?" Of course the filmmakers now have the audience eager to learn what Lebel knows; but instead of disclosing the information at this moment, Lebel adds, "It was silly of me not to have seen it before. Am I right in thinking the president has no engagements outside the palace today, tomorrow or Saturday?" The Minister replies, "Nothing." Lebel gives the hint-breaking news, "And what is Sunday, August 25?" A Close-Up of the Minister plays out the great cliché: "Of — *he smacks his left palm to his forehead* — course! Liberation Day!"

The Parallel Editing in *The Day of the Jackal* is especially effective because it balances an ongoing structure of back and forth "reporting" between the Jackal, international intelligence agencies and Lebel, in a concert of Dramatic Irony.

Here are two illustrations of "letting the audience *know* a character knows something" that are far more inventive.

THE VERDICT

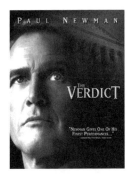

Chapter 16 , "A Meeting" & Chapter 17, "The Admitting Nurse" @ 1:33:10

Attorney Frank Galvin and his partner Mick review the "insults" directed at Galvin by one of the surgical nurses who has refused to testify in a medical malpractice suit, as they try to figure out who she is protecting:

> GALVIN
> You guys are a bunch of whores. You don't care who you hurt... you've got no loyalty.

> MICK
> One of the nurses?

> GALVIN
> Who? They're all testifying. Everyone who was in the operating room is testifying.

> MICK
> Okay? Who wasn't in the operating room?

Mick leaves the small office to get a glass of water from the cooler in the ante room. He disappears behind the doorway frame of Galvin's office. Galvin sits and the camera lowers behind him.

                    GALVIN
          The Admitting Nurse?
Mick returns with his water.

                    MICK
          What did she do?

                    GALVIN
          She took down the history…

                    MICK
          The history?

In Medium-Shot Galvin, with a cigarette in his right hand, reads from the document:

                    GALVIN
          Yeah. How old are you? How many children do you have?

The ending inflection is clear signal that there's more to read. Galvin's eyes look up from the document; he leans back in his chair and draws one more inhale on his cigarette. Ah-ha! He now knows something. He gets up in a quick motion that sees him press the cigarette into an ashtray. He takes his jacket and coat, along with the single sheet. He walks in the direction of Mick, the camera panning left with him as he moves into a Close-Up. Galvin hands Mick the sheet — the camera comes to rest — as he exits the office, closing the door behind him. Mick reads from the document:

                    MICK
          How old are you? How many children do you have?
          When did you last eat?

The reference to eating has everything to do with the plaintiff's claim that "the wrong anesthetic was given" to Galvin's client.

Here is another. Without dialogue!

Chapter 17, "The Admitting Nurse" @ 1:38:06

The "discovery" of an Admitting Nurse seems to dead end. She can't be found!

A Medium-Shot, of Galvin's office door, watches a small bundle of mail coming through the slot and dropping to the floor. A pan right begins: It calls attention to the silence of the office; it accentuates "early in the day" as the pan passes a wide interior doorway, allowing us to see light from a street side window shining across a wall, and especially reflected off of a leather couch upon which sleeps Galvin's lady friend and assistant, Laura. The camera continues its right pan; before it comes to rest, we hear the sliding sound of a metal cabinet drawer. The pan ends on Galvin in the background. He is holding a six-pack ring of Bud. In the foreground of screen right sleeps Galvin's partner Mickey, on another couch. Galvin frees up one can of beer and goes for the mail. With the beer can tucked under his chin he begins sorting through the mail. A New England Telephone Company bill fills the frame. In a Close-Up, Galvin stares down at his telephone bill. He takes the beer can out from under his chin. *Galvin has "figured" something out!*

François Truffaut grants a double — or is it triple — bit of Dramatic Irony?

THE 400 BLOWS

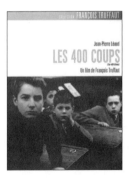

Chapter 2, "Antoine's Home Life" @ 0:24:07

Antoine and his friend have been cutting school. After an afternoon of games and other amusements, the two boys, in an Extreme Long-Shot, walk along a street. Another Extreme Long-Shot brings our attention to a kissing couple, near center frame in the busy Paris setting. The sound of heavy traffic is maintained across the cut. A Medium Long-Shot brings us behind the "kissing woman," her blonde hair blocking the face of the man. A Medium-Shot in profile now reveals that the woman is Antoine's mother; the man is not the boy's father. A cut to a Medium Long-Shot catches Antoine and his friend.

We see that Antoine notices (a cut brings us back to the Medium-Shot of the profile kissing couple) his mother and the "other" man. Mother spots Antoine, and immediately turns away. Antoine, in the Medium Long-Shot, hurries his friend off.

In eight seconds there are six cuts; an inter-cutting back and forth of the Medium-Shot of Mother and the Medium Long-Shot of Antoine! Both Antoine and his mother quickly catch on to what the audience knows. And what the father does not!

subplot

Film's narrative often snags itself when it attempts to duplicate a literary form by way of a *detailed* or *precise* adaptation, or when it imitates literature's capacity to carry subplots. A novel can more easily handle character histories — sometimes presented as flashbacks in movies — or add-on characters that remain non-interfering, because literature can proficiently give simple justification in a word (or two) to describe secondary connections without an implied assurance, or need, of follow-up. In cinema optional extras usually cause obstacles to the rhythmic current of the story.

Offering a seeming contradiction to the proverb "one picture is worth ten thousand words," David Mamet, in *On Directing Films*, gives examples of screenwriting that can't — and ought not — be filmed!

Before giving subplot examples — durable, debatable, or flawed — from a few of our fifty DVDs, let me make use of a subplot that would have been better deleted from its adaptation. I think the example, from *Brokeback Mountain*, is instructive, "seeing" as it is easily inconsequential, even if superfluous in literary form, while in the film it is a definite intrusion. It is, in its brief visual display, made conspicuously crucial by burdensome questions it brings up, and markedly so, as no trace of an answer is ever supplied.

In Annie Proulx's story, Ennis emphasizes to Jack the great threat the two would face should they become partners in ranching and love, "these two old guys ranched together down home, Earl and Rich — Dad would pass a remark when he seen them... I was what, nine years old and they found Earl dead in an irrigation ditch." Ennis describes the pitilessly mutilated body of Earl adding, "Dad made sure I seen it. Took me to see it. Me and K.E."

K.E. is Ennis' older brother, and on the preceding page in the novella he is introduced in response to Jack's, "I never figured you to throw a dirty punch." As a child Ennis had suffered under K.E.'s surprise attacks, "slugged me silly every day." His dad was adamant, "you got to take him unawares... make him feel some pain." Ennis let loose a series of his own take-by-surprise punches. K.E. is an avoidable subplot *even* in the Proulx story, but in the film's flashback presentation he is utterly pointless, and harmful!

In literary form Earl and Rich contribute but a trifling, except perhaps to the story's disadvantage: They nurture a strong inclination to be reading *their story*, rather than the plot-in-progress about a relationship-in-progress. Even Dad is of small value. It can be inferred — biologically — that each and every character we encounter has a mom and dad. Neither ancestry nor progeny guarantee character believability! The whole bygone tale is surely a dispensable warning — to Jack and the reader — of the all too common loathing of homosexuals in way too many locales. But! My point here is that Ennis' *telling* in Annie Proulx's book "sneaks on by" with modest mindful notice, "stealing" zilch from the narrative flow.

In the movie's flashback we *see* Dad, young Ennis, and K.E. They are, in image, clearly and too fully in attendance! Why — even if the filmmakers can't resist the flashback — include K.E.?

It is not unusual to find a barely endurable subplot which furnishes back-story exposition. Here's an example in which the *subplot characterization* also serves as an unnecessary machination in foreshadowing.

TOUCH OF EVIL

Chapter 4, "Tanya" @ 0:16:48

Taking time out from a murder investigation, Captain Quinlan stops in to visit an old flame. A pianola plays, as he wanders into a house on a trash-strewn street. The building is neighbor to an oil rig tower.

Tanya (pronounced Ta'- na in the film), smoking a small cigar, advises, "We're closed." Quinlan doesn't budge. He takes a bite of a candy bar. Tanya doesn't recognize her "old friend, Hank Quinlan": "You should lay off those candy bars."

Chapter 15, "All Used Up" @ 1:34:10

With his partner Pete and Vargas "closing in" on Quinlan, he visits Tanya and the pianola. Tanya still smokes a small cigar. Quinlan insists that she read his, "future" for him. "You haven't got any… your future is all used up." The contrivance of Tanya is particularly apparent because the time of the story is so conspicuous: In little more than a day the dramatic intentions are redundantly obvious; the mysterious gypsy is a cliché.

Remember how far into the total running time of *The Exorcist* the story actually begins, and Vincent Canby's annoyance? Subplot(s)!

THE EXORCIST

Chapter 5, "On the Set" @ 0:13:01

A film shoot is underway in the Washington, D.C. area. A college campus demonstration provides the scene's overall chaos. Chris MacNeil holding a copy of the screenplay exits her location trailer to grumble to the director: "Burke! Look at this damn thing. It just doesn't make sense." It is ironic that MacNeil grumbles just prior to the director being asked, "Is this scene really essential?" The film pauses in redundant subplot!

A movie in production as subplot also includes Father Karras, a character fundamental to the story's plot and dramatic necessities, who happens to be in the crowd of onlookers.

Chapter 6, "Chris' Walk Home" @ 0:14:58

Here I begin to feel Mr. Canby's irritation: Chris' walk home unites dubious sub-plotting with labored foreshadowing. Note the "disturbing" motorcycle sound, the windswept habits of strolling nuns, the bogus mystery of spying Father Karras — the audience saw him view Chris, and now we see her spot him — as he tries to bolster a self-doubting priest while a jet airliner roars overhead, and, of course, the film's musical theme endeavors to hold all this together. Each and every subplot develops into supplementary subplots.

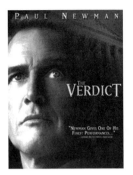

Chapter 4, "A Client" @ 0:15:40

Frank Galvin has been given a medical malpractice case as plaintiff's attorney. Following his first meeting with the family of his client the scene shifts to the office of the archdiocese of Boston, the "representatives" of the Catholic Hospital, a defendant in the case. The bishop is being briefed about the opposition via a dossier on Galvin.

The scene illustrates Dramatic Irony: The audience knows that Galvin's adversaries are canny — maybe even uncanny — and likely capable of anything to defeat him. It is also an example of Irony: A representative of the Church behaving less charitably and far more calculating than the teachings of Jesus.

The Cape Cod Casualty Company's adjuster summarizes Galvin's biographical information mentioning that Frank "Married Patricia Harrington, 1960." We see a picture of Patricia; and learn that after joining Stearns, Harrington, Pierce that same year, Galvin later found himself in legal jeopardy, resigned from the firm, and was divorced in 1970.

In literary form — a novel by Barry Reed — the telling of this information holds a strong appeal; it provides authenticity. But the appeal is prompt and perfunctory; it reinforces a plausible world while not meddling in the central plot, or premise.

Patricia Harrington does *appear* again…

Chapter 9, "Laura" @ 0:40:08

… in a frame on an end table in Frank's bedroom.

Frank and Laura — a beautiful woman who Frank has enjoyed noticing in his favorite neighborhood saloon — return to his apartment. With drinks in hand they awkwardly embrace. Laura sees Patricia's photo. Frank turns the photo face down. Laura smiles assuredly, "That's all right" and begins unbuttoning her blouse.

Frank's legal (predicament) history easily affixes to the central plot; his marriage doesn't, especially because that subplot adds a supplementary sub-subplot about Galvin's relationship to his father-in-law. It certainly isn't necessary for Patricia's photo to be in his apartment.

Chapter 8, "Hound's Tooth Clean" @ 0:50:13

Frank Serpico's relationship to Laurie begins as a subplot that can effectively link to the story's central necessities. Instead it establishes a character who functions as little more than a doubly redundant sounding board for already obvious exposition.

Laurie and Frank laugh and smooch, interrupted by a telephone call. Captain McClain is on the line. Frank has sought the Captain's counsel and assistance in transfers to "clean" precincts. Frank asks the Captain to "hold on a minute please, sir," connects a listening device to the earpiece of the phone, and hits the Play/Record buttons on a cassette recorder.

McClain tells Frank that, as he'd offered, he's met with Inspector Palmer, who assured him "that the 7th Division is as clean as a hound's tooth."

Frank thanks McClain, and is barely off the telephone when he reports to Laurie, "McClain says that Palmer says that the 7th is as clean as a hound's tooth." Frank doesn't respond to Laurie's unease — and relevant question in story time and deed — about his recording calls, "When did you start doing that?"

Chapter 11, "Priorities Outside the Department" @ 1:10:34

Following a scene in which Frank (and so too the audience) learns that Detective Bob Blair's contact, Jerry Berman, is going to the Mayor's office to report Frank's experience with widespread police corruption, and the department's inaction, Frank and his English sheepdog return home.

"Well? Tell me what happened," asks Laurie. "That guy is gonna go to the Mayor." Frank lifts a laughing Laurie and shouts, "To the Mayor!"

At **1:11:26** a cut takes us to a Close-Up of Jerry Berman; his head down, "I couldn't be any more embarrassed. It's like a personal defeat. However, there are priorities." Jerry explains the city's concern about the potential of a long hot summer of unrest and rioting, and that the Mayor cannot alienate the police. At **1:12:14** Frank arrives home to report to Laurie, "They're all rotten. Chickenshit. The whole fucking system's corrupt."

Let's see the lovely and promising start of Frank's and Laurie's relationship. I think it irresistibly kept Laurie from removal:

Chapter 7, "A Note from Joyce Max" @ 0:47:40

First, what does the title mean? Who is Joyce Max? That's what it says in the DVD's Scene Selections and the accompanying insert, though the reference in the opening scene of the chapter is to "Jewish Max," a guy who includes Frank in his bribes to the 93rd Precinct.

Frank sits in his backyard garden, refreshed with breakfast and strong coffee. With his dog Alfie alongside, Frank listens to opera. The above-angle Long-Shot allows us to see over the property's wall to a neighboring yard. In this shot, Laurie exits her back door. She holds a bucket of paint, a can of thinner and rag, her blue top lightly spattered with white paint. The dialogue makes patent the charm of the scene:

> LAURIE
> Is that Bjoerling?
>
> FRANK
> No. It's DiStefano.
>
> LAURIE
> I was sure it was Bjoerling.
>
> FRANK
> You could hear it better over here.
>
> LAURIE
> That's an invitation, right?
>
> FRANK
> Right. For coffee.
>
> LAURIE
> I'll have to take a rain check. I'm due at the hospital.
>
> FRANK
> Why don't you call in sick? Perfect place.

                    LAURIE
Not me.

                    FRANK
What are you dedicated or something?

                    LAURIE
That's right. I'm dedicated. Most men can't stand it.

                    FRANK
Well, what do they know?

                    LAURIE
I like your garden.

                    FRANK
Hey! Love my garden.

                    LAURIE
Okay! I love your garden.

                    FRANK
You know what they say, don't you?

                    LAURIE
No, what do they say?

                    FRANK
If you love a man's garden, you gotta love the man.

This *Serpico* scene tenders an example — most especially in post-production — of the lure to "hold onto" moments of charm, delight, and whimsy no matter the remaining gratuitousness of a character's inclusion.

Be sturdy! Don't permit subplots — in events and/or characters — to injure the story's form.

transitions

First, a little background on "little" transitions: with the widespread use of various digital post-production programs in both hardware and software, students can instantaneously "polish" their projects with a variety of effects: fade-outs, fade-ins, dissolves, etc.

In the "old days" even little effects took time to organize, review, order, and have completed by an optical department; and so, as a result of work demands, these effects were consequently left to be decided upon after an overall structure was close to completion. Visual transitions selected very early in the editing process are usually a result of ego demands and its associated fear. While the effects might rescue the young filmmaker with "awesome" (self-serving) imagery, at best they provide little more than pretentious costuming. Worst of all, they likely represent lots of lost opportunities!

Alexander Mackendrick posted a notice in his classroom: Process not Product. He believed the best learning would occur if students concentrated less on hurrying to complete their projects — "here's the product" — and more (much more) on enjoying and appreciating the discoveries in the process.

There was, and still remains, an advantage to taking time to make choices that achieve story clarity within an eloquent rhythmic structure. That "time" comes from living with the material in raw form for as long as possible.

A grand epic to search and study optical (little) transitions:

THE BRIDGE ON THE RIVER KWAI

Chapter 5, "Officers' Meeting" @ 0:18:50
The end of the first day in the prisoner of war camp: Colonel Nicholson expresses his commitment to maintaining order within the ranks of all the newly arrived British POWs. He insists that the morale and survival of his men depends on their following the orders of the British officers and not that of the Japanese.

A *dissolve* of three seconds fades-out **Chapter 5** with a simultaneous fade-in of:

Chapter 6, "A Point of Difference" @ 0:20:59

In a Long-Shot the Japanese camp commander, Colonel Saito, exits his quarters and approaches the assembled British prisoners under Nicholson's command.

The *dissolve* — a unique convention of cinema — certainly makes clear in this instance the overnight time lapse between the two chapters. The three-second dissolve probably comes close to the maximum length (72 frames) before a dissolve "reads" as a double exposure: two images concurrently visible.

As Chapter 5 is a night scene, and Chapter 6 is a bright daylight (the next morning) scene, let me offer by way of questions — not to avoid conjecture, or a difference of opinion in the selection of a dissolve, but to emphasis process — an alternative possibility for the transition between chapters. What would a Fade-Out from the night scene, with a hold of a couple of beats in black, and then a Fade-In to the daylight scene look like? Since Chapter 5 is a night scene, fading to black might be a more "natural" fit than a dissolve: the last light of the day eases away.

What about a Fade-Out from Chapter 5, and a long *dissolve* from black to the daylight scene? Depending upon the incoming scene's patterns in light, a *dissolve (out) from black* can create a more subtle and intriguing entrance to the new scene.

Optical effect options can be screened in the digital timeline *without* immediately adding them to the assembled sequence: Create a "transition test" sequence for your timeline, which not only allows you to view the options in transitions, but displays variations in the very clips and moments that join. Even in the "old yesterdays," optical possibilities could be screened by way of test versions provided by an optical department: a print of the SeLected OPticals, or SLOP print.

Chapter 6, "A Point of Difference" @ 0:23:28

Colonel Saito has ordered enlisted men and officers under Colonel Nicholson's command to do manual labor. The British Colonel refuses his officer's participation and reads from Article 27 of the Geneva Convention. Saito slaps Nicholson and throws the Geneva Convention booklet to the ground. Nicholson retrieves it and with blood running over his lips....

NICHOLSON
Since you refuse to abide by the laws of the civilized
world we must consider ourselves absolved from our duty
to obey you. My officers will not do manual labor.

Saito accepts the challenge and orders *all* to work. The British soldiers remain at attention, until Nicholson orders his Sergeant Major to "take the men to work."

SERGEANT MAJOR
Battalion, take up tools!

Here we have an uncomplicated cinematic moment, and a non-optical effect transition. In the continuous Long-Shot, the men in ranks begin to retrieve the hand tools in front of them. The sound track carries the *time* of bodies in motion, and tool "clangs," across a Medium-Shot of Saito — slightly less than two seconds in length — so that the next cut to an Extreme Long-Shot has all the men armed with assorted tools and ready for work. The sound provides a convincing transition across three distinct compositions; and with simplicity, allows for a compression of real time.

I mention this straight cut *transition* because soon after another compression in time is needed, and a dissolve is used: @ **0:27:18**.

Colonel Saito has come close to ordering the machine-gunning of Nicholson and his officers for refusing manual labor. He eyes the bright sky, and with hands on his hips turns to go to his quarters, leaving the British officers and one of his own standing in the hot sun.

In an Extreme Long-Shot Saito climbs the wooden steps to a shaded porch and exits the scene through his door. An elderly aboriginal sits half-naked at the door; he pulls and eases a rope, in redundantly rhythmic motion, working a fan in Colonel Saito's office.

A cut takes us back to the Long-Shot of the British officers. The Japanese officer removes his field cap, wiping his hand over his head. The shot dissolves to a tilted low-angle Medium-Shot which looks up at Colonel Nicholson against a sky in full hue; the flaming sun in upper screen left creates refractions in spots and streaks against the sky. This shot then cuts to an Extreme Long-Shot of the camp's grounds with the British officers still standing — and perfectly still — in the tropical heat of the day.

The various set-ups provide more solutions to compress (a *transition* in time) the hours under the sun than does the dissolve: the Close-Up of Saito's fan puller, the Medium-Shot of the machine gunners in the truck, the POWs along the outer wall of the camp infirmary, and/or the individual shots of Nicholson's officers.

Simply — at some point — having Saito's officer *no* longer visible on the ground generates a passage of time.

Perhaps *dissolves* developed into a much too easy transition solution in *time* and *space* configurations. At the least they became the predictable favorite of filmmakers and their audiences: cinematic clarity without distinction.

SERPICO

The sound of the *tool* "*clangs*" as a transition is reminiscent of image and sound magic in **Chapter 7** of *Serpico*. But let's call the chapter what it is: "**A Note from Jewish Max**" @ **0:47:24.**

In Long-Shot, Frank starts his hi-fi stereo LP turntable. He moves toward the camera, picks up a "breakfast" tray as the divine voice of a tenor begins. Frank readies to exit his back door: "Alfie, come on." He never fully leaves the blurred glass of the door, and he doesn't even close the door behind him, when a cut takes us to the above-angle shot in the garden. There is no "match" in visual time: Frank is already seated at a small white café table, his right arm raised as he checks on a hanging plant. There is an audio "match." The music continues in real time; however, a transition is achieved by a change in level and equalization of the music. The opera is quieter, and filtered to "say" that it is playing inside Frank's apartment.

There are several beautifully designed transitions in *Z*.

Z

Chapter 24, "A Witness" @ 1:07:00

A witness to the political assassination of The Deputy — a popular political figure and peace activist — has agreed to meet with the authorities. He is clubbed across the head as he walks along the street. Nearly unconscious, and surrounded by a gathering crowd, a Close-Up of his face, his head sideways in the frame, resting on the iron grate of a storm drain, cuts to another Close-Up of his face — this time upright — his eyes open. A white sheet is pulled up to his chin, and a white pillow can be seen behind his head. The camera moves out to reveal an ice pack atop his head, and bandages covering his wound. The witness finds he is alone in a vast ward of several dozen empty beds.

At **1:08:38** the witness has visitors. The Chief of Police and his henchman challenge the witness' veracity and medical history: "You fell and hit your head." "You suffer from epilepsy?" "Let's say you were influenced!"

An officer stationed at the hospital window warns, "General, they're coming." The three visitors exit frame left in a Master-Shot. The camera moves in to a Medium-Shot of the witness in profile; he sits up in bed, the ice pack balanced on his head. The exiting visitors' footsteps fade as a *cut* takes us to a Medium Close-Up from in front of the witness. It appears that he is still watching the leave-taking.

The witness speaks: "I'm a bachelor and live with my ma." The camera moves out accompanied by the sound of a stenographic machine. A voice asks, "Profession?" There are *new* visitors already there taking the witness' statement!

Pedro Almodóvar conjures up his own magical *transition*, though the DVD's chapter title interferes with the story's distribution of information.

Chapter 12, "Dr, Roncero, Alicia's Father" @ 0:38:58

Benigno is at work. He is caressingly massaging co-matose Alicia's inner thigh. A door latch sound attracts his attention to screen right. Benigno says, "Mr. Roncero." An Off-Camera (OC) voice responds: "Good Morning."

Into this Master-Shot steps Mr. Roncero. He moves from screen right between the camera and the bed so that we are behind him. Mr. Roncero is holding an appointment calendar. A Close-Up brings us to a front view of him as he (looking downward) checks the calendar. His eyes peek upward, clearly attentive to Alicia's thigh, then upward a bit more to Benigno, and down to the thigh. A Close-Up of Alicia's thigh — as a POV — displays Benigno's thumbs smoothly sliding up and down Alicia's inner thigh, almost slithering into the folded sheet. A cut to Mr. Roncero's Close-Up catches his eyes' shift upward again to Benigno, and then down to the calendar. Mr. Roncero appears uncomfortable, or is he tempted by the sensuality of Alicia's leg and Benigno's work?

Mr. Roncero brings up a visit with Benigno, and an appointment — never kept — to discuss Benigno's sexual orientation: "If you like men or women." Mr. Roncero is a psychiatrist? Benigno claims that he no longer has a problem. The Master-Shot (from behind Mr. Roncero) now shows Benigno rubbing a lotion into his palms, and beginning a moisturizing massage of Alicia's exposed leg. Again we return to Mr. Roncero and his eyes glance up and down, settling on Alicia.

A new Master-Shot, the camera now on an axis to the right of the previous Master, reveals a female nurse working with Benigno to adjust Alicia's position in bed.

NURSE
Was her father here?

BENIGNO
Yes. He asked me if I was a faggot.

Time has passed in front of Mr. Roncero, and right before our eyes!

Mr. Roncero is a psychiatrist *and* Alicia's father. Was his interest in Alicia's thigh an indication of paternal concern for his daughter's well being "at the hands" of her male nurse?

In *Touch of Evil*, the recently revised version from Orson Welles' fifty-plus pages of notes, a curiously confusing *dissolve* presents students, and professionals alike, an exigent quandary:

TOUCH OF EVIL

Chapter 6, "Following Vargas" @ 0:28:00

"Uncle Joe" Grandi, the local border hoodlum, follows Mike Vargas — Mexican narcotics agent — and his new wife Susie into Texas. The Vargas' are met by a squad car carrying Captain Hank Quinlan and several of his detectives. Quinlan and Vargas have a meeting planned so as to begin an investigation into the murder of an American businessman. One of Quinlan's men is to drive Susie to the nearby Mirador Motel.

Grandi's car gains on the detective and the now asleep Susie, although an earlier combination of shots does (oddly) represent that Susie knows there's a car following. The very talkative detective spots the hoodlum's car in his rear view mirror, but nevertheless looks back over his right shoulder as well. A cut occurs as the detective is looking back. At **0:30:26** an Extreme Long-Shot, which looks across the slightly titled desert landscape, shows Grandi's car in the distance, and almost immediately with the cut, the sound of squealing brakes hits our ears. The crane-mounted camera lowers so that we see the Vargas car and the detective exiting his car to confront Grandi, whose car pulls nearly alongside.

A break in the 180-degree rule cuts to a hardly needed low-angle Long-Shot as Grandi's car — now facing screen left — comes to a stop. What turns out to be the Mirador Motel can be seen in the background, up the hill in the right portion of the frame.

The detective orders Grandi, who somehow thinks to turn off the radio, out of his car. Grandi offers complaints as he is led to the Vargas car.

A *dissolve* then reveals the sleeping Susie being wakened by the detective, now leaning into the car from the driver's side, "Wake up Mrs. Vargas. We're here." Mrs. Vargas starts out of the car with a disappointed look at the craggy run-down Mirador. The detective assures her, "This is all the motel we got this side of town, ma'am." As the detective stands away from the car door — his left arm leaving the steering wheel — the camera lifts to a higher angle, and we spot Grandi in the distance, his back to the camera. Susie shuts the passenger-side door, and now she sees Grandi, "Oh, no!" Grandi turns, "Oh yeah."

Here we have a sequence of shots worth probing, particularly since the transition, by way of a dissolve, makes matters screwy!

We have an opportunity to take honest advantage of sleeping Susie by using a Fade-Out rather than a dissolve; perhaps the detective's wake-up call preceding a Fade-In to the "Susie, Detective, and Grandi" shot. However helpful the Fade-Out, a central problem remains: Why doesn't Susie wake up when the detective slams the car door and shouts orders to Grandi? Or when Grandi protests? Or when Grandi and the detective climb into the Vargas car — unseen, but it must have happened — to drive the short distance up to the Mirador?

Could it be that Welles' notes were followed to a *Transition*? Welles himself — I'd bet — would have set aside his notes when confronted with the scene's confusion. This is a good example of an (optical) *product* with little appreciation for the discoveries of *process*. The two shots (clips) between the "Detective Spots Grandi's Car" in Medium-Shot, and the "Wake Up Mrs. Vargas" Long-Shot, might better serve the sequence if they had found their way onto the "editing room floor." A final two suggestions to consider:

1. Delete any hint that Susie sees the Grandi car. After all that she's experienced the previous night it is unlikely she'd keep her mouth shut about being followed, and...

2. Don't end the Medium-Shot of the (driving) detective while he's looking back to the Grandi car. Instead, let him be looking ahead for several beats before the (possible) little transition of a Fade-Out. You can, I'm sure, list some other promising choices.

This next transition illustrates that "everything old is new again," or vice-versa:

Chapter 6, "Investigators Arrive" @ 0:17:19

Michel, reading the newspaper, walks down a flight of stairs into the Paris Metro. On his heels — known to the audience — are two detectives who just missed him at the Inter-American Agency, where Michel collects his mail, and conducts various illicit deals. Light jazz accompanies the scene on an otherwise simple, if not blank, track. We see the two detectives hurry into a Metro station, and the camera zooms out and pans right, crossing the Champs-Élysées, past the Arc de Triomphe to the other side of the avenue as Michel comes-up from the Metro. The music stops. A Medium-Shot brings Michel to a cinema. Posters and photos of Humphrey Bogart are on display for *The Harder They Fall*.

A Close-Up of Bogart is inter-cut with a Close-Up of Michel, hard at work puffing his cigarette: Note the wisps of smoke passing in front of the Bogart photo. The two men make strong eye contact as Michel removes his sun glasses. A soft, cheerful whistling escorts Michel's thumb, back and forth, across his lips. Michel exits frame right in a Medium-Shot. The camera pauses at the theatre's glass doors; a soft-edge iris close assures that we'll see the two detectives reflected in the glass. They look left and right for Michel. An iris open — to the next scene — completes the transition from several seconds in black.

Breathless made a critical contribution to the films of the New Wave; it is bold and daringly progressive in its shooting and editing styles. Yet it takes good advantage of a silent-era device to see Michel off to the next scene, while keeping us advised that detectives are still on his trail.

I'll preface the next illustration, an example of classic film *transition* with David Mamet's advice about scene structure in cinema: "Get in late and get out early." This admonition links up nicely with Dede Allen's concern about '"entrances and exits."

Chapter 3, "Material Witness" @ 0:14:29

Samuel, an Amish boy, has witnessed a murder while in the public bathroom in Philadelphia's Pennsylvania Station. The killers don't know he's there. Samuel presses himself into the corner of a stall. He emits a small whimper. One of the killers hears, and begins checking. The killer, gun at the ready, makes his way along the line of stall doors. Samuel barely escapes detection by sliding under the divider and into the previous stall just as the killer breaks the latch with a jolting kick. A tilt up from the toilet shows Samuel balanced on the bowl. A slow move in toward his face accents the silence. The boy's eyes are wide; his teeny breaths scarcely discernible. Samuel — and the audience — concentrate on the ever quieter shuffle of foot-steps, as the killers leave the bathroom.

Chapter 4, "John Book" @ 16:12

A cut brings a Medium-Shot in soft focus. We are behind a police officer, noted by the handcuffs visible on his nearly silhouetted form. The audio switches from the hush of the bathroom to the muffled static of a police radio. Now, heavy and definite footsteps are heard. The police officer moves off — note his turn first to screen left and then to exit right — clearing the frame: We see Samuel in the protected embrace of his mother; they are sitting on a waiting room bench. An echoing message comes over the public address system, acknowledging with certainty that Samuel and his mother, and the police, are still in Penn Station.

This straightforward, no-frills cut is unambiguous in information: It is dramatically significant, and emotionally engulfing! It astonishes in its innocence and unfussiness; it is pure cinema.

In *The Art of Dramatic Writing*, Lajos Egri explains that melodrama and soap opera are predictably void of any (plausible) occurrence that prompts a character to decisions, actions, or obstacles. According to Negri, the key to quality drama has to do with the storytellers' understanding, presentation and inclusion of *transitions*. *The Verdict* supplies a brilliant lesson in this larger transition: A Story/Character/Dramatic transition:

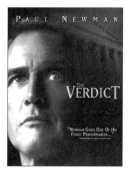

Chapter 5, "Dr. Gruber" @ 0:23:06

Frank Galvin, an alcoholic Boston lawyer with few prospects and a reputation in decline, enters a small and meager hospital ward to visit his latest — and only — client. He is equipped with a Polaroid camera, and expects a display of hospital bed photos will secure settlement money for him and his comatose client: quick and easy work for a take of one-third!

Galvin loads flash cubes and snaps a picture. The camera ejects the print; the mechanism combines with the client's "hissing" respirator. Galvin moves to the opposite side of the bed, placing the undeveloped picture on the gray institutional blanket at the foot of the metal framed bed. He flashes another picture, this time pausing to "see" his client who is attached to life-support tubing and cylinders. Galvin moves back to his first position as he places the second ejected undeveloped picture alongside the first.

Now, in Extreme Close-Up, Galvin brings the camera to his eye. He lowers it, staring at his client to the rhythmic "blows" of the respirator. He looks motionless at the Polaroid camera. A cut brings us to a Close-Up of the developing images. The shot holds for more than twenty seconds as the lifeless woman (two of her) comes into sight. Galvin sits onto a bed. A magnificently daring contrast comes to our ears: Giggling! Two nurses are on a break. They chat as they pass in the hallway. One of them sees Galvin: "Sir, you're not allowed to be in here." Galvin sits, overcome and not answering. The nurse approaches him, "You can't be in here." There are more than a few lingering beats that convey Galvin's *transition*: Recognition that this case — he later emphasizes that *"This* is the case" — holds nothing less than his redemption.

His Close-Up waits during respirator breaths of nearly eight seconds; and Galvin responds in a solemn voice: "I'm her attorney."

showing

Karel Reisz and Gavin Millar target their concern about the frequently under-utilized art of *showing* in their updated *The Technique of Film Editing*: "The tradition of expressive visual juxtaposition… has been lost largely since the advent of sound… [this] neglect… has brought with it a great loss to cinema."

Edward Dmytryk, in *On Film Editing*, simplifies the notion: "A demonstration is better than an explanation." It is the profound difference between the impact of cinema and the necessities of theatre; especially so of radio.

A classic example — a *telling* difference — can be found in John Osborne's instructions in the screenplay, and seen in the finished presentation of the 1963 Academy Award–winning film *Tom Jones*.

What has become known as the "Eating" scene is perhaps the most memorable in the film — and it could be the least in the screenplay.

TOM JONES

Chapter 9, "That Woman Mrs. Waters" @ 1:17:46
Tom has rescued Mrs. Waters from a lascivious British Officer. They have stopped at a country inn. The scene begins with the two seated and already served the opening course. Bold jumps throughout the meal's time *never* show the food arriving at the table, instead back and forth cuts between Tom and Mrs. Waters reveal the next course. Individual (separated) Close-Ups of the two, with only a couple of integrated actions — grasping a wishbone, and seductively offering an oyster — break the space between them. The scene builds to a sumptuously erotic visual tête-à-tête of immense charm and sexual glee.

It is a good and surprising lesson to *read* the scene as written:

DINING ROOM. NIGHT.
Tom eats a tremendous eighteenth-century type meal while Mrs. Waters watches him, obviously entranced with him. As his appetite is slowly satisfied, so she gets to work on him, and his eyes and attention slowly shift from his food to her.

The scene can be read in about ten seconds, and doesn't include Mrs. Waters' eating. The film's version runs some three minutes and fifteen seconds; both eat and *demonstrate* voracious appetites!

In 1929, Dziga Vertov's *Man with a Movie Camera* tested the communication of visual phenomena "to create a truly international film." It was *not* aided by titles, script, actors, or sets. It is considered the first "complete separation of cinema from literature and theatre" and, of course, it would not play well on radio.

I could not help thinking about Vertov's "experiment" during the first moments of *Osama*. Director Siddiq Barmak studied filmmaking in the Soviet Union. He was at first ambivalent — he was angry and distressed by Soviet occupation of his native Afghanistan — but did finally accept a scholarship. Barmak's film embraces the work of early Russian cinema, incorporates his self-possessed talent, and opens in deference: A man with a movie camera. The process turns out to be the product:

OSAMA

Chapter 1, "A Demonstration" @ 0:00:04

A Close-Up of a rusted can is not simply the image which begins the film; it is quickly disclosed that it is a point of view (POV) being *filmed* at that very moment: A tourist — or is it a journalist (?) — is out and about the streets of a village in Afghanistan.

A boy swings the rusted can, producing protective smoke to "keep away the evil eye" and "all misfortune." The boy, an inexperienced clairvoyant whose magic does not work, is, however, accurate in his foreboding. The story spreads out from the rusted can; the camera finds the protagonist and antagonist(s) of the principal plot. What the images show are disastrous for the man with the camera.

A simple device: Begin in Close-Up and ever newer information can't help but be distributed as an ever larger world is *shown*:

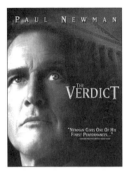

Chapter 2, "A Hearse Chaser" @ 0:01:41

We see a Close-Up of a waiting hand on the left, and two hands (on the right) search for a ten-dollar bill, which is then passed to the left. The camera tilts upward following a sweet-breath atomizer into a Medium-Shot of Frank Galvin. He sends a mist into his mouth, and flexes his eyelids as open as he can get them. Galvin turns toward the camera, passing by on screen right. The camera holds as Galvin walks away, and into an "increasing" Long-Shot of a funeral parlor; the deceased in an open coffin rests in the background. The camera begins to follow Galvin to a Medium Long-Shot as he is introduced to the seated widow ("Mrs. D., this is Frank Galvin; he's a good friend of ours, and a very fine attorney") by the "hand" that took the money.

Rosemary's Baby contains an inspired scene that offers a triple demonstration: The unique power of (word-free) cinema to invoke participation in a character's curiosity and anxieties; demonstration of showing rather than telling, and a visible "clue" to the scene's post-production "puzzling" discoveries. The scene confirms Ingmar Bergman's poetic statement, "I touched wordless secrets that only the cinema can discover."

ROSEMARY'S BABY

Chapter 23, "The Name is an Anagram" @ 1:28:18

The Chapter — and scene — begins in a Medium Close-Up of a glass cabinet. Rosemary enters frame right and removes a Scrabble board and tiles, turning toward the camera before walking away and into a Long-Shot. It is interesting that it is not a common move — isn't it odd that Rosemary doesn't simply turn to her right before walking away from the camera? It does afford us a quick glance at the Scrabble game. I not only call your attention to this choice in production because of the better visibility the move provides, but also because of the relationship between Rosemary's getting her Scrabble set and the Chapter title.

In the previous Chapter, "All of Them Witches," Rosemary is given a wrapped book, and a message, "the name is an anagram." I recall a hubbub in the theatre as people whispered to their movie-going partners, "What's an anagram?" Rosemary's peculiar reverse turn, that allows the audience to see the Scrabble board, brought many whispers of "Oh!" or "Ah-ha!" The game showed the definition.

The spilling of the tiles — and in particular, the Close-Up of the spelled out, ALL OF THEM WITCHES on the dark wood floor — elicited the last happy whispers as everyone now remembered the answer to "What's an anagram?" This three-opportunities-to-define anagram is but the first courteously engaging device in the story-*showing*. Let's not forget that a riddle to solve, and participating in the physicality of playing-out the puzzle, "moves us" to the edge of our seats!

As the camera pans with Rosemary, the opening shot supplies the scene's Master-Shot. It is in this shot that we see the Scrabble tiles "poured" onto the floor. A curious cut now reveals Rosemary's assumed starting point for the anagram: the title of the book. What is curious about the cut from the Long-Shot to the Close-Up? The cut occurs @ 1:28:34 and does not, in any way, imply some preternatural powers which have in one fell spill arranged the correct spelling of the book's title. No one suspects that Rosemary performed a miracle, or that the filmmakers poured Scrabble tiles day after day, or month after month, patiently awaiting that one spectacularly precise result. Why is there no such confusion in the structured choice? For one thing the spilling tiles' sound ends in the Long-Shot, and most decisive is that after the tiles pour from their bag — held upside down — Rosemary slants the bag forward as she brings it to her side. This relatively quick gesture, along with the ending of the reverberating "click-clacking" of tiles hitting the floor, makes clear the "space" in time. It is a paradigm of film's solemnity that it is capable of constructing (in deletions) bold, yet precise transitions.

The scene is constructed in eight set-ups and three failed attempts to solve the riddle. Delicate selections in Close-Ups of Rosemary in concentration, and the subtle sounds of shift-sliding tiles, allow for the very few moments — only at the start of puzzle solving — that we actually see the tiles being arranged... and rearranged.

Considering that Rosemary's dearest friend Hutch has "sent" her a death-bed warning it is less than reasonable that she'd attempt but three tries before calling it quits, "Now that really makes sense... poor Hutch."

Rosemary's words notwithstanding, the director and editor recognized a problem, and solved it by *showing* rather than *telling*: They changed the original order. They re-positioned HOW IS HELL FACT ME last in the order of three. This makes available the shot in which Rosemary's hand opens to reveal a "T" left over; *showing* that Rosemary is getting colder, not warmer (closer) to a solution. A great choice made possible by the fundamental nature in cinema of fragments/separation.

When Rosemary realizes that the anagram is not to be found in the title of the book, but rather in a name referenced in the book, and underlined, she reaches for and picks up the book, bringing it to her. You will notice that in the lower left corner of the screen, a portion of arranged tiles are visible: ELF SHOT... The second failed attempt, not the third!

PSYCHO

Check in. Relax. Take a shower.

Chapter 3, "Forty Thousand Dollars" @ 0:06:36
Marion Crane returns to her place of employment after a lunch time hotel rendezvous with her lover Sam. You'll note Mr. Hitchcock — a usual guest appearance — in a white cowboy hat, out on the street in front of Marion's office.

Crane's boss, Mr. Lowry, soon returns from his lunch with a wealthy "oil lease" man who will be paying $40,000 in cash for the Harris Street property. Marion, suffering a headache, asks to leave work early to "spend the weekend in bed." and agrees to Mr. Lowry's request that she put Mr. Cassidy's $40,000 "in the safe deposit box at the bank" on her way home.

A dissolve @ **0:10:40** brings us to **Chapter 4, "Stolen Money"** and Marion's bedroom. She enters screen left, already dressed down to her undergarments. She turns away from the camera after looking toward her bed which sits in the foreground of the frame. She reaches into an open closet which is centered in the composition. The camera tilts downward, moving in as it rack focuses from Marion at the closet, to an Extreme Close-Up of a white envelope on the bed. The envelope is packed with Mr. Cassidy's cash. The absolute silence of the scene breaks with the sudden note of hauntingly apprehensive music. The camera pans left and rack focuses on a filled suitcase at the foot of the bed. "Say" no more!

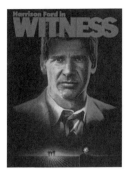

Chapter 5, "Positive I.D." @ 0:25:49

Detective John Book spends the day with the Amish Mother and her son Samuel — the sole witness to a brutal knifing in the men's bathroom at Philadelphia's Pennsylvania Station. Samuel has viewed a line-up: No suspect spotted. The three share a lunch break at a street-side hot dog and hamburger joint.

The next cut is a Close-Up of Detective Book. His right elbow is on his desk, his face resting in that hand, tucked under his ear and cupping his jaw. At the instant of the cut, Book's left hand turns a page from a large mug shot ledger. There is an ever-so-slight, but perceptible, pause before a cut reveals, in Close-Up, Samuel looking down at the newly turned page. Samuel shakes his head indicating no recognized face. In soft focus, Book's left hand comes forward turning another page. The next cut is a Medium-Shot of Book and Samuel, Book still resting his head in his right hand, his left back, and past Samuel's shoulder. Samuel sits framed within the arms of the detective.

Here is a fine illustration of visual inference: John Book's posture/body language at the opening of the scene makes it clear that he and Samuel have returned to the precinct a *good while* ago; and most especially, that Book's been turning mug shot pages without luck... for some time!

Cut-Aways/Inserts are synonymous terms which onomatopoeically imply "of little importance." particularly when placed against the prevailing authoritarian sound of Master-Shot. But! In the art of *showing* they are decisive.

Here are a couple of terrific examples:

THE LONELINESS OF THE LONG DISTANCE RUNNER

Chapter 20, "Caught" @ 1:22:13

In a heavy downpour the detective arrives at Colin's house. It is attention grabbing that the detective is without an umbrella. This is a decision *showing* merit: The rain must have begun only a short while ago, "catching" the detective in the downpour, or the detective is so dedicated as not to be sidetracked.

Colin answers the door and the detective informs him, "I've got some news for you. You've been identified." The police have thoroughly searched Colin's house looking for money stolen from a neighborhood bakery. The detective interrupts Colin's silly bantering, "Stop messing around. I want to know where that money is." In perfect synchronization to Colin's response, "Money... ha-ha... you should have said," the rain washes the stolen bills out the downspout located to the right of the door. The audience sees the crumpled bills begin to emerge — just as the detective is about to turn to leave — and in an instant, as the detective's eyes glance down, spotting the soaked money, Colin swings out the doorway, his feet tapping and twisting in a hide-the-money "dance": a wonderful integration of the characters, the dialogue and the Cut-Away of Colin's shifting shoes, staging any number of ballet positions. For several beats of audience delight and anxiety the detective is frozen by the ludicrousness of his very good fortune, and Colin's dismal luck.

In his 1984 book, *On Film Editing*, Ed Dmytryk describes a scene from *The Verdict* which he fervently anticipated would bring revitalization to Eisenstein's theory of montage. Dmytryk points out that while not pure montage — there is dialogue — the decisive moment does prove cinema's extraordinarily simple powers:

THE VERDICT

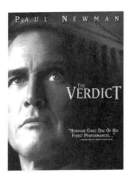

Chapter 18, "A Spy" @ 1:43:08

Attorney Frank Galvin has come to New York City to confront the nurse who admitted his client to the archdiocese's hospital in Boston some four years earlier. The client, now in a permanent vegetative state, was given the wrong anesthetic. It is clear to Galvin that the nurse (Kaitlin) has knowledge that will convince the Boston jury to deliver a verdict for the plaintiff. No longer a nurse, Kaitlin works for Chelsea Child Care. She is surrounded by children when Galvin "meets" her in the playground:

> GALVIN
> Oh! You're the one they said was a nurse.

> KAITLIN
> Who told you that?

> GALVIN
> I don't know… Mrs.…?

> KAITLIN
> Mrs. Simmons?

> GALVIN
> Yeah!

> KAITLIN
> I used to be a nurse.

GALVIN

It's a wonderful profession. My daughter-in-law's in it.
What did you do? Did you stop?

KAITLIN

Yes.

GALVIN

Why'd you do that? Will you help me?

Read Galvin's last two phrases again. The phrases hold no relationship in their structural order, their literal meaning, or in their inflections. The first phrase ends @ **1:43:36**, and "Will you help me?" begins @ **1:43:54**. There are eighteen seconds between the lines. The pause, or — as screenwriters might direct — "*a very long beat*" disqualifies the moment as radio or even theatre.

During this *very long beat*, Kaitlin's gaze shifts downward from Galvin's face; she has noticed something. In Extreme Close-Up, we see, INSERTED in Galvin's overcoat's left pocket, a New York to Boston Eastern Airlines Shuttle ticket. Still in the *very long beat*, Kaitlin's eyes again meet Galvin's. He knows she has seen the ticket, and he — and we — knows that she understands why he has come.

Galvin steps toward the camera, and Kaitlin, and asks his last question. A cut to a Close-Up of Kaitlin starts with her eyes shut. They open, but she gives no answer.

The Cut-Away/Insert makes it possible to avoid expository dialogue detailing the circumstances surrounding the current trial and every other fact about the case, all of which the audience has lived with for more than one and a half hours. Most vital of all, it establishes Kaitlin's long anguish, and likely expectation that this day would finally arrive... and the audience is eager to find out: What will happen next?

Far too often such shots as the *New York to Boston Airline Ticket* are thought of as useful "fixes" to get out of a troubling or lengthy camera run, or other post-production jam. Stefan Sharff unfortunately joins the ranks in accepting such a patch-up function for the Cut-Away. In his chapter "Familiar Image" in *The Elements of Cinema* he writes: "When fragmentation into shots became prevalent, a need arose for extra connectors to smooth over 'difficult' spots whenever, as a result of mistakes or mismatching, continuity shots did not go well together. They were also useful to help with deletions and condensations of action... and help ease changes in picture size and composition."

A Cut-Away/Insert is usually a Close-Up, or Extreme Close-Up, which shows what a character is doing or seeing, or shows the audience what the character should, or will, discern. The Cut-Away/Insert is, in all practicality, a point of view (POV) shot, and is therefore integral to the visual and emotional participation of the audience. This aspect of composition is central to film's ability to *show*; and distinguishes cinema from theatre: Story is determined in image, not in the spoken word!

atmosphere

This heading wittingly concludes the STORY chapters. Initially, I didn't expect to include this topic. PLACE, the next section, begins with a chapter entitled "Light," and I figured that would fully incorporate "atmosphere." After all, the distinguished cinematographer Sven Nykvist, aesthetically — and sensibly — linked the two with his observation, "[T]here is nothing that can ruin the atmosphere as easily as too much light."

Working, reading, interviewing, and screening fashioned a newfangled thought: While "atmosphere" is readily portrayed by way of location, light and condition — creating a *mood* — it is also an essential link to *story*. But! I began to consider that there is another, and perhaps even closer link between story and "atmosphere" than *mood*. It is less immediate to any scene, and therefore more comprehensive: It is the *tone* of the total work.

I am in effect separating the two synonyms of "atmosphere": mood as "feeling of ambiance," and tone as "distinctive demeanor" — the *tenor* or *resonance* of a film. This link to *story* is more than a means to define genre. It challenges the filmmaker's intuition: What impact does the overall milieu have on the audience? How do I maintain consistency? Can (seeming) contradictions work to the story's advantage?

So I thought to position this chapter as a way to reconcile a last thought about STORY before new ones begin with *light* on PLACE.

Let's look at two scenes from *Butch Cassidy and the Sundance Kid*. I think together they express a rationale for the filmmakers' choices which maintain the *tone* of the story: *atmosphere*.

Chapter 10, "Second Hit on the Flyer" @ 0:31:26
The Hole in the Wall Gang led by Butch and Sundance is just beginning a train-robbing outing when they recognize the voice inside the locked boxcar that holds the train's safe. It's the voice of the Union Pacific Railroad agent Mr. Woodcock. They've met during a previous robbery: **Chapter 6, "First Hit on the Flyer" @ 0:15:38.** Woodcock exhibits the effects of the dynamiting of a boxcar he guarded earlier: arm in a sling, cuts, bruises and a (cartoon-like) black-eye. Butch and Sundance trick Woodcock into sliding open the door. They find a massively modern safe.

> BUTCH
> (gestures toward the safe)
> Woodcock, what'd you have to go and do something like that for?

> WOODCOCK
> Well, Butch, you blew the last one so easy.…

Butch asks a gang member for more dynamite, and an enormous explosion blasts Butch and Sundance backward into the air and onto the ground, splinters the box car, and launches heaps of money up to the sky. While gang members scramble about catching the raining bills, Sundance laughs, "Think you used enough dynamite there Butch?" No one is killed — or even injured! An important choice to adhere to the movie's overall tone: adventurous, daring, and joyful banter.

The last chapter of the film successfully continues this tone by selecting an adventurous and daring final image of Butch and Sundance, which follows their enduringly silly — no matter what — repartee:

Chapter 24, "The Shootout" @ 1:39:03
The two men ride into a small Bolivian village. A stolen white mule in their possession is recognized by its branded mark, and reported to the local police captain.

The two men begin a meal at an outside table.

                    BUTCH
          The specialty of the house… and it's still moving.

Even though, via Dramatic Irony, the audience is made aware of an approaching peril we are nevertheless startled by a gunshot blast that demolishes Butch's
plate. The two run for cover, bumping each other as they flee.

                    BUTCH
          Well, that settles it. This place gets no more of my business.

A pause in the shooting prompts:

                    BUTCH
          I bet it's just one guy!

Sundance removes his hat and holds it out from the cover of a wall. A half-a-
dozen shots hit the hat!

                    SUNDANCE
          Don't you get sick of being right all the time?

They are trapped inside the small eatery, and nearly out of ammunition. Sundance offers to make a run for the mule and more of their ammo.

                    BUTCH
          This is no time for bravery… I'll let you.

In the end Butch concedes that Sundance can't be the one to attempt a run to
the mule:

                    BUTCH
          Hell! I'm the one that has to go. 'Cause I could
          never give you cover. You can cover me.

Butch does make it — through a terrible hail of a hundred shots — to the mule and back. But, both fall wounded into the eatery. Yet there is, in the face of overwhelming odds and certain death, still a teasing — as ceaseless as the Bolivian gunfire.

> BUTCH
> Is that what you call giving cover?

> SUNDANCE
> Is that what you call running?

Our two "heroes" are gasping and bloody and trapped! The audience learns — a good case of Dramatic Irony — that now, joining the police siege, are several Bolivian army companies ready to get the "dos banditos yanquis."

Back at the eatery, in a high-angle Long-Shot, Butch and Sundance load their pistols. The sun is now low in the sky and Butch is spotlighted against the roughly textured and stained interior wall.

> BUTCH
> I've got a great idea where we should go next.

> SUNDANCE
> I don't want to hear it.

> BUTCH
> You'll change your mind when I tell ya.

> SUNDANCE
> Shut up!

The teasing continues over a beautifully framed Medium-Shot, while Sundance gets a bandana from his pocket to wrap Butch's bloodied hand.

> BUTCH
> Australia! I figured secretly you wanted to know... so I told ya.

Bruised, bloodied and gaspingly difficult breathing doesn't stop the two in their camaraderie and cockeyed optimism.

> BUTCH
> They speak English so we wouldn't be foreigners. They
> got horses in Australia. They got thousands of miles... we
> could hide out in. A good climate... nice beaches; you
> could learn to swim....

Finally, the two get to their feet and run into the plaza firing. They are not stopped by bullets: a freeze frame stops them. They remain on their feet through barrages of gunfire. An off-camera (OC) command of "Fuego! Fuego! Fuego!" commences repeated cascades. The gunshots and commands fade slowly as sepia tone replaces the color "photo" of Butch and Sundance. Gently rolling notes from a saloon piano fade-in, and the picture moves away, away and away; the final image in wide, high-angle Extreme Long-Shot presents the town plaza, stopping so as to conceal the walls and rooftops packed-full of Bolivian police and soldiers.

A good concluding creative choice: The movie's long established *atmosphere* holds the story to its truthful historic end. There is more than a touch of sadness in the farewell, while sparing Butch, Sundance and especially the audience, the terrible *tone* of reality.

One of director Alexander Mackendrick's classic works faced a similar challenge. In this case it necessitated a way of playing out its "dark" *atmosphere* without losing its tonal resolve to a comedic genre.

A gang of thieves, made up of Professor Marcus and his unconventional "quartet" of co-conspirators — The Major, Louis, Harry, and One-Round — have gotten away with an enterprisingly accomplished armored car heist, only to be "caught" by a scrupulously ethical — and sometimes delusional — Mrs. Wilberforce.

THE LADYKILLERS

Chapter 12, "Fond Farewells" @ 0:41:48

The gang prepares to leave Mrs. Wilberforce's rental house. They depart with a steamer trunk of the loot. Some of the stolen bills are in One-Round's cello case. As Mrs. Wilberforce sees them out she is incessantly "entwined" in Professor Marcus' lengthy wool scarf. The gang awaits One-Round as he thanks Mrs. Wilberforce for "the nice tea and everything." The door closes, catching the cello case strap.

One-Round tugs on the instrument case. He is advised to "ring the bell, brain. Don't just stand there!" But before Mrs. Wilberforce can answer the door, One-Round tries to free the case with an abrupt yank; it breaks, spilling the money and the (crime) beans, just as Mrs. Wilberforce opens the door to find One-Round on his knees surrounded by lots of loose bills.

The gang hurries from their getaway car to help One-Round gather-up the money. Professor Marcus closes the door with an encouraging, "It's alright, Mrs. Wilberforce, everything's under control... Goodbye."

Mrs. Wilberforce re-opens the door, and Professor Marcus's hand re-closes it with an unambiguous "Goodbye." The gang scrambles back to their car; in the midst of herky-jerky starts and brake screech stops, they come to the deduction that they "must do something;" Mrs. Wilberforce can identify them!

How is the story's humorous tone — albeit dark to very dark — maintained, when in their efforts to "do something" the gang not only fails to rid itself of Mrs. Wilberforce, but its members do each other in?

Chapter 17, "A Spark of Decency" @ 1:06:52

The gang draws matches — the short match is to "do in" Mrs. Wilberforce. The Major is chosen. But while others try patiently to wait, the Major sneaks out a window with the cello case of loot.

Chapter 18, "Rooftop Accident" @ 1:08:42

The Major is spotted on the roof by Professor Marcus, and pursued by the gang. The Major forces One-Round from the steep slant of the shingles, and eventually tosses the cello, which falls with perfect synchronization into Harry's hands, as Mrs. Wilberforce exits her kitchen door. Take special note of all the vaudevillian slapstick, Chaplin-like "designs" within the sequence.

The Major, trapped by Louis, slides himself along the rooftop peak, till he is out of roof. A painfully piercing train whistle, smoke and chugging from the rail yard below, leads the camera to the pleading Major, and Mackendrick cuts to a Close-Up of the cello being put into a large coffin-like crate — for safe storage — by Mrs. Wilberforce. As her shadow clears the box, we see it is an elegantly carved chest.

Sounds of crashing, assorted "boings" and rattles brings us back to the rooftop. Louis sits alone and adjusts his fedora.

Professor Marcus asks if The Major is hurt. Harry can't get the words out, and Louis responds, "I shouldn't think he felt a thing."

Chapter 19, "Alliances" @ 1:13:59

The gang gathers for The Major's "departure." Professor Marcus leads Louis and Harry through the backyard plank gate to a wheelbarrowed Major. Harry drops a yellow daffodil onto the body.

Enjoy the wonderfully incongruous image @ **1:14:28** of One-Round and Professor Marcus in wheelbarrow procession, along the roadway above the rail yard. Smoke billows from a coal-fired engine below, the sounds incorporated with the acerbically somber funeral score.

In *Dr. Strangelove*, the *atmosphere* is more than hinted at in the film's subtitle, *Or: How I Learned to Stop Worrying and Love The Bomb*.

DR. STRANGELOVE

Chapter 1, "Start" @ 0:00:01

A disclaimer, in a roll title, appears ahead of the Columbia Pictures' emblem:

"It is the stated position of the U.S. Air Force that their safeguards would prevent the occurrence of such events as are depicted in this film. Furthermore, it should be noted that none of the characters portrayed in this film are meant to represent any real persons living or dead."

The disclaimer and narration about a doomsday device in the hands of the Soviet Union follow the Columbia Pictures' logo, and unnecessarily stagger-starts the story. What might rightfully be considered the "real" opening does "launch" the film's genre — a black comedy — and overall *atmosphere*: a scorning satire of outlandish apprehension. A Depression-era song, "Try a Little Tenderness" in a World War II–era rendition with a sing-along chorus of orchestra members accompanies the head credits drawn in a cartoon-like line, and superimposed over a U.S. Strategic Air Command B-52 Stratofortress bomber being "affectionately" re-fueled in the sky. The audience is well settled in for the nightmarish derision of this Stanley Kubrick classic.

Sound is an obvious ally of *atmosphere*: music and effects. We'll begin with an illustration in music. Music has accompanied movies since the earliest days of the silent era. While it is deservedly credited with signaling the emotional demeanor of character and scene — whether directly or contrapuntally — it initially "played" a role in calming the likely anxiety of audience members sitting in a darkened room with dozens of strangers, doubtlessly disturbed by the clattering of the film projector's motor.

Music can, as well, classify *projected* — as in anticipated — *atmospheres*:

THE LONELINESS OF THE LONG DISTANCE RUNNER

Chapter 1, "Opening Credits" @ 0:00:37

The opening contains a voice over (VO) narration. It is the voice of the protagonist Colin Smith giving brief context to the film's title. The last line barely ends as the first of the head titles appear, cueing John Addison's score. The music is, in structure, an overture which unmistakably describes the story's multifaceted tones. It is melancholy — or perhaps *lonely* — and courageous, adventurous and perilous.

Let's continue with an illustration — using music and effects — with an important link to our *fragment* topic. This example encompasses a sensational solution to the difficulties encountered in the work environment of production. It doesn't only offer a "fix," it concentrates the scene's atmosphere and spirit.

THE FRENCH CONNECTION

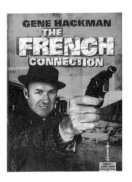

Chapter 5, "A Table Full of Suspects" @ 0:10:36

Detectives Doyle and Russo stop at The Chez for drinks. Lustrously sensual ladies entertain the packed club with a vivacious arrangement of "Everybody's Goin' to the Moon." The song explodes throughout the club. It all but drowns out the hub-bub of the crowd. With Russo at the bar, Doyle patrols the place. He greets the "cigarette girl" with a kiss — they speak, but no word is sounded — and takes first notice of a particular table. Doyle begins making his way back toward Russo. A camera pans to "that table" taking its cue from Doyle's head turn, and the point of view (POV) indicates "that table" is still on his mind. Doyle returns to the bar and orders a drink, his request in lip moves only: How could anyone be heard over the vigorous performers? At about **0:12:20** with Doyle in Long-Shot holding his drink and eyeing the table, the audio balance begins a swap, and continues over a POV of "that table." On a Close-Up of Doyle we become aware of a single ear-ringing tone that eventually obscures the jazzy song before it too disappears into a modest ambient sound of the club's patrons, *just in time* for us to hear Doyle's and Russo's dialogue.

In the course of production the words of the detectives entering The Chez and greeting the bartender, and the cigarette girl, would have been clearly recorded. The lively singers would likely have been filmed and recorded to play-back. Combining all of these in post-production created some trouble! How can we — over such a jazzy number — hear Doyle's pronouncements to Russo: "I make at least two junk connections at that far table over there in the corner" and "That table is definitely wrong"?

A beautifully poetic, dream-like solution is found in the audio segue: We can hear the necessary dialogue, and it cogently stages Doyle's concentrated hunch about "that table." It then allows for an effective return to the song and its conclusion prior to the detectives' continued discussion; and Doyle's all-night plan: "What do you say we stick around and give him a tail?"

The French Connection serves as an illustration in the creative process of establishing a film's *atmosphere* via music. The film's score demonstrates a creatively smart bond to a pivotal sound in Doyle's quest to "bust" the bad guys.

Chapter 6, "The Tail" @ 0:16:36

The hectic illumination of Times Square at night cuts to a full frame neon sign of Ratner's Deli Restaurant on Delancey Street at dawn. A slow pan left from the Williamsburg Bridge brings us to Doyle's and Russo's car. All is quiet but for a steady hollow-airy ambiance and Russo's sarcastic, "Relax. You're having fun, ain't ya?" At **0:16:50** composer Don Ellis hits with two separated identical notes. The notes are a deep gnashing-like arrangement. Though Doyle's face is obscured by the windshield and 7:00 A.M. drizzle, we can make out his form, especially by the brim-up fedora on his head. Russo, in the passenger seat, is clear. His window is open and he watches. A cut back to Ratner's with a tilt down catches "the greaser with the blonde" exiting for their car. The gnashing notes now begin to shape a "melody." And, as Doyle and Russo follow their suspects, an instrumentation surrounds the gnashing notes and they are transformed into music: The sound is rounder and protracted.

If we jump ahead — way ahead — in the story to:

Chapter 26, "120 Pounds" @ 1:28:28

…we find Doyle, Russo and police mechanic Irv discouraged and bewildered. They've brutally dismembered the suspected Lincoln automobile. Doyle was certain they'd find a large stash of heroin. They haven't!

Russo checks Irv on the weight of the car, and finds a discrepancy in the owner's manual of 120 pounds. Russo insists that Doyle's "gotta be right." Irv, waving his can of Coke insists that he's "ripped everything out of there except the rocker panels." Doyle rushes forward, his face in Irv's, filling the camera lens, "Come on, Irv, what the hell's that?"

A cut to a Close-Up, lit by a work-light, shows hands with small tools loosening and removing screws, and a chrome-plated rippled metal panel. A boldly blatant cut to a tighter Close-Up reveals a power chisel, positioned at the edge of the panel-less car body. The chisel cuts through auto body metal — its gnashing-raspy sound is the inspiration for Ellis's atmosphere. Hands bend the piece back, breaking it free. Beneath are blue bags of heroin! Doyle was right… and he is pleased.

An altogether unusual — especially at the time — but wise decision was made for *Rififi*.

RIFIFI

Chapter 12, "The Arrival" @ 0:43:51

Orchestration of overwhelming suspense/thriller music greets Tony on a nighttime Paris street. He checks out cars to steal. A nice touch is added, in that the first auto he moves toward is at the same time approached by the returning owners.

Soon Tony is off in a quite easy to take vehicle. He picks up his three associates waiting with all their gear on the steps of a metro station. The group has carefully cased, and double-cased, the Mappin & Webb jewelry store, and adjoining hotel with rooms above the jewelry store. They have planned a daring robbery. At **0:46:10** the men ring the concierge bell at the hotel. They tie and blindfold the man and woman owners, and bring them upstairs in a lift — the score in a time-keeping suspenseful manner — to the "selected" suite from which they'll enter the store below. The chapter ends with the music diminishing into silence at the quiet close of the door.

Chapter 13, "Do Not Adjust Your Volume" @ 0:47:15

Flashlights guide the way about the room, and to the seated and bound couple. The thieves at work with precision in time and tools incrementally increase an atmosphere of agonizing stress. But rather than utilizing music as a usual enrichment of such an atmosphere — there is no speaking — the filmmakers' choice here is suggested in the chapter title: The ambiance of the Place and the labors of the Character(s) generate all of the atmosphere needed at this moment in the Story.

Chapter 16, "Car Trouble" @ 1:11:06

Tony drops his accomplices at Mario's and drives off. A dissolve takes us to a high-angle shot looking down to water as the heist gear, packed in two large plaid suitcases, plummets in a crashing splash, followed by the cane umbrella which was used so skillfully to catch the battered floor of the hotel suite before it dropped into Mappin & Webb triggering the alarm.

Tony leaves the stolen car along the river. A heavy-duty "putt-putt-putt" engine sound, and single horn blow from a passing river barge, fills the scene. Another dissolve brings us to:

Chapter 17, "Back to Mario's" @ 1:11:58

Music begins: A swirling anxious melody meets a Master-Shot and a door buzzer. Mario walks quickly toward the camera — Jo and Cesar watch from an adjoining wide doorway — into a Medium Close-Up. He opens the door, and Tony enters. They appear, all of them, to be "home free."

I offer a suggestion: The "putt-putting" barge sound would so easily and gracefully segue into the music's return.

The New Wave films launched, in good part, by several prominent critics turned filmmakers in post-war France — François Truffaut and Jean Luc-Godard among them — expressed an altogether new *atmosphere*.

Martin Scorsese's comment, "I had no idea what was happening... [the film] is too hip for me," gets us to a New Wave example so provocative in production, editing, and structured rhythm as to transform the work into an *attitude.* Writing about *Breathless* in the *Chicago Reader*, Jonathan Rosenbaum observed, "Gritty and engaging... the quintessential existentialist movie in style as well as attitude."

BREATHLESS

Chapter 1, "Car Thieves" @ 0:01:51

Michel has stolen a car from the Marsielles waterfront. He heads out to enjoy a ride in the country. He sings, "La-la-la–lalala." He sings of "amour." He looks over his shoulder out the back window, "No way he's overtaking me in that stupid bus." He looks out the windshield singing across four POV jump-cuts. He speaks about his plan to "get money and ask Patricia, yes or no", and a jaunt with his love to "Milano, Genova, and Roma." At **0:03:38** he turns on the car's radio. He finds a pistol in the glove compartment. He pretends to shoot passing motorists, "pow-pow-pow" and even the "nice" sun, dancing its light through the roadside trees. He aims out and up to the sun and real gunshots ring out.

A cut takes us behind Michel — the gunfire was only pretend — as he comes upon slowed traffic: "Women drivers are cowardice personified."

"When I first saw *Breathless* in the 1960s, I thought 'Wow.' Just in the first five-minute sequence in introducing Jean-Paul Belmondo's character (Michel) as this petty thief, every rule was violated... the discontinuity of what was going on; even screen directions were mixed," film editor Richard Chew enthusiastically explained. "I thought either this guy (Jean-Luc Godard) doesn't know what he's doing or he's so confident that he has the grammar of film down that he's trying to show us a new way to use the material he has to tell a story."

Chapter 2, "Michel & the Cop" @ 0:04:31

Michel decides to pass a line of cars which have slowed at a roadway construction site. Motorcycle cops come after him, and a series of jumps in action and direction get Michel off the road to adjust his "jump-start" wires. One cop passes, but the next comes back to Michel, who is standing at the front of the car with the hood raised. A series of genuinely fragmented images nonetheless informs that Michel shoots the cop, and with an accompanying over-the-top suspense track he runs across a field into a Fade-Out.

In keeping with examples of establishing and maintaining the tone of a film, let's have a look at one which, at first viewing, I felt over-startled the settled atmosphere. The *tone* of *Dog Day Afternoon* might be expressed as a *presenting mind-set*. I considered that too severe an altering came to pass. Of course, when watched again — and again — the change in *tone* no longer feels so apparent; the experience of several screenings does ready the *tone* change. I did respect that the shock of the altering event held powerful advantages, but wonder (still) if holding the benefits of both components could have been achieved. See what you think.

DOG DAY AFTERNOON

The robbery should have taken 10 minutes. 4 hours later, the bank was like a circus sideshow. 8 hours later, it was the hottest thing on live T.V. 12 hours later, it was all history. And it's all true.

AL PACINO
in DOG DAY
AFTERNOON

Chapter 1, "August 22, 1972" @ 0:00:20
The choice of the Elton John song played over a bright New York City day establishes a tone that is optimistic and cheerful.

Chapter 2, "The Robbery Begins" @ 0:05:32
Sal sits alongside the bank manager's desk and takes an automatic weapon from his attaché case. Sonny, with a blue bow ribbon-tied "flower box" fills out a bank slip. Stevie suggests, "Maybe we should take something smaller." Sonny "reminds" him that Sal's "started already. He's got the gun out."

There is a *tone* of amateurish incompetence which generates a good and beneficial dose of anxiety in the audience; but the anxiety and the robbers' ineptitude rouse chuckles. Then @ **0:06:46** Sonny slowly walks toward a teller. He holds a check and deposit slip; carrying his "flower box," @ **0:07:00** a series of three cuts shows Sonny in a bizarre battle with the flower box lid as he tries to gain control of his rifle hidden inside. This moment is magnificent. It easily encourages grins and laughter while it implements a slapstick *tone* which is reinforced. Stevie announces, "I can't do it, Sonny." Sal and Sonny are confused as they try to speak around the bank's square pillars. Sal has to prompt Stevie to not take the getaway car to go home. "We need the car, take the subway" and "Stevie... the keys!" Sal's rifle butt is briefly entangled in a large potted plant. Stevie exits only to rush back to warn Sonny, "There's a girl under that desk over there." Wonderfully amusing; and yet, difficult as it always is, it is performed with a deferential affection for the characters.

Chapter 11, "Travel Plans; Maria's Boyfriend" @ 0:43:38

Sonny and Sal are trapped in the bank by a regiment of New York City police and detectives. Sonny decides that he's been thinking of their situation in the wrong way. The robbers are not really trapped. They control the bank staff, so they hold hostages, and Sonny and Sal should be making demands of law enforcement. "I'm flying to the tropics... Fuck the snow... ready to go to Algeria? We're all going to sunny climes."

In a Long-Shot the camera pans left. It follows Sonny to the teller's counter and frames Sonny and Sal in a Medium Close-Up. Sal holds his rifle upward, the stock resting on the counter.

> SONNY
> You gotta understand something. If we leave the country
> there's no coming back here. If there's anybody you want
> to talk to... say goodbye to... do it now.

> SAL
> (takes the suggestion into a long consideration, and whispers)
> No.

> SONNY
> Is there any special country you wanna go to?

> SAL
> Wyoming.

> SONNY
> No Wyoming. That's not a country. That's all right...
> I'm gonna take care of it.

Chapter 14, "Riches; A Star Is Born" @ 0:59:32

Sonny gets word, "Your food is here." Two Long-Shots show onlookers and cops with coffee and sandwiches.

Sonny exits the bank in a Medium profile shot; the camera pans left, ultimately, in Long-Shot, framing the sunny side of the street, across from the shaded bank. The camera is behind Sonny, as a pizza delivery kid follows Detective Sergeant Moretti's instructions, and carries a stack of take-out boxes to Sonny who, despite Moretti's insistence that the food is paid for, enthusiastically stuffs the delivery kid's pocket with five-dollar bills from the bank. Sonny eventually flings fives up and down the street to the "partying" chaotic crowd.

Chapter 28, "Sal? Ready To Go?" @ 1:58:42
The hostages and robbers have arrived at Kennedy International Airport, and their plane has taxied alongside the limo-bus that brought them.

> SONNY
> They gonna have any food on board?

FBI agent Sheldon comes up to the front passenger side of the bus.

> SHELDON
> There's your jet. We get one more (hostage) now. That's the deal.

> SONNY
> Right. Okay... who goes?

> BANK MANAGER
> Sylvia?

> SYLVIA
> Maria.

Maria exits the bus and stands facing inside.

> MARIA
> I'll pray for you... Sal? Because this is your first plane trip don't be scared, okay?

She hands Sal her rosary beads.

SONNY
Hey! I just realized I didn't eat all day... Is there gonna be any food on board?

SHELDON
There'll be hamburgers on the plane. Ready?

SONNY
Sal?

SAL (hardly clear)
Wha...

SONNY
Ready to go?

SAL
Yeah.

SONNY
Okay. Let's move it.

FBI AGENT/DRIVER
Sal? We don't want any accidents at this point right?
Keep your gun pointed up.

Sal obeys instantly. The FBI agent/bus driver opens a small secret compartment in the driver's side arm rest. A revolver is hidden there.

SHELDON
Ready to get out first?

FBI AGENT/DRIVER (taking the revolver)
I'm ready.

Sheldon reaches into the bus and grabs hold of Sonny's rifle. The agent/driver turns and shoots Sal once... right in the middle of his forehead; then puts the cocked revolver to Sonny's left temple.

SONNY

Don't shoot me.

Yes! There *is* visible and verbal warning — the agent's hidden gun; the rosary gift; "Sal? Ready to go?" — something terrible could happen. Does it prepare the audience? Does it infuse a change in *attitude*? Does it overcome the protracted *atmosphere* of festive extravaganza? Should it?

PLACE

Let's begin in the first place! The initial choice for any location starts with the selection of the film frame. The profile of each frame is revealed on a screen by its Aspect Ratio: A mathematical expression of the relationship between the horizontal and the vertical. A square, no matter the measurement of any side, would be expressed in a relationship of horizontal to vertical, or width to height, as 1:1.

Screen size and ratio do impact a presentation — some films "do better" viewed on smaller (home) television screens, and some can be harmed — many multiplex theatres have reduced screen size in comparison to the older, single-screen movie palaces. On the other hand, television screens have been getting larger and larger, and do match a more accurate cinematic aspect ratio.

Producing a synchronous sound film (composite print) required a designated space along the edge of the perforations for an optical (audio) track. With the horizontal line separating each frame widened to produce a picture that would be wider than taller, in an effort to more closely simulate human vision, the early standard aspect ratio (Academy Aperture Ratio) became 1.37:1.

DVDs are most often released in the aspect ratio of a film's intended place. VHS tapes, unless in "letterbox" version, are scanned, or formatted, to "fit your screen."

This means that the film was screened — often by an editor — and various "portions" of the projectable image (place) were selected to be the center of attention, and then optically re-photographed — frame left, right, center; half-left, half-right, or a pan across the frame — so as to be certain the selections would be visible on the smaller, squarer shape of home sets (4:3). You can "see" why so many filmmakers are ambivalent about permitting this. Formatting alters the film's indigenous place, making the composed locations alien, or even outlandish.

The fifty DVDs selected for this book present their locations in a variety of aspect ratios, some in a *wide* variety. They are worth studying for their perceptions of space, influence of the horizon on composition, and the movement of camera and actors "in" the scope of the screen. Here are a few to explore.

Chapter 12, "Germany's Retreat" @ 1:21:07

A horn sounds the rout of the Teutonic Knights. You'll note, in this "square" of early frames (1.33:1), that the composing "signals" the vertical. Both the figure with the horn, and the banner bearer in the background, indicate frame top to bottom. Watch the next several cuts to observe the consistency: Even across the expanse of the frozen Lake Chudskoye, there is a low horizon and so a high sky.

BURNT BY THE SUN

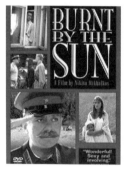

Chapter 4, "Pulling Rank" @ 0:12:27

The film is shot in an unusual 1.62:1, permitting a well-mannered world of the horizontal and/to vertical. Colonel Kotov has been "pulled" from his steam bath to stop advancing tank maneuvers across a wheat field.

The opening shot of Kotov does hold him below the center of the frame, but there is no loss of the field's expanse. The next cut keeps a rather low horizon, but it certainly is not an obvious compositional technique. Kotov's ride along the line of tanks also allows a decent stability — perhaps a bit over-influenced to frame height — between the vertical woods of the background, and the outraged farmers in the foreground. Note how effortlessly the "portraits" play. At **0:14:02**, Kotov and a tank commander run to "watch" fighter planes overhead. The camera tilts upward and pans right as Kotov runs into a Long-Shot. The aspect ratio provides a practical balance in composing the wheat field, the farmers, Kotov, and the plane fly by in the sky.

Chapter 16, "The Last Supper" @ 1:11:00

The 1.66:1 aspect ratio finesses the horizontal somewhat more than the vertical. Viridiana gathers a group of local beggars and provides for them at her deceased uncle's estate. The peculiar group has the "run of things" for a day. Three of the "estate guests" prepare for a formal dinner; they discuss portrait paintings and their subjects. A pan right (horizontal) "fits" better than the composing on the (slight pan back) tilt down to the three; their torsos cut off on the verge of the obvious. The pan left which follows one woman to the glass silverware and table linen cabinet works ably. A fine transition takes us from the envious words of a beggar-guest, "To die without eating off of such wonderful linens" to an Extreme Close-Up of the table top: Scraps of food, soiled plates, and a centered goblet of wine, resting on a folded lace napkin, specify an already consumed meal. A hand reaches for the goblet and tips it. The spilled wine initiates a dolly left which passes the dinner guests seated at the table.

Take note of how beautifully effective is the ever-so-slight high-angle composing from the end of the table @ **1:15:28**, while @ **1:16:30** is one of the most celebrated shots of any Buñuel film — a "muse" for the chapter's title.

8½

Chapter 2, "A Walk in the Park" @ 0:05:42

Another unusual ratio (1.78:1) is handled smartly by director Federico Fellini and cinematographer Gianni Di Venanzo.

As the view of space becomes increasingly horizontal, Medium-Shots of characters become ever more difficult and critical. The (circling) leftward pan and move limits Medium-Shots, displaying Long-Shot backgrounds and Close-Ups. A cut and pan right does the same.

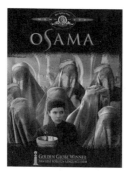

Chapter 6, "Prayer Time" @ 0:29:25

A twelve-year-old girl is disguised as a boy, named Osama, so that she and her mother might survive the brutal Taliban regime. Osama and a generous shopkeeper perform "ablutions" along the water's edge. The Close-Up of their arms and water vessels carry across the more extreme horizontal format of the 1.85:1 aspect ratio. When the two enter a small building for prayer you'll notice that the Long-Shots are frequently higher or lower than eye level, helping avoid the potential for vertical clumsiness in wide-screen compositions. At 0:31:00 the camera looks slightly down and along a row of men bent over with faces to the matted flooring. A cut to a Medium-Shot is well designed for the horizontal dominance of the screen, by using a narrow depth of field — the area in focus is restricted — so that the rising black-bearded Taliban is to the center-right of the screen, framed on both sides and behind, by figures in soft focus, while a vertical post on screen right "reduces" the extent of the aspect ratio.

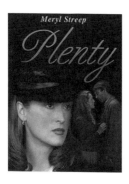

Chapter 5, "Raymond Brock" @ 0:18:27

At 2.35:1 you can see the many hindrances that arise when working across a severe horizontal place; I wonder about the appeal for filmmaker and audience.

British Foreign Service officer Brock makes his way through the chaotic streets in post-World War II Brussels. He is engaged outside the Grand Hotel and asked to take charge of the sudden death of a British guest in the lobby.

You'll note that the opening shot of a busy street, with loud truck traffic of the American Army, and nuns "book-ending" parochial uniformed girls across the screen, fits suitably but for a small awkwardness that occurs with lower bodies nearly cut off. Brock enters frame left and walks into the background occasionally (more or less) badly framed. Watch the next shot, as Brock moves toward the camera, and I think you'll notice the trouble inherent in the frame top to bottom relationship.

The scene outside the hotel is comprised of three set-ups. The first and second provide good illustration in the post-production trouble of such wide-screen framing: A Master-Shot of people and traffic moving across to screen left, uncovers a car being "examined" by two policemen and a civilian. The civilian looks to screen right and acknowledges Brock. Just prior to the second shot Brock appears, entering at the far right of the frame. Take special note of the cut! At the incoming moment of the cut to a Medium-Shot, Brock is not in the frame; he actually enters in this shot as well. The extreme nature of the aspect ratio requires far greater concern for the impact the scope of the frame holds for the editor. It does not take a very quick eye to see that the cut creates the illusion (of course it isn't an illusion at all) that Brock has "backed up" for an instant. This is what comes of "matching" the realities of a location, rather than the spatial needs of the frame. Here the horizontal formatting needs an *addition* of two or three more frames in the outgoing Master-Shot, and a deletion of the same in the *incoming* Medium-Shot; with a "tweaking" of Brock's "Good morning." The greeting should better assist the cut; even if a trifle (or more) out of synchronization.

At **0:20:02** a fully bordered frame in black, but for the delicate curves of two small windows, demonstrates how superfluous so much of the left and right of the frame is. We recognize Brock in the little right window, and two soldiers open the (black) back doors of what turns out to be the inside of an ambulance: A larger illuminated field, and much modified aspect ratio, easily "records" two attendants carrying the body into the ambulance.

The universal standard for the physical size of the film area between the perforations was established by Thomas Edison and William Dickson in 1892. Each frame is four perforations in height, and 35mm (1.38 inches) in width.

William Kennedy Laurie Dickson was born in France, and in early adulthood immigrated to the United States fervent to work for Thomas Edison in his Menlo Park, New Jersey laboratory. Dickson, an amateur photographer, was intrigued by early efforts to make moving pictures. In 1891 Edison filed a patent on the Kinetoscope viewer, which had been created, along with a film strip camera, in 1890 by Dickson.

Eventually Dickson founded his own company, and developed a camera and projector called the Biograph, which allowed films to be displayed for a gathered audience, unlike individual viewing on the Kinetoscope. The company, the American Mutoscope and Biograph Company, released its own films and eventually became a major movie studio of its time.

Film editor Walter Murch recently synchronized a short fragment of film for the Library of Congress. It shows Dickson playing a violin into a large megaphone while two other Edison men dance. The sound had been recorded on an 1890 cylinder; making the seventeen-second sync sound film the oldest in existence.

Doesn't it seem sensible, accurate and right that William Kennedy Laurie Dickson be recognized as the creator of motion pictures?

light

Somewhat genesis-like, the first directors commanded "Lights... camera... action!"

8½

Chapter 1, "Come Into the Light" @ 0:00:25

The DVD's chapter title gives justification I could not resist for my placing this scene at the outset of *Light*. The opening shot fades-in from the briefest of credits: Our protagonist, film director Guido, is caught in a traffic jam. His car has not quite made it to the light at the end of a tunnel. Guido is clothed in black, wearing a Fellini pork pie hat, also black. From our position in the back seat, it appears that Guido is much more bounded in darkness than any other motorist.

The heavy, almost scratchy ambiance, with its incessant, though muted, tin basin-like banging, signals a nightmarish day, made additionally ominous by freeze-frame pauses on passengers in other vehicles.

Guido wipes his windshield with a cloth, and a wispy locust sound fades-in, nearly concomitant to smoke starting to infiltrate the car. Guido's breathing becomes panicked; he pounds and kicks against the doors and windows. His hands desperately smear and scratch across the windows, creating squeegee sounds. Finally, Guido floats free and soars upward into a breezy sky... upward into light! The light announces open, secure, and inspired.

A film student's early production encounters are often light deficient. At the School of Visual Arts — and at many others to be sure — the standing exposure (and joke) is ƒ2.8. That is an aperture begging for light, in suspense if something identifiable will emerge in a frame.

8½ administers a fine exposure test.

Chapter 1, "Come Into the Light" @ 0:05:10

Guido enters the health spa's lavatory. The camera tilts upward from the lower curve of a mirror as it rack focuses to his reflection in Close-Up. Guido's face is a deep gray, separated from the background by vertical borders of lighter grays to a near-white on screen left.

Guido reaches into frame right — his hand in the soft focus of distance, lens selection, and low light — to pull on the light. The "click" of the switch brings craggy illumination to his face, his eyes in dark sockets, his nose casting its shadow from upper lip to chin; the right side of his face shaded so unkindly as to create a mime-like pallor.

A cut brings a Master-Shot, and a superb display of quick flashing increments of increasing light, from a dim moody menace of long shadows to a bright on-high throw of illumination that all but eliminates gray.

The images captured on film are the resulting reaction of silver halide — which has been bonded to a base of celluloid triacetate — infused by direct and reflected light. The pictures produced in the "tarnished" silver particles can then be projected via a beam of light onto a light reflecting screen so to enter the lens of our eyes — absorbed by the sensory membrane retina — initiating an all-embracing response: *Light* is the magic of movies!

Upon viewing D. W. Griffith's *Birth of a Nation*, President Woodrow Wilson is said to have remarked, "It is history written in lightning."

Our eyes supply more than three-quarters of the information gathered by our five senses. You might say that sight enlightens us! It comes as no surprise that the extent of our solace and security is closely linked to our eyes. That link is of course only possible with light. Darkness, and the anxiety it promotes, is not merely the absence of light. The lower the height of a light source, the more blatant the resultant shadows. "Artificial" light used to illuminate interiors, or light produced by fire, which yet provides warmth and comfort, still hint at a potential threat to the primitive aspects of our brain. Is there any wonder that the Old English word deorc (dark) meant gloomy, cheerless? The Indo-European form, dherg could mean dirty; this is the likely source of the word *dregs*. Let's not forget the Dark Ages, or darkness as a foreboding metaphor, as in *ominous* and *secretive*.

The Exorcist is a genre film — advertised as the "Scariest Movie of All Time" — that easily illustrates the exaggeration in contrasts of light and dark so that we can "see" the visual relationship to Story, Place, and Characters.

THE EXORCIST

Chapter 3, "Face to Face" @ 0:08:44

Father Mirrin, in Extreme Long-Shot, arrives in a jeep at the site of an ancient temple. Two men, armed with rifles, cause us alarm as they rush toward the priest. They clearly recognize him as he peacefully gestures "hello" with a wave of his right hand. Note the slight turn of Mirrin as he is about to move off, and the cut back to the soldiers as they begin to walk toward the *shadows* of the archway from which they had appeared. The next cut of Father Mirrin — a Tracking Long-Shot — effectively deletes time from the previous shot. We see the priest walking left to right amid the ruins of the temple. You'll also note that the cut begins with Mirrin not yet visible behind fallen columns; the few beats of Mirrin hidden assist the intelligibility of the time deletion. There is, as well, a simple segue across the cut making use of footsteps. The tracking shot is not precisely horizontal, but rather, it brings Mirrin and the camera to each other, so that by the end of the shot Mirrin is closer, and therefore larger in scale.

At **0:09:18** another Extreme Long-Shot frames Mirrin in a large field of collapsed structures — a grotesque wall on screen right. The camera zooms out, as Father Mirrin makes his way from the *shadows* into a *bright sun* — the camera zoom, and Mirrin come to rest at the same time — a cut to his Close-Up happens simultaneously with a surge in wind; his hat brim twists as *darkness* covers his face. A back-lit point of view (POV) shot *silhouettes* (a dark outline of form) a stone demon. A terrible swirl of music *highlights* the evil figure; *sun rays* yield red arching flares of light: A foreboding!

The uneasiness of "being in the dark" might explain the ever-increasing comfort in the opening of *Catch-22*. Before there is light there is darkness — and silence! The film begins in black:

CATCH-22

Chapter 1, "Help the Bombardier" @ 0:00:06

The head credits are white in a military-stencil font. The black is not merely a background for the credits. It turns out to be an end to darkness: a new morning. Incrementally the darkness gives way to approaching light, and an image: A sun rises over a rocky landscape on the Italian Mediterranean. The light invites dawn birds, and they call to time-lapse photography which hastens the sun's light striking the water in a glowing beam which moves backward from the foreground to meet the light at its source. Our comfort in light, setting, and sound is obliterated by a staggeringly contrasting cranking, belching, and yowling of B-25 engines as the Army Air Force bombers ready for a WWII mission.

One of the boldest illustrations of movie darkness "appears" at the outset of *Plenty*.

PLENTY

Chapter 1, "Main Titles" @ 0:00:18

Over black, and accompanied by full orchestration, are yellow titles. The filmmakers play on our discomfort with darkness; it augments secrecy and danger. At about **0:01:24** in the left quarter of the screen a face begins to appear. It is some distance away so it is small, and we can make out that it is looking upward. At about **0:01:48** another face becomes apparent, just to the left of the first. By **0:02:00** we see that the two faces are to the right of a line of others; all are looking skyward from the edge of woods. A whisper and the faint drone of an airplane's propeller engine are heard. There is more whispering; and now lights blink from the woods.

There is light beaming from the projection booth, but hardly a thing is visible on the screen. Then a Close-Up of a lantern blinks a signal; its light refractions create a near dissolve Close-Up of the protagonist, Susan Traherne. A full frame of the sky barely precedes a "whump" of a parachute opening and jolting with the force of caught air. Things in the *night* are beginning to make *sense*. The darkness depicts a supply drop to resistance fighters in Nazi-occupied France. As best I can recall the theatre viewing of the film, I feel certain that the DVD release has modified the *darkness*; there is far less effective difficulty in seeing.

The flashlights in the dark illustrate light as *focal point*. Our eyes will follow the light; indeed, they will be attracted to it.

THE FRENCH CONNECTION

Chapter 25, "Tearing It Apart" @ 1:25:23
A work-light prompts a series of bold cuts as detectives and a mechanic, in a police department garage, callously tear — and break — apart a Lincoln automobile as they rummage around for suspected hidden heroin. You'll note that the previous scene's last image @ **1:25:22** displayed a single headlight of a police vehicle. This chapter opens with the garage work light practically positioned — in the incoming frame — where our eyes have been focused on the headlight in the outgoing frame.

From **1:25:38** the theme of light as an influence on cuts quickens, so that between **1:25:48** and **1:26:33** the idea of light as focal point, and focal point as initiator of cuts, is even more *focused* and observable.

The etymology of *focus* is rich with associations to light, optics (eyes), design and attention.

Focus with its synonym *focal point* derives from the Latin for *hearth*, as in *fireplace* or *flame*. The link to hearth also leads to *central point; center*, and a *point of interest*. Light as focus/focal point is perhaps more obvious in the craft of theatre. The eyes of the audience are essentially focused — brought to attention — by spots of light. Light might be a more intricate matter in cinema, while neverthe-less taking its cue from the stage. The theatrical use of light as focal point in mise-en-scène is bluntly illustrated in *The Ladykillers*.

THE LADYKILLERS

Chapter 4, "The Gang's All Here" @ 0:13:28;
Chapter 5, "A Spot of Tea" @ 0:14:45
The gang is together in the apartment rented by Professor Marcus from the elderly Mrs. Wilberforce. Gang member Louis distrusts the "getaway" planned for the armored car heist that uses innocent Mrs. Wilberforce to escort the stolen money. Especially take note of the light and effective discrepancy in the first two cuts: Reverse Master-Shots.

Initially we are behind the reclining Professor Marcus and all of the gang members' faces are spotted in light. The second shot @ **0:13:36** captures Marcus as the focal point in light, frame location, and a composing that quickly directs our eyes because the gang members "surround" the Professor. But you'll see that this reverse "suddenly" puts One-Round and Harry in the dark, and, in so doing, this *mismatch* guarantees clarity of focal point.

In "**A Spot of Tea**" the gang hurries to answer the door knocks of Mrs. Wilberforce who, appreciating the lovely string music, has graciously arrived with tea for all. The gang gathers their instruments in hand, and Professor Marcus opens the door. Mrs. Wilberforce, again in a Master-Shot, steps forward into the glowingly illuminated doorway as the unmistakable focal point of the composition — no doubt assisted by the action of the door opening. The gang, in this set-up, frames Mrs. Wilberforce. Then an amazing and wonderful choice is revealed on the next cut, and another reverse Master-Shot: The gang members with all of their *faces in light* appear in a new arrangement. They are now in a single line; all of them on the right side of the frame. Very theatrical and simul-taneously cinematic in its clarity of focal point, and boldness of an alternative to reality!

Our eyes "feel" like watching people — we'll seek them out within the frame. We prefer to consider a face, and specifically people's eyes.

While light is central to mood, information and focal point, on occasion fascinating conflicts must be reconciled.

BREAKER MORANT

Chapter Index 9, Chapter 38, "The Verdict" @ 1:31:26

George Witton returns to his cell after hearing the verdict and sentence from his court martial. The camera, and the audience, observe the scene from inside the cell. Witton enters the doorway and approaches the camera. A guard closes the door, greatly reducing the light within the cell. A barred window of bright light, on the right side of the screen, holds our attention. This box of light might easily be the focal point of the composition. A guard passes the window so that Harry Morant — another court martial defendant — can be taken from his cell to learn the court's verdict and his sentence. Harry pauses in the barred light, fixing the collar on his tunic. The light — somewhat theatre-like in its "spotting" our focus — might create a tension in the composition but for a first-rate factor: The edge of Witton's cheek-bone and rim of his collar are lit with an illumination equal to the radiance of the window. A fine balance exists between focal point by light, and focal point by character's face: and eyes. If you watch this scene on a smallish screen, try covering the light which touches Witton's face, and I think you'll see that having the light makes all the difference.

Sven Nykvist's remark about "too much light" and "atmosphere" brings up some fundamental points. Light is not primarily to guarantee an exposure; atmosphere *is* impacted by light; atmosphere is an essential link between scene and story, and a central contribution of the cinematographer and production designer. Nykvist has also commented that it is curious how "infrequent [is the] mention of atmosphere in screenplays."

There are three basic "presentations" in light:

Key Light – A central source of illumination.

Fill Light – A balance to bring illumination to shadow areas and soften excessive or harsh contrasts.

Back-Light – Illumination which assists in the visibility of objects providing spatial clarity between foreground and background.

All three can be arranged in whole or in part, and can be organized and modified by various permutations: Direct; Reflected (Bounced); Flood to Spot; Diffused; Scrim or Flag.

"Consistency" in lighting makes good sense given film's inherent separation, and the post-production necessities of assembling individual *fragments*. But it is not required that each shot bring an identical result. As set-ups display a scene in Master-Shot, there is a concern that production equipment not be visible: Scrims, flags, lights, reflectors all must be out of sight! This is generally a fortunate proposition because it is in the Medium-Shots and Close-Ups that a "match" — of sorts — need only be *implied* while aesthetic considerations become paramount.

THE LONELINESS OF THE LONG DISTANCE RUNNER

Chapter 20, "Caught" @ 1:24:20

The scene is made up of three set-ups: a Master-Shot which begins with a dolly following parallel to the reformatory's governor and coming to a stop as the governor addresses Colin about his health and running; a Medium-Shot of Colin, the axis slightly adjusted right of the Master-Shot; and a Medium-Shot of the governor with axis slightly to the left.

You'll easily notice that the day is bright with the sun angling from screen left across the figures so that shadows are long, and strong contrasts from light to dark are apparent. Yet the Medium-Shots have softened the contrasts. While they do make for a more pleasing arrangement in key and fill light balance, they are perhaps more obvious than should be expected. There's a difference in back-light which high-lights Colin's hair in his Medium-Shot, but vanishes on the Medium-Shot of the governor. The softening of contrasts is especially needed and successful in the Medium-Shot of the governor. His hat would otherwise create unappealingly harsh shadows. You can see these in the Master-Shot, though they bother us little. What is consistent — in illusion — is that the sun is shining from behind Colin (screen left), and this "keeps" our eyes a bit settled.

Black-and-white film is rated for its responsiveness to illumination — ASA, ISO, EI or DIN — and values in contrast and granular visibility. Color film is rated both in light sensitivity and in either daylight or tungsten. Both are measured in degrees Kelvin: 5400K–5600K (daylight) or 3200K–3400K (tungsten): the higher the temperature in degrees Kelvin, the more blue-white the light, the lower the temperature the more orange-red the light. There are conversion and correction filters that "take the film" through a broad range of color temperatures (available light) to "match" the demands of different film stocks, and artists.

The Kelvin scale is named for the nineteenth-century physicist William Thomson, 1st Baron Kelvin (1824-1907). At age ten, he began studies at the University of Glasgow; published two papers by seventeen, and graduated from Cambridge University at twenty-one. At twenty-two he was awarded the chair of natural philosophy at the University of Glasgow. His work assisted in the development of the Second Law of Thermodynamics, and in 1848 he invented the temperature scale named after him.

Thomson was chief consultant for the laying of the first Atlantic cable (1857–1858); he contributed to the determination of the age of the Earth and the study of hydrodynamics; published more than 600 scientific papers, and received dozens of honorary degrees. He remained at the University of Glasgow until his retirement in 1899.

Let's screen a colorfully brilliant illustration of choices in light and pro-duction design, and costume: objects as visible scrims (in primary colors) to diffuse the back-light which is key to the illumination.

Chapter 3, "Attractions" @ 0:22:35

Tianging — in a low-angle Extreme Long-Shot — hangs pale blue and red dyed silks to dry. The sky is a backdrop of formless white light. The back-light, softened and diffused by the hanging silk, and (likely) diffused and/or reflected light initiated from the opposite side, permits full visibility of Tianging, rather than a view in silhouette.

Ju Dou, in Medium-Long-Shot, gathers wet, red dyed silks as if collecting a skein of knitting wool, with over and under gestures. She wears a pale blue top with a red tie in her hair. Note the bright yellow sunlight on the wall and large post, and the gentle shadows cast by the waving silks from above. As Ju Dou turns to look toward Tianging, you'll notice a busier shadow "billows" onto the pole. This "matches" Tianging's gathering of silk at the incoming of his Medium-Shot. Tianging sees that he is being eyed, and quickly turns away.

Ju Dou now turns to face the wooden platform upon which Tianging works, and so motivates a point of view (POV) Extreme Long-Shot looking upward to Tianging. Ju Dou enters into her POV from screen left, her hair and shoulders highlighted from above. Here is something not to be overlooked. Ju Dou does not leave the frame in the previous shot, and so her entry in the next provides "brand-new" information: Ju Dou draws near the working Tianging. Instead of the more typical approach which would have us follow Ju Dou as she moves across one frame to another — one space to the next — a minor, though vital, "surprise" occurs.

The next cut, a low-angle Medium-Shot of Tianging, provides a good illustration of light diffused by way of a scrim. Watch the variety and intensity of the illumination as Tianging alters the diffusion as he hoists the silk (a scrim) and thereby blocks and softens the flooding light in the sky.

Here's an example that splendidly illustrates the flexibility in choices — back-light as key light and a predominance of "non-corrected" blue light — and serves as a good introduction to our next chapter.

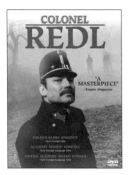

Chapter 8, "Duel of Dishonor" @ 0:37:09

Schorm and Kubinyi are scheduled to an early morning duel in the gymnasium of the military academy. Redl arrives to find Schorm — unable to sleep in the throes of frightful anxiety — already there.

The scene opens in Master-Shot. A haze of light from a row of windows along the back wall of the gymnasium puts Redl and Schorm in silhouette. Yet the second shot, a Close-Up of the two men, displays their faces with adequate detail. The mood is maintained — certainly crucial across the assorted set-ups — via illumination gently reflected back from the windows' source; and providing fill-light detail to the dark side of the space.

Following Kubinyi's arrival, a Medium-Shot returns Schorm to the screen. Note that while he is back-lit — a row of windows contrasts his dark hair offering a separation — the back-light is the key-light; and Schorm is neither in silhouette nor is he gently illuminated in reflected light. The overall ambiance is maintained within a realm of light between the first and second shots.

setting

This chapter might have been entitled *Location*. Allow me to take a more "spacious" account. While permitting a consideration of specific interiors or exteriors — the Place of a scene — it grants a look at the *epoch* in Character and Story.

Cinematographer Néstor Almendros and Director François Truffaut faced an intriguing dispute in their collaboration on *La Chambre verte* (1978; U.S. title *The Green Room* or *The Vanishing*). According to Almendros, "Truffaut had [a] weird idea [for] period movies." Their quarrel resulted from differing mental pictures each insisted should be evident to the other, and provides an answer to the question, "How is history best 'translated' to film?" While collaboration means alliance, teamwork, and cooperation, it does not preclude clashes. Collaboration requires an attempt to set aside idiosyncratic preferences and egocentric excitement in favor of the project's advance. Any dispute which yields a benefit is commendable.

Almendros challenged the notion held by Truffaut and, at one time, a great many other filmmakers that historic pieces — the past of long ago — ought to be filmed in black and white. Truffaut believed that color was anachronistic. Almendros, who "knew the past through painting," and so in color, was unquestionably doing his job with valued devotion. The cinematographer's foremost responsibilities are in the service of the material — the screenplay — not to the director. The same can be said for the film editor: *Material* in the post-production process is the photographed images, and the editor's paramount commitment should be to those images. It should be said that this should be true for all the cast and crew!

In the end *La Chambre Verte* was shot in color! An admirable clash benefited the film.

Colonel Redl is a period piece; the story takes place over some thirty-five years leading up to the First World War. The filmmakers use a small medley of stock footage from the time; a time of only B&W cinematography.

COLONEL REDL

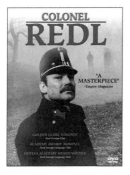

See Chapter 27, "A Piece of History" @ 2:17:12. The overall "environment" is drawn from a selective simplicity of color. Exteriors (natural light) are mostly in blue — see **Chapter 2, "Cadet School" @ 0:05:02** — while interiors (artificial light) are, for the most part, rendered orange. See **Chapter 3, "Winter At Grandmother's" @ 0:07:46**. These chromatic choices "appear" to embrace an accurate "feel" for the epoch and locations.

If daylight-balanced film (balanced for 5400 degrees Kelvin) is exposed in artificial light (3400 degrees Kelvin), an overall cast of orange will prevail. Conversely, if tungsten-balanced film (artificial light) is exposed in natural light (5400 degrees Kelvin), the film will hold an overall cast of blue. Filters do exist which convert daylight to tungsten, and tungsten to daylight. Not surprisingly, the filters are in blue (No. 80) and orange (No. 85).

Add the collection of laboratory and optical techniques, and weeks of photographic and/or digital tests, and filmmakers have hundreds of choices available!

I encourage students to solve problems with a search for *variety*; many work best in differing combinations. In the worlds of medicine, economics, and politics, experts often seek a one-and-only answer to complex problems. There cannot be a sole solution — most especially not in the world of art — because nothing is absolute!

In this regard let's turn to *Butch Cassidy and the Sundance Kid.*

This nineteenth century — the epoch — story was depicted in black and white and color. The opening of the film renders the era as if viewing a faded photograph of yesteryear. The opening sequence continues the visual theme of the head credits, in which a projector runs "distressed" film clips of Butch and Sundance's Hole in the Wall Gang busy "pulling" a train robbery, and chased by a posse.

BUTCH CASSIDY AND THE SUNDANCE KID

Chapter 2, "Butch" @ 0:02:56

A hue of brownish gray — sepia tone — composes a series of Close-Ups. Butch checks out a local bank, and sees — watch how Butch's eyes motivate the brisk cutting of the bank scene — that it has the latest contraptions in security. "What happened to the old bank? It was beautiful!" Butch asks the uniformed guard. "People kept robbing it," to which Butch responds, "That's a small price to pay for beauty!"

Chapter 3, "Sundance" @ 0:09:02

After a card-cheating dispute in the local bar, Butch and Sundance gather their winnings and exit. A dissolve takes us to a Long-Shot of the two men riding off toward the light of the background sky.

Chapter 4, "Hole in the Wall Gang" @ 0:09:09

Another dissolve fades-out the sepia, and fades-in full color. The first dissolve, which ends Chapter 3, is traditional and evident. Two distinct images are joined by way of a simultaneous fade-out of the first and a fade-in of the second.

The dissolve that brings color is not evident because it takes place within a single image. The original image of Butch and Sundance — and the entirety of the production — is in color. A b&w positive master (Pan Master) was made from the original images shot with color negative film. A positive color master (Interpositive) was also made. An optical department then re-photograped the two master elements onto a new color negative, with a simultaneous fade-out from the Pan Master, and fade-in to the Interpositive. In other words, because the dissolve occurs upon itself — the image does not change — only the introduction of full color is observed. The sepia is created in the newly produced color negative (Internegative), from the re-photographed (b&w) Pan Master: You can choose any number of monochromes.

I bring this up, not to offer *training* in optical effects, but to *school* the reader in the collaboration of post-production. This is mentioned to advise against a "one or the other" mind set.

This can bring us to Settings as Location and Mood:

THE GODFATHER

Chapter 10, "How's the Italian Food in This Restaurant?" @ 1:23:25

An Extreme Long-Shot: 1940s-era automobile headlights shine onto a Bronx street, casting a green hue to a slightly wet pavement. A long black limo brings Michael Corleone, Sollozo, and Police Captain McClusky to Louis' Restaurant. The vehicle pulls up to the curb, but before it comes to a complete stop, there is a cut to the interior of the car: Michael in Close-Up. There is a lovely touch to the incoming moment of Michael. His body tilts a tad, responding to laws of inertia. This shot will be followed by the previous Long-Shot along the curb. The eyes of characters are so essential a factor in focal point that I'll aim your attention to the conspicuousness of the cut from Michael back to the Long-Shot. Michael's eyes shift downward some two to three frames before the cut, reducing the good motivation to the cut back to the Long-Shot which shows the men exiting the limo. The downward shift of his eyes also incites our eyes to watch with a new alertness, and no sooner does this happen than the cut occurs. Ed Dmytryk refers to such "glitches" as "mental hiccups."

You'll notice the Christmas-like complement in light between the red of Louis' sign and the interior's illumination. Uncorrected fluorescent light is often greenish.

The next cut is, notwithstanding the location and chapter title, delicious! Street traffic and a nearby elevated train rumbling continue across a jump in time. An Extreme Long-Shot finds the three men already seated and a waiter approaching from the background with a plate of raw vegetables and a bottle of wine.

The apprehension in the scene rests in dramatic irony: The audience knows that Michael is supposed to kill both the corrupt police captain and the Corleone family's Mafia adversary. We know that a gun will be waiting for him in the restaurant's bathroom, and so we feel a re-charged tension when Michael says, "I have to go to the bathroom. Is that all right?" The filmmakers then build upon this by Sollozzo's frisking of Michael. McCluskey checked him for a weapon earlier in the limo.

At **1:26:54** a reverse Long-Shot offers a perfect lesson in location setting and mood: Michael is nearly silhouetted as he stands alongside the table. But he holds his form, separated from the background by the red neon of Louis' window sign, and the highlight off his hair. The tablecloths reflect light so that the table tops — rectangular and round — frame the three men, and create a rich, engaging depth to the dining area. McCluskey is lit by a light to the upper left of the frame, and by light reflected by the napkin he's tucked under his chin. Sollozzo's dark form is accented by the earth colors of the walls. An overall "feel" for post-WWII New York is reliant on autos, objects, costumes, and make-up, but it is made exceptional by the production designer's and cinematographer's simple earthen palette: A deep yellow-umber in "flesh-tones" and place, with vividly controlled splashes (an oxymoron?) of red and orange light, make plausible the epoch. A meal out and "using" the bathroom — in preparation for a double killing — provoke a paradox in the ordinary, and a disturbing vulnerability. Note the simplicity of the set-ups in the bathroom, the time taken to feel for the gun, and the recurrence of the elevated rumblings.

Let's stay with bathrooms and their peculiar sway.

Psycho, the 1960 Alfred Hitchcock thriller, was reported to have been the first American mainstream movie to show a flushing toilet.

PSYCHO

Check in. Relax. Take a shower.

Chapter 10, "The Shower" @ 0:46:12.

The selection of the Bates Motel bathroom for the cruel murder scene, altered shower-taking habits for years afterward. Is there another setting so immediate in promising susceptibility?

In keeping with our sudden bathroom settings, let me conclude this chapter with a masterful example that crosses the threshold into the next chapter's sphere.

ATLANTIC CITY

Burt Lancaster · Susan Sarandon
A Louis Malle Film

ATLANTIC CITY

Nominated for 5 Academy Awards

Chapter 5, "White Christmas" @ 0:20:26

Dave arrives in Atlantic City with the dope he's filched from a phone booth drug-drop in Philadelphia. Needing help finding local customers for the stolen cocaine, he elicits the help of Fred, the operator of Clifton's Bar.

Dave follows Fred… to the bathroom? Yes! It is, for now, Fred's private office! A patron, already making use of the place, is unsympathetically escorted out by Fred. There is irony (a joke on Dave) in the choice of the setting, but it is not without its threat. We learn from Fred that word is out about the dope lifted from a Philadelphia phone booth. Dave naïvely confirms the news, hoping that by "cutting" Fred in, he'll be secure.

Fred controls the *setting*, moving, with the camera, toward Dave to take a "taste," then moves — the camera following with a pan right — to check out his eyes in the mirror on the opposite wall. Fred walks to the far end of the bathroom to "use" the toilet. His face above the stall wall, he pees, and lets Dave in on his "business philosophy." The audience views all four walls of the setting, and Dave, the desperate amateur dealer, pleadingly tails along seeking cocaine-interested clients.

Fred finally relents and writes a phone number on the back of a business card: "I'd love to help my friend." But, instead of passing the card to the eagerly waiting Dave — "I don't do business with you" — Fred flushes it down the toilet. Dave scuttles to the bowl, reaching deep and just catching the card. "Shit!" He wipes his hand — on his jacket — and the card, both drenched in water and urine.

The *setting* imparts a poignant foundation. It links the Place and the Characters, sustains Dave's vulnerability and prompts his association with Lou Pascal, and, in doing that, it augurs the plot of the Story.

The connections to the three sections of this book are not limited to *Atlantic City*. With all my bathroom talk, I did not mean to suggest — nor recommend — that particular facility as key to cinematic settings, but only to emphasize the significance in selecting locations. The location is the Place from which we can derive mood, action and the temperament of performance; and so Character and Story.

space

Film is a two-dimensional presentation of images which have been produced in a three-dimensional setting. From our childhood discovery of single-point perspective, summoned in drawing after drawing of railroad tracks vanishing on the "horizon" of art room pads, we, as grown-ups, remain fascinated by the illusion of genuine space displayed "in" the surface of paper or up on a movie screen. The "deception" is an essential element in cinema's attraction — it is mesmerizing to our eyes! I found an ideal model of my childhood railroad track drawings.

HIGH NOON

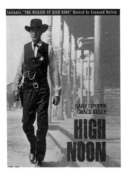

Chapter 12, "Church Meeting" @ 0:45:50
Director Fred Zinnemann's arrangement exceeds a mere fascination with creating depth. The context cannot be evaded — the menacing wait for Frank Miller. Zinnemann contrasts the inescapable *advance of time* — the hands and swinging pendulums of clocks, conveying danger, due from out of a (distant) past, arriving at noon, en route along the *unmoving tracks.*

Even though the tracks are at a standstill, their relationship to perspective and our perception results from their scale as well. That is, the wooden horizontal ties and the vertical gauge of the rails appear to condense — become smaller — the higher they "climb" in the frame. It is this that creates the spatial illusion of depth. Our visual reference does *not* imply a quickly diminishing tower rising vertically.

The impact of scale, and visual references, bestow wondrously unlimited distance "within" the fixed, flat surface of the silver screen.

THE VIRGIN SPRING

Chapter 8, "Three Goatherds" @ 0:30:58
Karin's horse whinnies, and the sound is heard by three herdsmen at rest in a glade.

At **0:31:17** a shot of two of the brothers gives initial hint to scale and space: The younger (clearly still a boy) is larger, though smaller! Our visual reference "tells" us that he is closer, but closer than whom? Closer than the older brother! The older brother is smaller and therefore farther back. Back from what? The screen is flat!

I don't mean to be either annoying or obvious, but watch as the camera pans left to focus on the third brother; so large is he that his face nearly fills the frame. You will admit that this shot is brilliantly engaging. The elements that produce "space" are understandable and reasonable, but the shot is not any less astonishing.

Lenses provide an immediate and discernible rendition of space: Expansiveness, compression, depth, object relationships, focal point, and altogether they fashion a composition. Lens choices can permit easy — if not quick — adjustments in focus, allow distances to appear greater than the eyes' (or camera position's) view, closer, or just about the same. This illusion or matching of distance is the basis for determining a normal lens, wide angle lens, or long lens. A normal lens (25mm focal length lens for 16mm format, and a 50mm focal length lens for 35mm) produces an "equivalent" distance from camera to subject. A lens that "increases" (expands) the distance (space) is considered wide angle, and a lens that decreases (compresses) the distance (space) is considered a long lens or telephoto. Zooming-in or zooming-out is nothing more than changing the focal length of the lens while continuing to shoot.

Watch the shot again, and you'll notice that the opening moment — on the two brothers — holds focus well "into" the background, but the pan to the third brother exposes a background out of focus. The camera's lens has been adjusted for distance during the pan left, so that the third brother will be in focus. The third brother sits closer to the camera, and if the distance setting on the lens remained as it was for the two brothers, the third brother would be out of focus — but "his" background would be sharp. The closer a subject is to the camera, the more critical is the focus. The further the subject is from the camera, the more likely it is that objects between the camera and the subject will be in (relative) focus, and even more likely still, the objects beyond the subject will remain in focus. This is a simple explanation of depth of field: the points in space between the camera and the "focused subject," and the points beyond that retain focus.

At **0:31:21** a cut takes the audience a good distance away from the three brothers. Take note that the foreground — the area in the lower frame — is in focus, and how decently focused is the background. I'll point out that the filmmakers know what design they have in mind, and so they've "cheated" a little bit. The third brother is going to rush the camera, and needs to be in focus when his face again fills the frame; the lens is already focused on a point somewhat in front of the brothers. A wide-angle lens is being used which produces the deep expanse of space — probably creating a distance twice the actual (a 20mm-25mm lens in a 35mm format) from camera to the brothers — and will be more forgiving of a minor ambiguity in distance setting.

Watch as the third brother does "rush" the camera: The two other brothers move incrementally out of focus. The depth of field narrows as the subject of focus is closer to the camera. Note the "distortion" in the width of the third brother's face, and the exaggerated distance from his face to his shoulders, and how the width across his shoulders appears too short for the proportions of his face. These factors result from the optical properties of a wide-angle lens: Spatial relationships are magnified *and* exaggerated, but, for this moment, in this story, a dazzling lens to choose.

The third brother looks back, and you'll note the distance setting has been adjusted (rack focus) as the camera continues to run. The two brothers in the background come into better focus and *they* rush toward the camera. Because they do not approach as near to the lens as did the third brother, they are less affected by the distortions of a wide-angle lens.

Focus and other aspects of depth of field are also impacted by light. The more light available, the smaller the aperture setting for exposure, and of course the opposite is true. The smaller the aperture setting (f:8, f:11, f:22), the greater will be the depth of field, and with that comes a distance setting that is less critical. While the combination of more light, small aperture, and wide angle lens sounds awfully appealing in its "easiness" and mercies, alternatives do exist, and they are the preferred choices for other moments in other stories.

A good illustration of this can be seen in Andrei Tarkovsky's short film *The Steamroller and the Violin*.

THE STEAMROLLER AND THE VIOLIN

Chapter 3, "Sasha's Adventures on the way to the Music Lesson" @ 0:07:14

A boy comes through a large and grand doorway. He has completed his lesson, and appears upset. His mother hurries to him and is relieved when she sees the grade the boy has been given. The mother encourages her son, "Don't cry. What's the matter dear? A 'B' is a good grade."

Watching them leave @ **0:07:55** is Sasha — awaiting his violin lesson — and a girl in pink. You'll note that Sasha is favored by the lens: He is in focus while the girl is "clearly" soft. Even when Sasha looks to the girl — and she smiles shyly — the lens is not adjusted to fix her distance to the camera so as to bring her into sharpness. There is something fascinating about this, because our eyes can't do it: They will focus in an instant when we shift our gaze. It is only when Sasha gets up to go through the large — and also out of focus — door in the background that the lens is adjusted so as to focus *somewhat* into the distance of the seated girl. As Sasha moves away from the camera toward the lesson room door, the lens holds the girl in focus. Sasha has left an apple — was it supposed to go to the teacher? — on the edge of the girl's chair. Tempted by the apple, the girl reaches and stops, startling a cat that was resting on another, cushioned chair. After the cut to the cat, a new set-up brings us back to the girl. The camera is now lower; framing ever so subtly upward. The apple is centered at frame bottom, and Sasha's chair is out of focus below it. The girl moves the apple — beyond tempting distance? — and the camera moves in and left. As the distance between camera and apple closes, and the lens is less wide angle (longer focal length) than that of the "three brothers scene," the light is less luminous, requiring a larger aperture (f:3.5, f:5.6) for exposure, and the depth of field narrows to the extreme. Nonetheless, a beautiful moment!

Let's look at another example of an appealing spatial presentation via an intentionally narrowed depth of field:

JEAN DE FLORETTE

Chapter 3 & 4, @ 0:21:44

This scene, in one set-up, begins with an Extreme Close-Up of hands at work on a writing instrument. Wood particles are rubbed into a small box. An inkwell, ashtray, lamp base, and writing tablet sit on the round table. The camera tilts upward with a simultaneous pan right, following the "pencil," to a Close-Up of Cesar Soubeyran. In the background, on screen left sits Cesar's nephew, Ugolin. But for Cesar's face, the entire frame is exaggeratedly blurred.

By reducing the illumination which "strikes" the film, a "reasonable" exposure requires that the aperture of the lens be adjusted to allow more light to pass through the lens: Remember that a lower-numbered f-stop (f:2, f:3.5, f:5.6) gives a *larger* aperture (opening), and contributes to a narrower depth of field; the higher numbers (f:8; f:11; f:22) give a smaller aperture, and increase the depth of field. Why the *lower/larger* and the *higher/smaller*? This is because the f-stop numbers represent a ratio of the focal length of the lens to the diameter of its aperture settings. As the aperture opening becomes ever smaller, the ratios to the focal length of the lens increase.

The acute blurring of the background is achieved by focusing the lens on Cesar and positioning Ugolin beyond the point at which the focal length of the lens combined with a larger aperture setting will limit the clarity/sharpness of the space beyond Cesar. You can relax a bit; there are charts and other "tools" that calibrate such permutations!

Beyond perspective in single (or multiple) vanishing points, scale of objects, their position in the frame, the lens choices, or illumination and aperture, lies a simple yet effective device for rendering space in two dimensions: overlapping objects.

Let's continue with *The Steamroller and the Violin*.

THE STEAMROLLER AND THE VIOLIN

Chapter 4, "A Lesson on the Violin" @ 0:09:05. Sasha, in Close-Up, has begun his playing. The music can already be heard as Chapter 3 concludes — the sound of his violin through the lesson room doors sitting soft in the background.

A pan left, with focus adjustments, crosses the pages of notes on Sasha's music stand and the music teacher's glass of water, which initially appears as shimmering light until the object comes into focus. The teacher admonitions her pupil, "Don't get carried away Sasha. And don't sway."

A Master-Shot portrays Sasha's pause. The teacher, an imposing woman, finally appears, moving from left to right, her figure crossing Sasha: She is in front — closer to the camera — of the boy. She instructs Sasha without eye contact, "From the top." Still in Master-Shot, Sasha begins again. The teacher's dark form now crosses from right to left, again establishing a spatial relationship through overlapping. This time her movement fully conceals Sasha, and as her form moves across the frame Sasha is revealed in Medium-Shot. The teacher is unsatisfied, "This is uneven. What's with you... once again from the top... let's go." Clapping to counts, the teacher's silhouette moves to the right yet again, turning the entire frame black, "Tempo, tempo!" Her overlapping brings Sasha in Close-Up; an out of focus, yet evident, metronome is plopped down in the right foreground of the frame, ticking the teacher's count for Sasha.

While the teacher decides, "What should I do with you? Too much imagination!" Sasha, @ 0:10:58, is much closer to the metronome as he gathers his things — the lesson is ended. He walks into the background, receding in size, a portion of the frame *overlapped* by the metronome.

Space can also be "constructed" via compositions within the film frame. Director Jules Dassin makes use of internal (borders and frames) spatial references.

Chapter 2, "Poker Game" @ 0:03:17

Tony le Stéphanois is out of cash. His poker-playing pals won't stake him, and so he announces that he'll "call for cash." He leaves the table in two shots: a Close-Up and a Master-Shot. A cut takes us to a Close-Up of framed glass. It is a large, translucent, rippled pane in the door of the "back room" card game. Tony enters screen right; he opens the door and looks back to the players. Perhaps the shot holds too briefly — a dissolve takes us to Tony's friend Jo le Suedois — but hitting the pause button on your remote will allow for additional time to study the composed space: The opening door reveals another room. It is in soft focus, yet it attracts the eye with a new and deeper space framed in the doorway, accented by Tony's Close-Up on the right side of the film frame.

Chapter 4, "L'Age D'or" @ 0:11:52

Tony encounters Mado, his long-ago love. She is seated with another man at a table in the club that bears the name of the chapter title. Note how two distinct pillars — one vertically etched, narrowing toward its top, the other a twisting spiral column — border the center of the film frame, and frame Tony's approach to Mado's table. Tony tells the "other man' to "Scram," and he and Mado leave.

Chapter 5, "At Home with Tony" @ 0:12:41

A dissolve from the previous chapter brings the audience to a door which is opening away from the camera. In shadow, Tony and Mado frame the background space of Tony's apartment. Tony accuses Mado of betrayal and infidelity; he orders that she remove her jewelry and fur coat. Tony stands in the doorway of the bedroom, and calls Mado to him. In an intonation both sensual and threatening Tony commands that "the rest of it" be removed. Mado undresses.

The wall on the right, bordered at the top of the frame by a wall telephone and a curved chair back on the left, frames Tony and Mado; they are ever more compactly framed within the doorway.

Chapter 6, "At Home with Mario" @ 0:17:36

Tony and Jo arrive at Mario's apartment to agree to the heist scheme. Mario's woman friend, Ida, who has been helping Mario with his bath, greets them at the door. Tony and Jo open the bathroom door; the two men, framed by the doorway, frame Mario in the tub. Upon hearing the good news, Mario cheerfully climbs from the tub. Jo has stepped into the bathroom, positioned between Tony and Mario, and Tony has moved toward frame left, more fully in the doorway, so that Tony, in his black suit, overlaps Jo, in his gray sport jacket, who overlaps the wet Mario who is pulling on his white bathrobe. The line-up of values and the overlapping of the three figures create a rich and sophisticated version of space, all framed within the bathroom doorway.

Finally, Ida appears and Mario encourages his "pet' to go to bed ("Warm up my side"), explaining that the men must talk. A cut to a Master-Shot gives perfect illustration to Dassin's spatial design via borders within the film frame. Tony and Jo, with backs to the camera, stand in the foreground — slightly right of frame center — framed by a variety of doors, the largest and centered double doorway frames Ida and Mario in the background; they are framed by no less than three doors leading the eye to frame right, and to the deepest space of the lighted bathroom. Ida says, "Good night" exiting away and through a door, as Mario walks forward through opened double doors, toward Tony and Jo, closing the two doors behind him.

Spatial relationships and the simplest notions of a "make-believe" three dimensions are enhanced by contrasts in scale, axis of camera, and lens choices. There are occasions when the space within a scene needs to be placed into service for a second time, or more. Beyond the craft of creating space is the art of employing that space for dramatic purpose in storytelling, or story*showing!*

In *Serpico*, Frank and Inspector Lombardo, working undercover, watch a storefront gambling operation. With the place guarded by lookouts, the two police officers decide to go to the roof of another building, and then descend a fire-escape, which will bring them to the street behind the lookout guarding curbside — at the gambling parlor's front door.

Chapter 15, "I'll Work with You" @ 1:43:54

Following a Long-Shot which gets Serpico and Lombardo scooting up a neighborhood stoop, a cut to Close-Up @ **1:44:36** brings us face to face with the storefront lookout. The camera tilts upward to the fire escape and the space between buildings. The next cut — visually so logical — takes us onto a rooftop as the two cops make their way high above the street. This shot follows right to left, and as Serpico reaches the roof's ledge, the camera continues moving: a tilt downward and to the left, as a point of view (POV) shows us the curbside lookout from high above. The next series of cuts offers additional spatial schooling. First and foremost in this chapter, a low-angle Long-Shot, with a view of the shaft between buildings — as in the tilt up in the "face to face" shot — is used as a mid-point cut, specifically illustrating the leap across the space between rooftops. This cut visually reinforces the fact that the leap is daring and dangerous because they cross the sky "high above the street." Second, note that the cuts from the first rooftop to the low-angle Long-Shot of the shaft between, and then to the landings on the next roof, always maintain, at the very least, a small bit of the "flying" cops in the outgoing and incoming frames. In other words, there is no incoming or outgoing frame, across the three-shot depiction of the leaps, that excludes Serpico or Lombardo; both three-shot successions keep the focal point — the leaping cops — and a grip on the audience's apprehensiveness up on the screen.

The art of cinema encourages a wondrous expansion of theatre's proscenium presentation. Camera placement permits the audience full access to the space of any location.

Here is a scene that, with simple brilliance, illustrates film's capacity to create the illusion of three dimensions, all the while projecting juxtaposed images in only two dimensions.

Index 8, Chapter 35, "The Prison Yard" @ 1:17:53.
Through the intercutting of relatively few set-ups
(likely five or six), this three-character scene discloses
the four compass points of its place.

Curiously, it begins with a Long-Shot which
graphically underscores two-dimensions: a "flat" view
of a stone wall nearly reaching the top (vertical) of the
frame, and running the full (horizontal) length of
the wide-angle shot!

Witton, Handcock, and Morant quarrel about
Handcock's testimony given at their court martial. Witton is incensed that
Morant and Handcock have kept the truth from their attorney, Major Thomas:

WITTON
Major Thomas has been pleading justifying circumstances,
and now we're just lying.

Handcock is outraged by Witton's naiveté.

HANDCOCK
We're lying? What about them? It's no bloody secret our
graves were dug the day they arrested us at Fort Edward!

Morant argues that circumstances require that certain secrets be kept:

MORANT
It's a new kind of war, George.

The movement (physical action) of each character, enhanced by their use
of objects (physical life), "propels" the cuts to smartly situated camera positions.
Witton uses a rock to scrape his initials on the wall; he turns to face a smoking
(the cigarette just lit) Morant, exiting his opened cell; he faces Handcock, who
moves away and opposite the wall.

Handcock, crouched, is shining one of his boots; he jumps to his feet
throwing the boot against the wall, followed by the shining paraphernalia as he

continues moving away from Witton; he stares in the direction of Morant, then Witton, and back to Morant before a last look to Witton, which sets-up a cut to the next scene.

Take note of the last shot which moves-in to Handcock. The camera is positioned with the wall behind it, not, as in the scene's opening, with the wall in front of the camera!

This scene is worthy of long study. It displays four directions in three dimensions (360 degrees), without visual bewilderment in the relationship of Character to Character to Place "within" the two-dimensional confines of the screen (180 degrees).

set-ups

This theme gets us back to *fragments*. Here is a deceptive inconsistency: A genuine analysis of a scene requires a model in deconstruction, and that is exactly what the crew must do so as to produce the necessary *fragments* to create a scene. I say "deceptive inconsistency" because a good director and cinematographer will not "think" this way! Let me explain.

Originally I intended to divide this theme in two. The second part would discuss coverage. Students — and more professionals than you'd imagine — confuse the two. Lots of set-ups do not necessarily make for good (adequate to exceptional) coverage, while interestingly, having few *set-ups* does not necessarily make for poor coverage.

Set-ups refer to the number of camera positions decided upon. That is, how many *fragments* will be provided for post-production, in order to assemble a scene? *Coverage* gets us closer to the function of the *fragments*.

Let's begin with a very practical assessment.

Chapter 14, "A Regular Princess Grace" @ 0:57:48

The scene opens on an Exterior Close-Up. A warning horn precedes a blast set off by a construction crew. The camera zooms back, and we see that we are in an interior of a restaurant; the blast was seen through a window. The camera follows a waiter to Lou's and Sally's table; Lou's voice gets to our ears before we see the two of them. Lou complains about the commercialization of the city: "Burger King casinos. McDonald's casinos. Pizzeria casinos. Jesus!"

This first shot is a set-up in Master-Shot. You'll note that the shot no sooner gets all the way back, than it begins a slow move-in. The move-in ends at **0:58:36.**

Lou "confides" that he's thinking of going "to Miami." Sally is thinking "Monaco." Lou's question, about Monaco being the place where "that Kelly girl from Philadelphia" comes from, elicits an affirmative series of head nods which takes us to the next set-up: a Close-Up of Sally. The construction of the scene now inter-cuts this Close-Up with (you guessed it) a Close-Up of Lou. You'll notice that there are moments when we are not seeing who is speaking. We see Lou when we hear Sally or vice versa. This is possible because the set-ups are not filmed in snippets of fragments. The camera holds on Sally throughout the conversation (dialogue) even when Lou is speaking, and so the opposite is true. This practical approach allows for a great variety of editing opportunities as they become apparent, to serve the needs of the scene, the story, and the performance. The Master-Shot as well was in all likelihood shot for the entire segment of the scene. There is a clear and good illustration for learning that comes from the scene being built in two distinct *segments*. You'll notice that at **0:59:34** a reverse Master-Shot, with the waiter again leading us to the table, gets the camera (this time) to the window side of the restaurant, and provides an improved "feel" for the *space*.

This second *segment* is played in the initially observed (similar to the first *segment's* opening) Master-Shot, and in over-the-shoulder set-ups of both characters. There *is* a cut to a Close-Up of Sally which is used for her protest to the waiter, "No fish... I want meat." It is very similar to the original

Close-Up from the first *segment* of the scene, but it is not from a selected moment from that segment's Close-Up, although it could have been. Take note of the Cut-Away/Insert of the silver cigarette holder, and one beautifully seductive Close-Up of Sally in the next to last cut: All together the scene is shot in nine set-ups.

The "good" director and cinematographer designed this practical succession of set-ups for this fairly long-running, dialogue-filled scene. They first took into account the total requirements of the scene, and envisioned the entirety of images which would provide as many options as functionally possible: good *coverage*. And! The over-the-shoulder shots and Close-Ups are of a different axis than the Master-Shots. In other words, set-ups are not simply *enlargements* of the view established in the Master-Shot. This allows for richness in perspectives across set-ups, and is central to having the audience move from observer to participant.

The usual protocol is to cover the scene in Master-Shot first. There are some practical work advantages for this, but there is also risk. Consider that there are far more aesthetic and functional compositions to be found in Master-Shots than in Close-Ups, and you'll realize that it is advisable to design your "tighter" set-ups first; and then adjust the camera axis for your Master-Shot. You can do this even if you shoot the Master-Shot first.

Without intending to contradict myself, let me offer a seeming paradox. Let's take a look at a scene that is completed in a single set-up, yet still takes *coverage* into account.

THE VERDICT

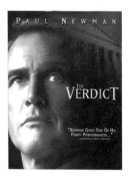

Chapter 8, "The Opposition" @ 0:34:34

Director Sidney Lumet has a sharpened sensitivity — prepared by years of experience directing dramas played out on live telecasts — to the essential function of set-ups.

The camera, and actions, permit a solo shot, or the plan for a functional, single set-up is the basis for the planned actions of the actors and the camera.

The scene opens in the Master-Shot *portion*, with Galvin and Mickey doing case research in a law library; @ **0:35:02**, in synchronicity to Mickey's standing, the camera tilts upward as it lowers, and follows him as he climbs spiral steps to the upper stack of books. Lumet has also integrated Mickey's dialogue with his walk, climb, and searching for a text. You'll note how seldom and slight are Galvin's head turns toward Mickey, even when they speak. The most severe of these occurs as Mickey descends the steps, becoming the focal point in the shot.

At **0:35:36** the camera — raised, and tilted downward to follow Mickey back to his seat — begins a move-in so as to finish the scene in a Medium Close-Up. Mickey shifts his posture at the desk, displaying a nearly full face shot. Galvin *no* longer turns — not even in the slightest — but talks to his partner, first with head down and hands clasped across his forehead, then as the camera nears its final position, he stares contemplatively in profile, hands clasped in front of his face, his right thumb emphasizing his words and concentration.

Galvin's profile eliminates any need for a reverse set-up.

There is an assumption that the set-ups decided upon should always (make every effort to) match actions. This originates in the belief that film production endeavors to duplicate realities across camera set-ups. Believe or not, there are circumstances when trying to match "real life" can and should be disregarded, as they interfere with function!

LITTLE BIG MAN

Chapter 11, "Death and Life" @ 1:13:26

Jack returns to the Cheyenne village of his (spiritually adopted) Grandfather, Old Lodge Skins. After an initial greeting and Grandfather's offer of something "to eat," Jack spots severe scarring on Grandfather's neck.

Though the scene is arranged in more than a dozen set-ups, the initial six make the point.

Jack enters the teepee and approaches Grandfather, and sits to share the offered food. Grandfather explains the scar, "It's a wound. It cut the tunnel through which light travels to the heart." In Long-Shot, Jack *leans forward* — his face drawing near to Grandfather's — and asks, "You mean you're blind?"

The next cut to a reverse, over Jack's right shoulder with Grandfather the focal point, does not have Jack in the lean-in position. If Jack's actions were matched for this set-up, Grandfather's face would be hidden by the back of Jack's head; and so unusable, without function!

It is also worth noting and considering that Grandfather seldom "matches" across most of the first eighteen cuts!

Alexander MacKendrick used a good hypothetical in his classes: A two set-up scene which clarifies (good) *coverage*.

1. A Master-Shot depicts someone entering a room and sitting in a chair.

2. A Close-Up of the chair, but without the someone sitting in it. Then, after a few beats, someone enters the frame and sits in the chair.

The "few beats" *represent* all the time it took for "the someone" to enter the building, enter the room, walk across the floor before sitting in the chair; perhaps even the time before — when "the someone" awoke, climbed out of bed, had breakfast, prepared to leave for — I think you get it!

Let's look at two examples from the same film. They illustrate Mackendrick's "hypothetical."

BREAKER MORANT

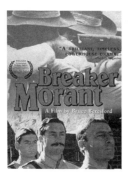

Index 1, Chapter 8, "Ambush" @ 0:10:31

The scene is shot in two set-ups: a Master-Shot and a Close-Up of George Witton. Notice that the Close-Up of Witton "repeats" the action of the Master-Shot. He enters the lavatory area.

It still amazes me how often the full range of action is only included in the Master-Shot. This seems to be another risk that comes from over-concentration and shooting priority given to Master-Shots. The Close-Ups and Medium-Shots are often *abbreviated* in actions. Think: What did this moment come out of, and what does this moment go into?

The repeat of the action in *Breaker Morant* has permitted a cut to Witton's Close-up while he is *still in motion*; a vital option in the cutting. "What did this moment come out of?"

A seldom considered, but accurate, prospect maintains that to cut to Witton in Close-Up, if the Set-Up began with him *already* leaning, would require an excessive wait in the Master-Shot to make the cut convincing. Witton's posture in weight and body language would be a sure give-away that he had not just taken his position, but has been leaning for a while, waiting for the camera and "Action!" The action would of course be only mouth-moving dialogue!

At **0:11:23** you'll note that a return to Witton's Close-Up serves an extra-splendid purpose: The sound of a door latch gets his attention, and he turns to face screen right, leading to the next moment, and the next scene in the continuous sequence. "What does this moment go into?"

Index 8, Chapter 35, "The Prison Yard" @ 1:17:53

Again the scene opens in Master-Shot, and it is Witton "entering" — the shot probably began with Witton out of the frame, the incoming frame of choice has him visible and moving left.

The cut to his Close-Up once again has him in motion. The Close-Up set-up began with the wall as "empty" background (MacKendrick's "empty chair") and on "Action!" Witton entered frame right and once again leaned, this time against the stone wall.

In Luis Buñuel's *Viridiana* the master director crafts a simple and effective design in *set-ups* to provide a good case study in *coverage*.

VIRIDIANA

Chapter 6, "The Wedding Dress" @ 0:14:52

Note the inflection (dramatic) transition *from* the Uncle's reference to his niece, Viridiana, "Sometimes I feel like hitting her," which is accented by his throwing the napkin onto the breakfast tray, *to* "Ramona, come here." This is a good example of what is indicated in screenplays as a "beat:"

> DON JAIME
> Sometimes I feel like hitting her.
> (beat)
> Ramona come here.

Frequently there is no scripted indication of a method to conduct the actor across the inflection change. Here the napkin offers an assist.

The housekeeper approaches Don Jaime from right to left, the camera panning with her. She crosses in front of and past Don Jaime, who is seated on the edge of his bed, and is therefore lower in the frame. He asks Ramona to sit beside him and the camera anticipates the housekeeper's motion to sit, lowers to near eye level, and simultaneously moves slightly right and inward, so as to compose a two-shot in profile: Uncle Don Jaime on screen right facing Ramona on screen left, looking right.

Don Jaime asks Ramona's help in convincing Viridiana "to [make her] stay a few more days."

A cut occurs at this moment: a Close-Up of Don Jaime, over the right shoulder of Ramona. It is unnecessarily conspicuous, in part because, while the set-up is accurate to the need of the moment, the fullness in coverage is either missing or misused, and because the dramatic requirements are overlooked in favor of a (sort of) "match cut" of the Uncle wiping his mouth with an embroidered white napkin. The next line should have signaled the pacing (beats) across the previous cut: "You're a good soul, Ramona. Speak to her."

Uncle Don Jaime is plotting and using Ramona as a co-conspirator to keep niece Viridiana, a religious novitiate, from returning to the convent to take her vows. The napkin (once again) can be viewed as a pause in Don Jaime's ploy to win the housekeeper's willingness to help. It assists his presenting himself — no matter how insincere — as a not well, vulnerable, and betrayed old man. The action with the napkin demonstrates that the Close-Up likely began with the napkin already at Don Jaime's mouth. Adding several beats onto the outgoing Master-Shot, and making better use of Don Jaime's eyes, along with more beats before his next line, would help realize that the Uncle is scheming.

The next cut takes us to a new Master-Shot: a Long-Shot past Don Jaime's left shoulder, with Ramona the focal point of the composition. The cut occurs *after* an undisguised bribe: "I know I needn't even offer you a reward... but if you succeed I promise I won't forget you or [your daughter] Rita." Note that the first phrase is said with eyes downward — returning the napkin to the tray — another effort to gain sympathy. Ramona's response, "But why would she listen to a servant?" is rushed, in that it does not allow Ramona to respond — if in reaction beats alone — to Don Jaime's generous, if illicit, offer.

But! The coverage is lovely in its simplicity. This new Master-Shot will hold to show Ramona getting up from the bed; and going to retrieve a "little blue bottle with no label… from a cabinet" in accordance with Don Jaime's request. Here too, the cut is several frames from working: Don Jaime's description of the bottle begins while still on the Master-Shot. This in itself does not create a problem; the "glitch" occurs some two to three frames after the start of the phrase, Don Jaime gestures upward with his head. Instead of watching Ramona, as we'd prefer, our eyes dart to Don Jaime's head move.

The next set-up in the *coverage* is an Extreme Close-Up of the cabinet with medicines and potions. We can see Ramona's shadow approach the cabinet just before she reaches inside; the camera dollies back — and left — to a Medium-Shot, in synchronization with Ramona's search for the "little blue bottle." Ramona finds a bottle and turns, holding the bottle for Don Jaime to see: "This one?"

A new Master-Shot, prompted as Ramona's point of view (POV) of Don Jaime across the room, serves to see him acknowledge the medicine bottle, and ask that she go back to work. In this shot, Don Jaime responds to repetitive skipping sounds from outside. He turns to look to screen right, gets up from the bed, and the camera pans right following him to a window. Note that as Don Jaime reaches the window, Ramona crosses the frame from left to right, between the panning camera and Don Jaime. This affords the set-up additional spatial appeal by way of overlapping bodies in motion — nearly creating a "wipe" across the frame — while incorporating the housekeeper's compliance.

Another set-up is revealed within a couple of frames of Don Jaime's right hand moving the window curtain aside: his POV looking outside and downward to Viridiana, wearing her novitiate robe, playing jump rope with Rita.

Finally, we have a set-up showing Don Jaime's gentle head tilt and yearning smile, in a low-angle Medium Close-Up, from outside (Exterior) looking upward and into the window.

Chapter 8, "Target Practice" @ 0:58:45

The scene begins on an isolated landscape with an immediately noticed tree centered in the frame. The shot serves important multiple purposes. It follows the opening scene to Chapter 8 which ends with the Jackal driving away from an outdoor market, after purchase of a handsome round melon. With the melon alongside him in the passenger seat, the Jackal revs the engine of his sports car to the scene's final frame.

The landscape creates a contrast to the full-of-life Genoa market street in image and sound. The commotion of pedestrians, buses, autos, scooters, and the waving clamor of a traffic cop ceases in an on-the-spot instant, supplanted by a scarcely audible atmosphere of small birds.

The scene might very well begin on the next cut; a Close-Up of the melon, wrapped in a stockinette (rete) rope, being painted with white markings. Several advantages occur with the landscape opening. It permits far greater possibilities in outgoing frame selection to exit the Genoa scene because the beats held on the tree create a suitable "feel" in time to get the Jackal, and audience, to the isolated pastoral setting without requiring images of driving; it adds an intriguingly unexpected tension. The peacefulness of this place — the near-quiet chirps of birds — hints that something fascinatingly dangerous is about to be disclosed. The curiousness of the painted melon makes that clear. The Jackal's drive with the melon in the passenger seat assists the forewarning of the melon as human: a face and target.

The matter-of-factness — and meticulousness — of the Jackal abets in the dismay of the final moments.

The Long-Shot, which follows the Close-Up of the melon, reintroduces the tree as space for weapon citing, and marksmanship, as the camera follows the Jackal from the trunk of his car, now with his new rifle and the melon's fully painted face.

This scene gives us a lesson in the A to Z of set-ups! While the final editing might be viewed as a series of cuts getting us from A-B; B-C; C-D, and so on, the set-ups demonstrate a mind-set and plan more closely resembling A-Z; A-G; A-L; C-M; C-W; H-K; H-Y, etc. The *set-ups* are providing an overlapping *coverage* of the in and out moments to previous and upcoming actions: "What does this moment come out of; and what does this moment go into?"

The set-ups (unedited) might include getting the paint out of the car's trunk (A-Z; A-G; A-L; C-M); placing the melon in the rete (A-Z; A-G; A-L; C-M; C-W); walking all the way to and back from the tree (A-Z; A-L; H-K; H-Y), and so on.

The cut @ **1:00:01** again uses the Long-Shot of the tree, this time with the melon hanging from a left-side branch. This is the most critical and smart repeat of the Long-Shot, especially with the camera zoom-in to the Jackal as he prepares for his first shot, and because, after this moment, the melon is depicted only in long focal length lens views — replicating the rifle's scope — which of course greatly reduces the distance — the space — from the Jackal to the hanging melon. This perspective can make it look like a very easy shot! The Jackal's expertise is "documented" in reinforcing the vastness of distance, and in his precise adjustments to the rifle's scope after each "hit" with regular ammunition.

Let me call special attention to the moment @ **1:00:11** to **1:00:26**. Here again we see how the eyes of the character influence the editing choices and rhythms. It might seem predictable given the context of the scene: marksman and target. But take note of the brilliant use of the Jackal's eye @ **1:00:23** as he calculates a last and minor vertical adjustment. After hitting higher but to the left, the Jackal looks through the scope, and @ **1:00:35** we see another cut to the melon, but this time — and only this time — there is no gun shot. This makes possible the next cut to the rifle as seen from the other side, without confusing the change in direction. The rifle is now pointing to screen right. The "special" bullet is loaded, and the Jackal takes aim.

The last shot of the scene (and the rifle) moves us to a (Master-Shot) reverse in distance. We are again, as in the *Set-Up* which brought the Jackal and melon to the "hanging" tree, behind and slightly below the melon, with the Jackal far off in the background. Using the special exploding bullet, the choice of a melon as a human head is accentuated when the demolished fruit sends "red meat" in all directions.

Here is a simple scene in coverage that illustrates the brilliance of Visual Logic in the design of *set-ups*.

Chapter 7, "Young In Never" @ 0:23:40

1. The scene opens in a Fade-In on a Cut-Away/ Insert of a small table. A man's and woman's watch together. A hand takes the man's watch. With this set-up the scene consists of six in total.

2. A Medium-Shot of the Japanese architect putting on his watch. His glances off to screen right will eventually get us to:

3. A Long-Shot of the French actress dressing in her nurse costume. This set-up represents the architect's POV. The set-up continues and follows the actress to the bed and the architect. She kisses and "plays" with his arm.

4. A Medium Close-Up from the foot of the bed; the actress is seen from slightly above and from behind her nurse's cap. The architect has been looking down to her, but at the moment of the cut he turns his head to have his face to the camera. This cut is ever so slightly awkward for two reasons: The "feel" that it does not derive from enough existing time in the camera run — "What does this moment come out of?" — prior to its incoming frame, and because our eyes are still too attentive to the actress and her "arm playing."

    The actress will move to the left into a position that lifts her and turns her to face the architect. The camera will pan left and move slightly right to better frame the two. The actress gets up from the bed and while the camera holds focus on the architect as his eyes follow the actress, we can see her arm, though it is out of focus as she takes her watch from the small table.

5. The actress enters frame right into a low-angle Medium-Shot; a rendition of a POV as the architect "might" see the actress putting on her watch. Her look to him motivates:

6. A Medium-Long-Shot of the architect on the bed — the actress' POV. The camera follows the architect up from the bed, to his jacket and to the actress. They leave the hotel room, and the "end" moment of this set-up leads to a set-up in the hall, which is assisted by the edit exiting the room with the door still open.

The totality of the design is beautifully simple, and so very practical as the logic of its visual connections from set-up to set-up impart the function in *coverage*. The characters' eyes motivate cut points to set-ups as point of view (POV), which carry the audience across the space of the room, and from observer to participant.

CHARACTER

Playwright Harold Pinter was the recipient of the Nobel Prize in Literature in 2005. In his Nobel Lecture, "Art, Truth & Politics," Pinter began with an emphasis on the curious — if not supernaturally enchanted — impulse for his work. "Most of the plays are engendered by a line, a word or an image."

Pinter gives examples: "The first line of *The Homecoming* is 'What have you done with the scissors?' The first line from *Old Times* is 'Dark.'" Pinter finds himself "compelled to pursue the matter."

Such insubstantial beginnings take on imagined, and tangible, form, becoming a vehicle for character interaction. "In... *The Homecoming* I saw a man enter a stark room and ask his question [about scissors] of a younger man sitting on an ugly sofa reading a racing paper."

Pinter initially gives letter identification to the characters, Character A, B, C and so on, but it must be noted that Pinter refers to them not as *my* characters, but as "*the* characters." The author is not asserting *ownership* of the characters, above all because Pinter's characters are a result of *their* impulsive intrusion into his life.

What is most relevant about Pinter's intuitive process is its search for a story contained in a portrait. Pinter hears a voice — a character — speak a line, a word. "It is a strange moment, the moment of creating characters who up to that moment have had no existence." A word provides character, and character inspires setting — in place *and* narrative.

What is noteworthy to me as a film editor and teacher attempting to understand, clarify, and shed light upon good storytelling is Pinter's ensuing vision. Someone enters "a stark room" and someone is sitting — I'm captivated by the "ugly sofa" — and reading. What we have is the basic machinery of character: Physical Action (*motion*) and Physical Life (*objects*). To these add selecting the actors, and we have the simplest, yet effective, requirements for indisputably alive and authentic people.

David Mamet has suggested that until we have cast an actor, and he or she is engaged with objects in a place, there is no character, or perhaps better put, the character will unaffectedly be revealed with the emergence of an actor doing suitable things in a suitable place. Director Martin Ritt corroborates Mamet with compelling excess: "Casting is 90% of a director's job."

In his memoir, *Images*, Ingmar Bergman gives examples of how his theatre "upbringing" allowed for necessarily modest expenditures in his (especially early) films. Mise-en-scène — Master-Shot only — carried entire scenes; knowledge of beats, dramatic transitions and blocking skill made Bergman's success possible. With minimal coverage, there is little to no post-production assistance for altering and enhancing performance.

It is worth screening Bergman's final filmed story *Saraband*. The influence of theatre is apparent and even celebrated: a separation — playbill-like signals — via titled chapters; characters address the audience; interiors dominate; exposition in dialogue, and a ceremonially formal structure, particularly displayed with character entrances and exits.

This *theatrical* impulse to "introduce" characters is convenient — often allowing an applause pause for the identifiable performer — as well as providing an immediate focal point for an audience viewing the story through a proscenium. In *The Homecoming*, Pinter "saw a man *enter* a stark room."

On stage, an arrangement of *place* is often abstracted and static: a distinction between the theatre audience as observer and film's as *participant*. There is, therefore, a strong inclination to "add" a quick dynamic within the setting: An actor enters! As theatre lights give focus to the audience, the most unadorned "entrance and exit" can supply an *on* and *off* action.

Because stories are about people, entrances and exits establish easy beginnings and endings to scenes, but in film they are often far too timid and arbitrary. Following characters from place to place is neither fundamentally cinematic, nor necessary to welcome screen stars, and variations in camera set-ups discount contribution to focal point.

Irene Dailey, actor, teacher, and founder of the School of the Actors Company, advised students that in order to find a character's objective for each scene, and super-objective — a Stanislavsky approach to secure a character's ambition, desire, or duty — for the life of the play, it is crucial to understand why the author has chosen to have us meet characters at this particular time in their lives, or what *pattern(s)* in their lives has been stirred, shattered or transformed.

One word comes to mind when I think of Irene's advice: *sequel*. I'll follow Pinter's example and "pursue the matter." It seems to me that if there is a *need* for a sequel (leaving out the obvious considerations determined by the movie business), then the filmmakers might consider an epic production, a multi-episode presentation for television or an ongoing TV series.

The reason that, with few exceptions, sequels are usually inferior renditions of time spent with characters that initially provided admiration, amusement, diversion, and/or revelation, is that (perhaps) there is a very specific purpose in the time, and the very precise events within that time, which embrace the vitality and premise for a character's story.

I believe that Irene Dailey was on to something! Find a character's life pattern and you'll likely discern the occurrences, opportunities, and obstacles that alter that pattern, fundamentally providing an understanding of the story's "why."

A tightly integrated combining of pattern and time/purpose meeting of the character is efficiently illustrated in *Central Station*.

CENTRAL STATION

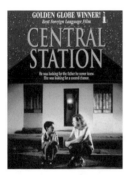

Chapter 1, "Start" @ 0:00:22

A pop-in from black brings a Long-Shot with a view along Rio de Janeiro's station platform; a train on screen right opens its doors to a rush hour crowd. A gently melancholy piano accompanies the crowd and a Close-Up of a tearful middle-aged woman, addressing her "darling" who has been sent to prison. She informs him (us) that, no matter all the years, she'll "be waiting... for [him]."

Following an image of the train station crowd, a Close-Up of an older man permits the audience another eavesdrop: "I want to send a letter to a guy who cheated me."

It is in this location that we meet Dora, and her current life pattern: She is a retired school teacher, serving the station patrons by taking dictation so that the illiterate can send off letters to lovers and cheats!

We meet *her* this day because *she* will encounter nine-year-old Josue, and her new journey in fact and metaphor!

Kolya grants more time spent with Frantisek's life pattern, and then combines a new proposition along with a new obstacle to advise the audience as to why we meet our protagonist now.

KOLYA

Chapter 1, "A Day at the Office" @ 0:01:16
Frantisek is a freelance musician. He enjoys "playing" with women.

Chapter 2, "A Talented Bachelor" @ 0:04:40
Frantisek is financially burdened. At **0:04:56** we see that he adores all women; at **0:05:16** we learn that he's on the financial edge; at **0:05:34** we hear how lonely he is; at **0:07:20** we see that he also freelances as a headstone restorer.

Chapter 3, "An Unusual Offer" @ 0:12:38
Frantisek owes lots of money. But! He can make a lot of money if he'll marry a single Russian mother so that she can stay in Czechoslovakia.

Between **0:16:50** and **0:18:45** we learn that Frantisek's mother has been told that she needs new rain gutters for her house, and that the information is correct! At **0:19:31** Frantisek sits in the cemetery, under a plastic tarp to escape the rain, and agrees to the arranged (fake) marriage.

Chapter 4, "For the Wrong Reasons" @ 0:20:04
Frantisek meets his bride and her little son Kolya, and it is soon very clear why the author has chosen this time in Frantisek's life!

It is not necessary to establish a character's life pattern from the outset of a story; chronology need not be the order. Character studies in obituaries offer a good lesson in storytelling arrangement. They are not chronological — see how far into the piece that the date and place of birth are referenced. Obituaries concentrate on life's personal achievements or disgraces, but for the most part, they are a story about a person's passing.

begin with the near-death time of their protagonists — in the case of *Amadeus* it is Antonio Salieri; Wolfgang Amadeus Mozart (and God) are the story's antagonists — and then construct a story in giant flashback.

However suitable the traditional obituary form, only a few entries are marvelously valuable in that structure: accounts of character, time, and events that are, by chance, a perfect fit for the form. Study and weigh those exceptions and you'll develop an appreciation for the distinctive in any story, place, and character.

Each of us can be self-observing and reflective, and are therefore inclined to "figure ourselves out" — we seek a degree of comfort via an ordered assembly of the world — and can be self-informed by the life adventures of the storytellers' *characters*. We irresistibly listen, read, and watch story after story after story… after story!

objects

During her off-Broadway performance as *Mrs. Klein*, a play by Nicholas Wright about the Freudian psychoanalyst Melanie Klein, actor and teacher Uta Hagen was interviewed on public radio. The host of the program, having recently attended the play, remarked how impressed she was by the actor's presence, focus, and convincing life on stage, in large part, she explained, "due to your engagement with props." Ms. Hagen quickly corrected the interviewer with immediacy and decisiveness. It was almost a scolding intrusion: "They're not props; they are *objects*."

Ms. Hagen's characterization, and *object* significance, was brought home to me — in fact, it was brought into my home. I received a telephone call from a former student, who, after an initial greeting, asked, "Guess who I met on Saturday?" I expected this was rhetorical and my former student continued, "Remember your breakdown of the 'Judge's Chambers Scene' from *The Verdict*?" (**See Chapter 10, "The Judge"** @ **0:42:37**.) "How you talked about the coverage providing a view of all the walls? How you talked about the physical life of the characters within the scene, and how it helped create authentic people, and an authentic place? I met Milo O'Shea!"

THE VERDICT

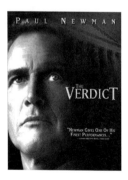

Milo O'Shea is the actor who plays Judge Hoyle. The scene brings together Frank Galvin (protagonist), Ed Concannon (legal adversary), and Judge Hoyle prior to trial. The judge attempts to press Galvin into a settlement before trial, "[To] save the commonwealth a lot of time and bother."

Upon entering the chambers at **0:42:58** Galvin finds Concannon already seated with a cup of coffee. He is reprimanded for being late, and not advised as to where to hang his overcoat. He clumsily makes his way to a chair, folding his coat onto his lap, made crowded with his briefcase. The use of these objects quickly addresses the bias of Hoyle, and foreshadows the trial-long conflict — both *dramatic* and *of interest*.

I had mentioned to the class that having Judge Hoyle eating breakfast in his chambers, then offering Galvin a hot cup of coffee — Hoyle gets up from his desk and pours the coffee for "Mr. Galvin" — to "convince" him to take the insurance company's settlement offer — "I myself would take the money and run like a thief" — is a terrific use of objects, making for a believable judge in his personal, comfortable and suitable place, as well as a Physical Action (motion) that demonstrates the subtext of the Judge's objective (in support of the insurance company, the doctors and their attorney) without an abundance of expository dialogue.

My former student recounted a Saturday evening spent at a friend's party, sitting on a couch alongside Judge Hoyle, i.e. Mr. Milo O'Shea. "I told him all about the scene and he was impressed. You'll forgive me," my former student confessed, "but I gave you no credit." I laughed my forgiveness!

"I just had to call to let you know what Mr. O'Shea explained about the scene, and how it got that way! Mr. O'Shea was in rehearsals for a Broadway play, and the day he was scheduled to shoot the Judge's Chambers scene the rehearsal ran late. A limo picked him up at the Broadway theatre and drove him to Astoria Studios. He told me that an assistant director was waiting outside, and rushed him out of the limo, complaining about O'Shea's being late while everyone was ready. As they approached the set O'Shea said that he hadn't had anything to eat and was very hungry. The assistant hurried him along, and said they'd feed him after the filming — 'Mr. Newman, Mason and Lumet are waiting.' Sidney Lumet's voice called out, 'What would you like to eat?' Mr. O'Shea placed his breakfast order with the director, and instead of court documents and folders in front of the Judge, there's eggs, toast, and coffee!"

This story brought to mind Sidney Lumet's comment of long ago, "All good work is a result of accidents." Yes! But you must be open to them, free to work in a "not too safe" collaborative environment!

I suspect that object engagement (Physical Life) is so essential a part of character because it holds a connection to defining man as the animal that uses tools. While this turns out not to be absolutely true — chimps have been known to use a branch to poke down into the opening of an ant hill to pull up edible insects attached to the jam-packed branch, and I've witnessed a friend's crow carry a grape along a 2x4 fence rail, then "cradle" the grape within a knot in the board, and eat the secured grape out of his invented little fruit bowl — it is a vital device offering richness of character and audience engagement.

Let's go back to *Kolya*: A collection of objects affectionately introduces our protagonist. The pattern of his life is integral to the tools of his life.

KOLYA

Chapter 1, "A Day at the Office" @ 0:01:18

A tilt downward from long church windows settles on a string quartet. A funeral inspires somber musical threads which accompany rack-focus shots of violin, cello, beer bottle at feet, and a whistling kettle, quieted by Franta's cello bow flicking its lid onto the floor. The scene also demonstrates the protagonist's teasing flirtatiousness: running his bow up and under the dress of the soloist as she sings the Lord's Prayer.

Chapter 3, "An Unusual Offer" @ 0:11:32

There is another tilt downward simultaneous to a rack-focus shot through branches and leaves, coming to rest on Frantisek all but surrounded by grave stones. He is applying gold-leaf paint to restore the chiseled name on a dark stone marker. Two gravediggers drive up to deliver "loads of new [painting] orders... Three in gold, two in silver."

Andrei Tarkovsky's short film is entitled with the story's — and the characters' — pivotal objects. Sergey and Sasha are, in fact, contrast, dream, and allegory.

THE STEAMROLLER AND THE VIOLIN

Chapter 5, "A Lesson on the Steamroller" @ 0:12:09.

Sasha's violin — the boy's accompanying object of beauty, touch, and auditory affection — has been rescued from local bullies by steamroller operator Sergey. The tough boys are outside of Sasha's apartment building when he arrives home after his music lesson. Sergey calls on Sasha to assist with a small repair on the engine. Sasha — like a surgical nurse — hands Sergey the needed tools.

Sergey then invites Sasha for a ride on the steamroller. This keeps Sasha under his watch, away from the bullies in the building's entranceway. Take note of the bullies "busyness" with objects of their own — some for mischief making. Sergey gives teasing answers to the boy's "driving" questions. Then, to the dismay and envy of the neighborhood toughs, Sergey lets Sasha drive the steamroller solo.

The steamroller is a somewhat unique tool/object, but characters inside, and using, an automobile is commonplace, and certainly not so far removed from the steamroller to require explanation. Operating machinery is the same as "operating" objects. Sometimes, as in the case of the automobile, the commonplace is both an *object* and a place. This is beginning to sound like a riddle.

Here's a wonderful example of such a place: an *object* as a *setting* in the service of character and story. In this case a selection in enthralling, and thrilling participation for the protagonist and audience alike!

François Truffaut's first feature,

THE 400 BLOWS

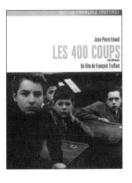

Chapter 2, "Antoine's Home Life" @ 0:21:36

Antoine Doinel and his friend skip school to find amusement at an arcade of pinball games — objects — and later at a *centrifuge ride*.

Antoine enters a small door with other riders while friend Rene watches from above. The ride also features a wonderful illustration in the good selections in the moments from very few camera setups: two Master-Shots, one looking down into the ride, the other up to the observers. Each uses camera moves to shift from Long-Shot to Medium-Shot and back; a Medium-Shot of Antoine with the camera tilting downward and upward as — showing his feet lifted off the floor — he attempts a spinning trick.

The shot of the watching crowd is also re-positioned upside down representing Antoine's point of view (POV) as he completes his trick, turning himself feet upward as the centrifuge spins nearly unchecked. The inter-cutting between shots has the audience laughing in delight, easily becoming participants of the belly-dropping whirls. Let Antoine spin us to:

motion

If engagement with *objects* (physical life) establishes our species, and therefore a plausible character, then *moving pictures* must subsequently assert the physical action of character: motion.

Watch the wondrous dance of character and camera.

JEAN DE FLORETTE

Chapter 3, @ 0:18:30

Cesar Soubeyran and his nephew Ugolin attend the funeral of their neighbor Marius. The audience, but not the other mourners of the village in Provence, knows all of the factors surrounding Marius' death, and Uncle and Nephew's plot to acquire the dead man's land with its precious source of pristine water.

The procession moves through the rugged hillside. Men (only) — most in black suits and hats — walk behind a horse drawn black carriage. Marius' simple wooden coffin is aboard.

The scene, in its entirety, stays in motion: dialogue exists simultaneously. Note the ease in combination of locked-down and moving camera: The second set-up @ **0:18:36** begins with the camera "still" and recording, then @ **0:18:42** it begins to track with the mourners, but then "slows" to allow the next rows to catch up.

In *Catch-22*, the first reference (and explanation) of the story's title occurs in an early scene in which all of the characters are in nearly non-stop motion:

Chapter 2, "Persecution Complex" @ 0:09:18

World War II Army Air Corps B-25 bombardier Yossarian has requested that the Mediterranean island base's Doctor Daneeka ground him, "I don't want to fly anymore... it's dangerous."

In an Extreme Long-Shot, Yossarian and Doc walk across the dusty busy camp of taxiing planes, trucks, tents, and stacked ammo. The camera pans right as the Doc explains that he cannot break the rules, "I can't ground anyone just because he asks me to."

YOSSARIAN
Can you ground someone who's crazy?

DOC
Of course; I have to. There's a rule that says I have to ground anyone who's crazy.

YOSSARIAN
I'm crazy!

DOC
Who says so?

YOSSARIAN
Ask anybody... ask...

As a B-25's tail wing passes screen right, a jogging figure of an airman approaches the two men.

YOSSARIAN (continues)
Hey Orr! Orr! Tell him!

A cut brings Orr into a Medium Shot. He is still jogging as he nears Yossarian and Doc.

ORR (stopping)
Tell him what?

YOSSARIAN (OS)
Am I crazy?

ORR
He's crazy Doc. He won't fly with me. I take good care
of him but he won't. He's crazy all right.

Orr jogs off to screen left. The camera pans with him into a Medium-Shot of
Yossarian and Doc. A bomber taxis from the background toward the camera,
coming up behind them. The noise of airplane engines force Doc and Yossarian to
speak louder. They have stopped walking. They *stand* side by side, but nonetheless they
continue in motion: Hand and arm waves, head turns toward the passing B-25, and
shoulder gesturing to aid in shouting, so as to be heard over the ever increasingly
loud engines.

YOSSARIAN
That's proof, isn't it? They all say I'm crazy.

DOC
They're crazy!

YOSSARIAN
Then why don't you ground them?

DOC
Why don't they ask me to ground them?

YOSSARIAN
Because they're crazy, that's why.

The left wing of the bomber now passes over the two, and the propellers generate
a small dust storm.

DOC

Well of course they're crazy. I just told you that! You can't
let crazy people decide whether you're crazy or not, can you?

The two start walking, the camera moves with them, and gets a bit ahead so as
to produce a longer view of the men and the airstrip around them.

YOSSARIAN

Is Orr crazy?

DOC

Of course he is! He has to be crazy after all the close calls he's had.

YOSSARIAN

Then why can't you ground him?

DOC

I can, but first he has to ask me.

Yossarian reacts by turning to Doc, and stopping him with hands to the chest.
This gesture also cues the camera to stop. The two are in Medium-Long-Shot.

YOSSARIAN

That's all he's gotta do to be grounded?

DOC

That's all!

YOSSARIAN

Then you can ground him?

DOC

No! Then I cannot ground him!

Yossarian waves frantic hands alongside his face.

YOSSARIAN
Aaarrghhh....

DOC
There's a catch.

YOSSARIAN
A catch?

DOC
Sure. Catch-22. Anyone who wants to get out of
combat isn't really crazy, so I can't ground him.

Yossarian claps his hands "in the know."
The men begin walking again; the camera moves with them.

YOSSARIAN
Okay! Let me see if I got this straight. In order to be
grounded I've got to crazy; and I must be crazy to keep
flying. But if I ask to be grounded, that means I'm not
crazy anymore...

The camera moves slightly right, and further ahead of Doc and Yossarian as they
come into the shade of the tail section of a taxiing B-25.

YOSSARIAN (continued)
...and I have to keep flying.

DOC
You got it! That's catch-22

YOSSARIAN
(runs to climb into the belly of the B-25)
Yyyyeeeeee....

A wonderful set-up reveals a Medium-Shot of Yossarian: He is upside down, his
dog-tags dangling across his nose, hanging from the fuselage portal in the plane.

The camera is mounted to the belly of the plane.

                    YOSSARIAN
         That's some catch, that catch-22.

A Yossarian POV of Doc, as he runs after the plane, is now also upside down.

                    DOC
         It's the best there is.

Just before the cut from this scene the camera begins pulling away from Doc.

Motion in a complex structure: an enormous and disorderly crowd; organized lines of police; various centers of action, and a vehicle which speeds into that center, becomes the focus of the conclusion of this scene from Z.

                              Z

Chapter 12, "Hit and Run" @ 0:30:22

The Deputy has concluded his talk about peace and democracy, and makes his way down a staircase lined with an overflowing crowd. A large black-and-white poster of him borders frame right; the international symbol of peace rests in the lower left corner of the poster. Loud applause follows him. He wipes his forehead of perspiration. Only a modest hall was permitted for this overwhelmingly popular figure, and, we've no doubt, the crammed hall has been uncomfortable. There is, as well, an uneasy feeling about the Deputy's safety.

The camera follows his movement out into the street. Loud applause is diffused by the chant of demonstrators gathered in the square to hear the speech over loudspeakers. Helmeted police stand at both sides of the square. People of the political left have already encountered organized assaults perpetrated by cronies of the police and military.

A POV shows the busy and threatening square. A cut back to the Deputy begins a camera move outward following him through the police line, and out into the square. Aides escort him past a line of clapping supporters. The Deputy calls out to the Police Inspector who is far across the square. The inspector turns away and disappears behind a line of police. The gap created by his departure closes quickly. The Deputy walks — calling, "Chief" — fully into the square, past the camera into a Long-Shot that takes us behind him. We can see the gang of right-wing agitators. The Deputy is vulnerable: Two young thugs approach, but though an aide pleads with a police official, no assistance is provided. The Deputy shows no fear, and the two young men turn and rush off.

For a brief moment we feel secure. But, as the Deputy shifts his eyes from the thugs to where the inspector was last seen, and passes the camera in Medium Close-Up — exiting frame left — his aide hurries forward as an annoying motor sound segues onto the modestly murmuring ambiance of the square. The aide rushes forward, initially into an out of focus blur, before coming into a near focus Close-Up. A weaving, small, blue, three-wheel truck is visible past the blue helmeted police. The aide, in Close-Up now, shouts, "Watch out!" The Deputy moves into a startled hesitating crouch, his face whirling. The truck moves toward the camera; a man in the back stands crashing a section of pipe across the Deputy's head.

This scene provides a perfect example for another of film's paradoxes: order, form and clarity in a presentation which portrays commotion and bedlam. It is not by chance — nor is it an easy task — that the audience can comprehend each and every moment in the frenzy of events. This scene supplies brilliant illustration of the director, cinematographer, actor, and editor collaboration: A grasp of the relationship of Place, Character and Action which advances a *functional* model of camera set-ups; and (later) an assembly in time and space that permits the viewer strong participatory emotion. No genuine emotional response is possible if the audience does not understand what is occurring. Or, as novelist Isaac Bashevis Singer said, "There is no art in confusion."

Let's screen a scene of small but lovely (and visually vital) motions.

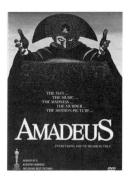

Chapter 12, "A Thing of Beauty" @ 0:51:23

Antonio Salieri steps slowly toward the camera, his eyes fixed beyond to screen left. He opens his hands in a questioning gesture: "How can I help you?" He comes to a stop.

A cut reveals his point of view (POV): In Long-Shot stands a woman; she unfastens a lace veil from her hat, allowing us to see that it is Mozart' wife. Salieri recognizes her: "Frau Mozart?" Again a cut takes us to her Long-Shot:

"I've come on behalf of my husband." She extends a large leather folder: "I brought you some samples of his work so that he can be considered for the royal appointment."

A cut back to Salieri makes this scene worthy of note: He takes two steps forward — toward Frau Mozart. Small gestures with his hands, and several tiny movements of his lips, before: "How charming, but why did he not come himself?" Salieri's steps, which likely bring him about a foot closer to her, initiate and *fully* motivate the next cut. It is (still) as in a POV, but Frau Mozart stands in a Medium-Close-Up!

Last in this chapter is an example that features *motion* as effective focal point, but by way of contrast: a simple application of space across the horizontal aspect ratio, and the internal illusion of depth by overlapping of people and objects, and most vital, a fine introduction into the wide realm of *dialogue*.

CENTRAL STATION

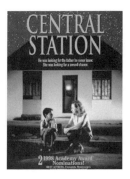

Chapter 5, "No Money, No Letter" @ 0:14:40

Another day of work at Rio de Janeiro's train station has ended for Dora; she moves across the frame from right to left. The camera holds her in focus with a short pan left that moves with her. Dora gets onto her train, standing between the two wide sliding doors; the train is too crowded to allow full entry into the car. Blurred figures move between Dora and the camera. At 0:14:51 Josue enters screen right in near total blur.

Josue has sought Dora's help: His mother has been seriously injured in a bus accident, and he wants Dora to write a letter to his estranged father. His blue T-shirt gets our attention when he stands still in the left border of the frame. If our eyes miss this opportunity, Dora's glance toward the blurred figure assures our notice. A cut to a Medium-Shot of Josue is Dora's POV. Blurred commuters move in front of and behind the boy.

While our eyes will ordinarily and invariably attend motion, here the contrast — the central characters are still — and the narrow depth of field leave no doubt as to the focal point in the compostion.

Josue's stare motivates a Medium Close-Up of Dora. She tries diverting her look, but makes eye contact with Josue just as the train doors begin to close. The last instant of the doors sliding shut is played across Dora's POV of Josue in Medium-Shot. A small gap in the door's rubber trim permits an intensely isolated, near freeze frame on the abandoned Josue.

It is not difficult in the least to understand their interaction; their eyes connect and do speak through the blurred "blowing curtains" of color, across the harried platform. Josue's "pleading" is made certain when he runs alongside the departing train, trying not to lose Dora.

dialogue

Alexander Mackendrick assigned exercises that "[explore] how film grammar can communicate most of the bare essentials of the narrative without the spoken word, [and thus] isolate just how much extra is added by the quality of the dialogue and the actors' performances."

I agree, and would suggest that dialogue not be stringently identified. Interaction and engagement between characters is less driven by the spoken word than by their demeanor, actions, and eyes: Let's see what the characters are saying! As in, I see what they mean. There can, and will, be words exchanged — and I am not advocating a return to the silent era — but learning the art of directing, acting, and editing demands a larger perspective. A few examples:

THE LONELINESS OF THE
LONG DISTANCE RUNNER

Chapter 16, "Smith Bonds with a Girl" @ 1:04:37
The sound of a Tory politician addressing the home audience on television precedes the first shot of the scene.

Colin and Mike sit in comfy-stuffy mix and match furniture in the darkened small living room watching the filled-with-platitudes "talk" on patriotism. They respond, at several points in the speech, with Winston Churchill imitative waves and shrugs. Colin gets up, and when he returns to his seat we realize, with a cut back to the television set, that he's cut the sound. The politician's hand and finger gestures and lip moves are all in silence, but for the ever-increasing chuckling of Colin and Mike. The filmmakers speed up the movements of the Tory as the two boys collapse in uproarious laughter.

With very few words — and those are not about a literal meaning — the scene constructs a *dialogue* between Colin and his friend — pals in alienation and anger — and in near wordlessness, the scene persuasively expresses Colin's discourse with his world.

When we expand upon the ordinary — and quite limited — definition of dialogue as two (or more) people speaking so as to communicate, we discover that cinema is likely a closer link to music and dance than to theatre.

I am reminded of Ingmar Bergman's "feeling" that when his films are at their best, "they are like a Béla Bartók symphony." And Walter Murch's comment that "Another way of looking at film editing is that it's a dance of eyes."

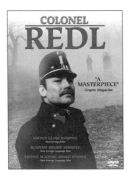

Chapter 22, "Duet For One" @ 1:47:56

At a masked ball in the palace of Archduke Ferdinand, Redl is introduced to a handsome young man. The two ride horses through the soft quiet of a deep snowy woods. A series of cuts — many boldly direct — begins a sensual dialogue by way of gallops, trots, and easy walks; horse grooming; closeness, and glances; exhalations and riding crop gestures against a snow covered tree.

A second scene brings Redl and his young Velocchio into a pretty piano shop. Velocchio "tests" the keys with a single note which is answered by Redl on another piano. A slow succession of notes and responses build as Redl removes his soft gray gloves, and a melodic duet develops across the piano shop. The scene is beautifully "played" in music and gentle moveabouts, with smiling, provocative peeks — all the dialogue that's needed.

Film editor Michael Kahn has a preference when he cuts a dialogue scene: "I like people looking at each other. I like eyes to meet." Again, let's have a *look*, but not say a word!

Chapter 2, "A Death in Marseilles" @ 0:02:56

A French undercover detective heads to his apartment with a newspaper and just purchased bag-less long bread tucked under his left arm. As he climbs the wide stone steps along the narrow, hilly, alley-like street which leads to the building, the sound of a radio (filtered and hollow) fades-in. The detective passes the camera, moving away and into the hallway — the radio sound clearer as if coming from a ground floor apartment — and proceeds to his mailbox. A reverse from inside the hall follows the action.

In soft focus a gloved hand, holding a pistol, rises into the left of the frame. The proceeding beats are a simple and perfect measure in non-speaking cinematic communication: an interaction motivated by eyes, and the context they propose.

1. The detective senses a presence in the hall, and in Close-Up he looks.

2. The detective's eyes shift downward…

3. In Close-Up we see the barrel of a pistol, its aim coming up.

4. Back to the Close-Up of the detective as his eyes shift upward…

5. We see the face of the man with the pistol; his eyes — in slight leer — look intently ahead. The eyes of the characters are locked! A slight gesture of the hit man's shoulder indicates a determined positioning of the pistol.

6. Back to the pistol's Close-Up. It fires.

7. The detective's Close-Up explodes in blood.

I get the feeling that you want talking? I'll give you talking! I'll also preserve the communicative wonder of eyes!

BONNIE AND CLYDE

Chapter 3, "What Armed Robbery's Like" @ 0:06:26

Take note that no words are spoken until we are approximately ten seconds into the scene. Dialogue should not drive, need not initiate nor conclude a scene. There's lots of soda pop guzzling!

>   BONNIE
>   What's it like?

>   CLYDE
>   What do you mean, prison?

>   BONNIE
>   No. Armed robbery!

At **0:06:46** Bonnie ends her answer and her eyes dazzlingly shift to Clyde. He contemplates, taking long, long beats, working the wooden match he holds in his teeth. Watch the inter-cutting between the two which enhances the eight seconds before Clyde gives his answer.

> CLYDE
> It ain't like anything.

> BONNIE
> Shoot. I knew you never robbed anyplace, you faker.

Clyde stares at Bonnie, and then ahead, making little throaty sounds; and reaches inside his suit jacket and takes out a pistol.

Bonnie's eyes shift downward to the pistol, half hidden under Clyde's arm. In a Cut-Away/Insert we see her fingers feel the barrel. We hear her giggly thrill. Clyde, in a Close-Up, is looking downward. His eyes then shift upward and right to Bonnie. A cut returns Bonnie in Close-Up, at that moment she looks to Clyde. More than twenty-five seconds have passed.

> BONNIE
> But you wouldn't have the gumption to use it.

Clyde never looks back to Bonnie. He stares far ahead.

> CLYDE
> All right. You just wait right here and keep your eyes open.

Note the pause after "All right."

The dialogue "portion" of the scene runs 1:15; but the dialogue itself takes hardly fifteen seconds. What would you do with the remaining sixty seconds if this were theatre or radio?

Here is an easily engaging scene. It makes use of speech, but its strength is derived from the music-like playfulness, which contrasts the context:.

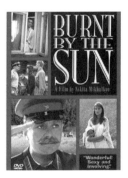

Chapter 23, "Helping Father Get Ready"
@ 1:49:20

The scene holds a sinister lure — a result of dramatic irony, and the contrast between Nadya's virtuousness and the reality of her father, Colonel Kotov's circumstance — known to him and the audience. It is 1936, the Stalinist purges have begun, and the Colonel is a target.

Nadya's concern for her father's drinking on an empty stomach quickly evolves to the moment at hand, by way of a *glance*, *silly sounds*, and a *grimace*.

> NADYA
>
> Where are you going?

It is upsettingly ironic that Nadya hurries her father, so that she might drive the car "as far as the bend."

The irony is nearly outdone by the father and daughter's embracing closeness. Their playful platypus game imparts an amusing adoration; their long hold-your-breath-humming contest with Nadya's frequent cheating is charming. The sound of humming intensifies an apprehension: a slow move-in to an old photo from happier and heroic days, showing Kotov with Joseph Stalin.

In cinema, dialogue is a tally of all methods that reach out to communicate. This offers a better model for screenwriter, director, cinematographer, actor, and editor.

Here is a selection that is (perhaps) a literal example of this notion, but it does illustrate my point, and efficiently incorporates the previous two chapters: Objects and Motion.

Chapter 3, "Teacher Meets Student" @ 0:16:00

Annie Sullivan arrives at the Keller's home in Tuscumbia, Alabama. She is eager to meet her new student, the blind and deaf Helen Keller. An Extreme Long-Shot shows Helen standing on the steps in front of the house as the voices of Captain and Mrs. Keller enthusiastically greet Miss Sullivan. Annie, nearly blind herself — she wears round dark glasses — has to be told, "There's Helen."

Several beats into the Extreme Long-Shot, Annie enters screen right and walks to Helen; she carries her wicker valise and purse. Annie slams the wicker valise onto the deck above the top step, and Helen is startled by the vibration. She reaches out and feels the wicker; her hand, feeling the top of the valise, touches Annie's hand. Gentle and separate key touches on a piano are cued to the Cut-Away/Insert of Helen and Annie "meeting" for the first time.

Helen examines Annie's fingers, then brings the hand to her nose to explore-sniff the new arrival. The Cut-Away, becoming a Close-Up of Helen, also spots an addition to the piano: strings. The camera pans right and follows Helen's search of Annie's face, glasses, eyes, and hat. Annie reaches out to embrace the girl, but Helen pulls away.

Wind instruments cue new efforts to communicate, and in the end, Helen, with tugs and a punch, welcomes Annie to her home!

Let's screen a dialogue scene that's a little different: a telephone conversation. You'll note that the editing rhythms create a visual pattern and pacing that precludes the domination of words alone, and the eyes still have it!

The robbery should have taken 10 minutes. 4 hours later, the bank was like a circus sideshow. 8 hours later, it was the hottest thing on live T.V. 12 hours later, it was all history. And it's all true.

Chapter 21, "Sonny and Angie Talk" @ 1:31:50
Sonny, now perspiring in the no lights, no air-condi-tioning bank, gets an outside telephone line to make one last call before a bus will take him, and the hos-tages, to Kennedy Airport and a flight safely out of the country.

> SONNY
> (to Sal)
> You know, I could call anybody, they'd put them on the phone.
> The Pope, an astronaut; the wisest of the wise. Who do
> I have to call?

This intriguing introduction to "who [he] has to call" is somewhat thinned by the chapter's title, and especially by dialogue @ **1:31:32** when Sonny first asks for an outside line.

> SONNY
> (into telephone)
> "I want to talk to my wife…"

There is a current inclination not to filter the off-camera (OC) voice "playing" through the phone. Contemporary films will, at times, reduce the level, or equal-ize the track (ever so slightly) so as to create a distinction between the on-camera speaker and the receiver-delivered lines, but presently many films do not alter the voice "inside" the telephone at all.

I will offer no rules on the subject, but see (and hear) if you don't agree the difference makes for a very big difference.

The scene is actually a cross-cutting of two scenes: the Interior of the bank, and the Interior of Angie's apartment.

At **1:32:33** a Close-Up of Sonny is framed by both his hands, the left holding the telephone, the right a handkerchief.

SONNY

I'm dying, you know that? I'm dying here.

ANGIE (OC)

Sonny, I blame myself. I noticed you've been tense,
like something is happening… yelling at the kids
like a madman…and then you want me to go on that ride…

ANGIE (On-Camera; Full Voice)

…the Caterpillar. From here to there full of those kids.
I'm not about to get on the ride. So you yell at me…
Pig, get on the fucking ride. Everything fell out of me.

The overlapping and simultaneous speaking are constructed in two (audio) tracks each for Sonny and Angie so as to permit the instantaneous adjustments between 1) their on-camera dialogue and 2) their off-camera dialogue.

Take special notice of Sonny's eyes @ 1:33:09 as he tries to get a "word in," and again @ 1:33:14 as he explodes!

This is a scene(s) of people talking to each other from *different places* — *trying* to talk, and attempting a final communication. The collaboration that "mixed" the words, and selectively blended the images, has produced an inspired and masterful sonata. The cadences elaborate sorrow, tragedy, and affection in all seriousness, and, in part, foolishness. It is an invigorating lesson in mystery, trickery, magic, and movie whodunit!

reactions

Actors often advise that the art of acting is in the reacting. In my book, *The Eye Is Quicker. Film Editing: Making a Good Film Better*, I include an entire chapter on the subject, "Reactions Speak Louder Than Words."

I hate to trouble you with another paradox, but: Reactions can simultaneously understate the visual (direct) action, yet engage the viewer by prompting imagination. In this way they initiate audience *participation* in the (indirect) action.

WITNESS

Chapter 3, "Material Witness" @ 0:12:07

Samuel needs to use the public restroom, and his mother reminds him to take his Amish black dress hat. He walks away from the camera to a lighted doorway in the background. A touch of foreboding accompanies him: the deep rumbling sound of a train below the mezzanine. The sound continues as Samuel enters the men's bathroom. He is "greeted" by a pleasant chap who is washing at a line of sinks.

It is a choice worth noting, that the Long-Shot of Samuel leaving the waiting area is joined to a Medium-Shot of the man in the bathroom. The man turns from the mirror to see who is entering, *reacting* to an echoing slam of the bathroom door.

The rumbling fades-out as Samuel enters a toilet stall at the back of the room. Footsteps turn Samuel's head, so that in Medium-Shot he faces us through a partially opened stall door. A cut to a Close-Up of the pleasant chap — he is rinsing his face, his body bent over the sink — also has him react to the footsteps; he turns from the camera (and sink), looking toward the bathroom doorway. An obscured figure crosses the frame, for an instant blocking our view of the "pleasant man" who is slowly turning to follow the new entrant into the restroom. Gentle, but nevertheless an uneasy reverberating sound of dribbles of water continues as the man returns to washing. The door slams again and the man reacts to new footsteps, again looking away from the sink. This time the camera tilts upward, following his motion. The mirror above his sink reveals another man stopping at a urinal. At **0:13:36** the two recent arrivals brutally attack the pleasant man. Take note how effective are the Extreme Close-Ups of Samuel's watching from the tiny gap of the stall door.

THE VIRGIN SPRING

Chapter 9, "Princess Karin" @ 0:34:28 & Chapter 10, "Tragedy" @ 36:40

As in *Witness*, the filmmakers use the reactions of an onlooker to the scene's escalating tension and horrid attack — in this case a Tore family woman servant who was to accompany daughter Karin Tore on her pilgrimage to church with the "Virgin's candles."

Bonnie And Clyde ends with a horrifying and prolonged (twenty-two seconds) machine-gunning. But, does it?

BONNIE AND CLYDE

Chapter 34, "Birds and Bullets Fly" @ 1:49:30

Watch what actually ends the film *after* the gruesomeness of the writhing bodies: A quiet move back and dolly right, past the bullet riddled car, stops with a view through the back window as Mr. Moss, two passers-by and the armed lawmen approach. The bodies of Bonnie and Clyde are not visible. A lowered submachine gun, a silent deep breath, and a cut to black ends the film.

Let's screen a nonviolent scene, lest you believe that excess is the central purpose of reactions. Watch and you can imagine.

Chapter 1, "Courage and Integrity" @ 0:08:32

Frank's first day on the job at his assigned precinct. He's partnered with the Patrolman of the Month, an old timer, but still uniformed police officer. A cut takes us from the precinct to a local luncheonette where the two officers have gone for lunch. Frank is introduced to Charlie, the owner and counterman. Charlie suggests "creamed chicken" and the older officer immediately accepts: "Sounds good to me." Frank naively — watch and you'll know what I mean — turns down Charlie's recommendation, instead ordering "a roast beef on a roll."

Three reactions on Charlie *disclose* the existence of a quid pro quo between the cops on the beat and Charlie's establishment.

A bold cut has the food already served the officers; Frank holds the sandwich bread open, disappointed to find, "It's all fat here."

Innocent Frank learns his first lesson about small-time corruptions in law enforcement. Take Charlie's lunch offerings — "Don't be fussy, it's free" — and in return there'll be no summonses for illegally parked trucks making deliveries to Charlie's place of business. Bet you imagined something was up from Charlie's reactions!

Alfred Hitchcock often made use of a simple, sequential structure that raised the curiosity of the audience. A character would "take a look"; a cut would show us the character's point of view (POV), and then a return to the character would demonstrate a reaction to what was viewed. But for every "rule" there's an exception.

In *The Sweet Hereafter* a choice in the order engages the audience in extent of concern, dismay, and downright horror that exceeds a result the "usual" structure might illicit.

THE SWEET HEREAFTER

Chapter 11, "That Morning" @ 0:54:22

An ominous dolly shot carries us down the aisle of the school bus from the front rows of seats to the emergency door window in the back. The shot appears via a dissolve from a tilt-up to a wall of school children, as Dolores, the neck-braced schoolbus driver, tells her story to attorney Mitchell Stephens. Her whimpering anguish carries well into the interior school bus shot, segueing into the film's hauntingly primitive melodies.

Though the story has not hidden the fact that the full schoolbus will suffer a horrible accident, the filmmakers nevertheless startle the audience with the bus driver's quick-steering adjustment at a moment when Dolores gives up her attention to the winter roadway, "Now you settles down back there," as she keeps an eye on "her children" in the rearview mirror.

The opening dolly shot is divided into two segments, the second coming after an aerial shot which follows the bus along a roadway empty but for a red truck that follows close behind. It is driven by Billy, the father of the two children waving (to him) out the back window. Billy's drive and cheerful waving is a regular morning ritual. The father smiles and lets his left hand leave the steering wheel to wave to his children. An instant after Billy starts his second wave, we "catch sight" of a change in his eyes. His hand reacts as well, freezing in a half-wave. A Medium-Long-Shot in a (not quite) POV discloses the source of the father's stricken reaction: The schoolbus goes into a skid, and crashing through a narrow guard rail it disappears over the snow-banked edge of the road. Along with the bus skidding and bump and bounce sound effects, the filmmakers add in an effectively exaggerated series of cries and fearful screams. A fairly quick cut — almost blurred by the severity of motion — to Dolores in the Medium-Shot is used again, inserted into the Medium-Long-Shot of the out of control school bus. She grapples with the steering wheel. An intense look of horror shows on the dad's face, the fingers of his left hand in a distressed twitch, as he brings his truck to a sliding stop.

Chapter 19, "The Widow" @ 0:49:28

Helene — the wife of the attacked and critically in-jured Deputy — has been brought to the hospital. She enters a meeting in which a doctor is updating her husband's condition for a group of government officials. The doctor uses a wall of back-lighted x-rays to illustrate the diagnosis and prognosis. There is a hollowness to the doctor's voice; a sort of thin-ness — near echo — in air that enhances the institu-tional location and impersonal medical presentation.

The dialogue is hardly ever heard in a view of the speaker. Not until **0:49:53** do we see (for certain) the doctor speaking on camera. A long lecture, of ghastly elucidations of skull and brain damage, precedes the moment: The audience is absorbed by the despondent, dark, entranced eyes of Helene.

Is there a better way to "play" this moment than on the reacting eyes of actor, Irene Papas? Have a gaze at:

Chapter 20, "Propaganda" @ 0:54:50

The Deputy is undergoing a third neurosurgical procedure. A guard, posted outside the surgical theatre, opens the scene in Extreme Close-Up. He turns to screen left as Helene moves toward the doorway of the hall leading to the oper-ating room, "It's not allowed, madam." Helene enters nonetheless. A response of such severity in her eyes "sees" the guard back off.

Watch *all* the eyes — Helene's, her friend's and aides' — as they make their way closer and closer to the doors of the operating room; a camera dolly in POV nervously turns a corner. The echoing order of the guard; the sliding door and footsteps — and a muffled repetitious "beat" of a respirator — augment the green tinged light of the tiled walls; adding to the unbearable failing hope.

The reactions are made evermore urgent and alarming as the scene con-cludes with but a partial view through the narrow horizontal window of the operating room door. The surgical team is focused downward to their critically injured patient; the Deputy cannot be seen.

The French Connection gives us an illustration of *fragments* joined to produce a scene that is intense, apprehensive, absurd, and a "lush" character prologue. And! A very good example of *reactions* to cinema marvel!

THE FRENCH CONNECTION

Chapter 3, "A Bust in Brooklyn" @ 0:05:57
This largely improvisational scene establishes life-like continuity from unqualified impossibilities. By juxtaposing shots, which pay special attention to the (reactive) eyes of the drug suspect, the filmmakers "conceal" some of the most brazen "mismatches" in film history. Especially watch detective Russo.

Here is an archetypal illustration of the extraordinary influence of reactions.

ROSEMARY'S BABY

Chapter 31, "What Have You Done to Its Eyes?" @ 2:08:28
Rosemary, with a large kitchen knife in hand, enters the Castavets' living room. Invited Satanic worshippers from across the globe have come to celebrate the baby's arrival. Rosemary slowly approaches the centerpiece of the gathering, a black cradle, shielded in black drapes. As Rosemary's hand reaches into the cradle so as to part the drapes, we notice the baby's blanket: black quilted satin. Shadows cast across her face disappear as soft reflected light more fully illuminates her. Rosemary's eyes indicate nauseated shock. She clutches her left hand across her mouth. The exaggerated quiet yields to a discordant arrangement distinguished by a woman's voice crying out in appalling agony. The cry is nearly in synchronization with Rosemary's look of terror.

In answer to the chapter's title — Rosemary's question — Roman Castevet explains, "He has his father's eyes." At **2:11:14** Rosemary screams "Oh God" and drops the knife; the camera follows its fall, and it sticks into the wood of the floor, standing at Rosemary's feet. Roman shouts, "God is dead." For barely more than a second, across Rosemary's face, there appears a double exposure of Satan's eyes — evocative of the ritualistic intercourse scene: **Chapter 11, "This Is No Dream! This Is Really Happening" @ 0:47:45.**

At **2:13:24**, as Rosemary is about to drink "plain, ordinary Lipton's tea," the baby begins to cry. Rosemary crosses the room and explains to Laura-Louise — a satanic cult member and neighbor — that she's rocking the baby too fast. Roman orders Laura-Louise to move away, and encourages Rosemary to rock *her* baby. As the guests assemble to watch, Rosemary begins a slow rocking of the cradle. The baby — through sound alone — begins to settle. Rosemary reaches into the cradle, and the baby quiets completely. She smiles as an ill-omened lullaby carries the scene, and the film, to its close.

No image of Satan's (and Rosemary's) baby is ever shown — and therefore never seen — and yet, thousands of people will pledge, even upon a holy bible, that they glimpsed the baby's face, and its red-horrific eyes.

Most "remember" seeing "those eyes" when Rosemary first peeked into the cradle, while many recall that it was when Rosemary surrendered to motherly instincts.

subtext

It might seem odd to include this chapter in the third section, *Character*, rather than in the first, *Story*. I have a simple and good reason, and a good illustration emphasizing that subtext is best kept in the realm of emotion, not intellect. In other words, subtext is most imperative as the character to character affection and/or aversion, and as such engages, and informs, the emotional life rather than the premise or message of *story*.

I do recognize that *subtext* as metaphor and theme is an enduring foundation in storytelling. Ideas and intellectual purpose are irresistible to our search for understanding and order. They will always inspire the artist, and occupy the audience, but I believe it best to maintain direct storytelling while avoiding willful intrusions of meaning. As David Mamet puts it, "Just tell the story!"

Here is my good illustration.

CASABLANCA

Chapter 36, "A Beautiful Friendship" @ 1:39:52
Ilsa and Victor Laszlo — a most-wanted resistance
leader — are escaping Nazi-controlled Morocco.
Their small plane taxis to take-off, when Major
Strasser arrives at the airport to stop them. Rick
prevents Strasser by shooting him. Immediately a car
packed with several Vichy French from the Municipal
Police pulls up.

Captain Renault announces, "Major Strasser
has been shot!" (@1:40:36). Take note of the next
"doubling" of reactions: Rick (apprehensive, looking toward Renault); Renault
(with a slight, but unmistakable smile looking toward Rick — you'll notice a
slim turn as his arms relax); Rick (still looking toward Renault, but somewhat
more confident).

Some six seconds — a remarkable number of beats — later, Renault
orders, "Round up the usual suspects!" The camera pans right and moves in to
a smiling Rick.

The eye to eye contact between Renault and Rick, "spied" by the audience,
provides *emotional meaning*: Whew! Captain Renault is going to protect Rick!

The original cut of this scene did not emphasize the "threat to Rick" beat
and, as such, furnished no "Whew!" The character to character *subtext* — and
audience alertness — was feeble.

As the Vichy police carry off Strasser's body, added Close-Ups of Renault
and Rick reinforced the subtext of camaraderie, and are a vital addition to a
successful ending — even with an unconcealed mismatch in the cut from Rick's
Close-Up to the above-angle Master-Shot as the Vichy Police drive away. The
emotion in *subtext* comes first, and triumphs!

The scene did (and still does) contain a patent thematic message: Captain
Renault pours himself a glass of *Eau Minerale Vichy Water* from a prominently
labeled bottle. The camera follows the bottle down into a trash basket, and
Renault's foot kicks it out of frame. But, this action, along with dialogue about
"[becoming] a patriot... a good time to start," and Renault's, "I think perhaps

you're right," without the unambiguous preceding *subtext* did not eliminate the studio's strong disappointment with the film's airfield ending. The studio believed both the airfield and the ending were foggy!

With *emotional* subtext in place the classic movie closes effectively: "Louis... I think this is the beginning of a beautiful friendship."

For those especially eager to maintain subtext as intellect and theme, I offer this combination.

OSAMA

Chapter 5, "A Job for the Boy" @ 0:28:40

In Afghanistan, under Taliban rule, women are not permitted to work, or to be out of their houses without a male escort. A desperate single mother disguises her twelve-year-old daughter to be her "son." She beseeches a shopkeeper to hire her daughter so that the family might survive on the small income. The girl is hired. Under the dangerous apprenticeship the girl obeys the owner's directives, necessary to protect her identity.

The Taliban comes down the street — no doubt frequently — to announce, "Prayer time!" The intruding voice is heard over a Close-Up of the girl. Note that her eyes shift in response to a (latch) sound, and motivate the POV of the Taliban in the shop's entranceway.

A cut to a Long-Shot — from *inside* the shop — shows the girl for a brief moment before a final section of wooden shutter covers the shop's window, and *shuts out the light.* Here is a significant *contrast* that generates a *subtext* in story metaphor: Shops must close for times of prayer, but the filmmakers "close the shop" with an interior perspective so that the "place" becomes dark. Contrast in light and dark? Yes! Here in metaphor — an *understated* (non-intrusive) intellectual *subtext* — under the merciless Taliban rule, religious observance shuts out the "light (knowledge, tolerance, compassion) of day."

This manner of *subtext* (more than equally) sticks to the story; the audience does not lose concern for the genuinely, not metaphorically, vulnerable girl.

Here is a marvelous scene to illustrate *subtext* as a portal to emotions which are instantaneously "legible" to the audience.

BALLAD OF A SOLDIER

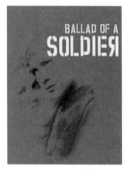

Chapter 3, "Six Days' Leave" @ 0:08:12

The scene opens looking out from inside a command bunker. A voice off-camera (OC) orders Alyosha Skvortsov to "report to the general."

Alyosha, a gangling Russian soldier, enters the bunker in a hurried crouch, safely dipping below the entranceway timbers. His eyes become larger, his mouth drops open, and he instinctively hops to attention beginning a salute, when his helmet clunks into the overhead supports. A cut to a Master-Shot reveals the general and his staff, and Alyosha in the soft-focused background gets off his hesitant salute. The general, with head bandaged, calls Alyosha to him.

It is the assembly of shots and the beats which surround the words which make the subtext emotionally unambiguous.

1. There are seven seconds between Alyosha's request to "exchange" his decoration for a chance to go home to see his mother and fix her roof, and the General's response in text. That time and the reactions between the General and Alyosha "say" that he's transgressed the military code of behavior. Will he face disciplinary action?

2. The General's question, "How old are you?" bestows compassion in its inflection — not in the literal meaning of the words — even though it elicits a literal answer. The interaction is only obvious and poignant in the subtext.

Chapter 2, "Family" @ 0:05:25

The arrival of the "nomadic couple" onto the board-walk and into the casino and oyster bar grants a simple illustration of a dialogue scene so structured, that the emotional connotations and significance — and eyes — drive the editing rhythms and con-structs an emotional subtext.

The sequence begins with obvious irony: the contrast in characters to place, and the lobby trio's rendition of the popular resort town's song: "On the Boardwalk in Atlantic City."

Note the musical introduction and opening lyrics, heard across the first (exterior) shot; a beautiful segue from the previous scene (stuffed bell clapper) and the startled flight of pigeons.

Let's read through the dialogue before we watch the scene. It will allow a far better appreciation of the inter-cutting of the five set-ups, and how it creates a *comprehensible subtext* that only *then* permits the plausibility of Sally's actions.

> SALLY
> Oh, Christ!

> CHRISSIE
> Hi. Oh, wow, it's really good to see you.

> SALLY
> I don't want you here. Get your asses out of here!

> CHRISSIE
> When do you finish?

> SALLY
> Look, you're not staying with me.

> DAVE
> Look Sally, we've got money.

SALLY
Oh great! You're in a hotel. Check in.

DAVE
We will have money.

CHRISSIE
Sally... Sal...

SALLY (to co-worker)
Can you spell me for an hour?

CO-WORKER
Yeah. Sure. Who are they?

SALLY
My husband and my sister.

For the story to work, let alone move ahead, Sally must bring Dave and Chrissie to her apartment. But! She also is justifiably pissed off at their showing up. She certainly let's them know — even if Chrissie *is* obviously pregnant. Sally is a decent person, but her husband ran off (who knows where they disappeared to?) with her sister, and now Sally's sibling is going to have Sally's husband's baby. "Oh Christ." Plenty of anger, and a need for a subtext in ambivalence! In this apprehensive exchange, the filmmakers must have the audience (in a *handful* of seconds) accept and *believe* in Sally's generosity.

Chrissie's helpless "Sally... Sal..." and teeny finger pats on the oyster bar counter, win over Sally, and us. Pay close attention to Sally and Chrissie's eye contact!

obstacles

Obstacles need not be derived from an adversary, nor do they need to be a pivotal or abiding hurdle. Each scene and sequence offers opportunity and hindrance. This is one of the defining traditions in which a story moves forward as an organized arrangement which sustains *story*, rather than *story* as an indiscriminate succession of events. Obstacles need only be an intrusion in a character's immediate objectives.

Let's look at several *Obstacles* with variations in significance, extent and twists.

BALLAD OF A SOLDIER

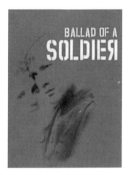

Chapter 4, "A Special Present" @ 0:11:21

Alyosha's heroic battle exploits have been rewarded with a six-day leave from the front to return to his village to fix the leaking roof on his mother's house.

Chapter 3 ends with a Fade-Out, but instead of a Fade-In to this chapter, the first shot "pops" in from black, a unique and effective *transition*: the opening shot, from the back of a jeep behind Alyosha and his driver, is "popping" with exhilaration, camaraderie, and eager anticipation. Played up with the addition of a patriotic Soviet score! Long lines of Russian soldiers, framing screen left and right, march in the opposite direction.

Alyosha's jeep cuts in front of a tank as it turns right, and past the camera in puffs of blowing sand. A dissolve finds the back of the jeep in need of a push, away from the camera to cross a river. Soldiers and tanks are crossing the other way; heading toward the camera. We might deem these mini-obstacles. This temporary halt in the journey reinforces a solidarity that will soon make plausible Alyosha's selfless acts that affect his foremost obstacle: time.

In fact, an example of one of Alyosha's *self-imposed* obstacles — though we might miss it as one — takes place immediately: Alyosha *agrees* to give of his time to make a delivery of soap to another soldier's wife back home.

It is by way of *obstacles* that anxiety and tension — sensed by a character or not — engage the audience. At times the source of an obstacle is less external than from a character's misinterpretations, or paranoia! Such sources create illustrations of *dramatic irony*, and so are no less a matter of tension for the audience: Any spoiler of serenity, harmony or repose is an *obstacle*.

THE TREASURE OF THE SIERRA MADRE

Chapter 14, "Sleepless Night" @ 0:43:14

A braying burro startles a sleeping Dobbs. The animal's sound segues to the rumbling of an orchestrated disturbance. Dobbs — in Close-Up — tries to return to sleep, but his glance to screen right initiates the camera's quick pan right to the empty sleeping gear of one of his gold prospecting partners, Howard. The shot holds several beats on the empty mat and blanket, when an unusual choice in action launches a reaction: Dobbs darts into the left edge of the frame. The lens does not adjust focus, and Dobbs is a "blur."

A cut to a Master-Shot from the back of the tent displays Dobbs, now sitting, his (other) partner Curtin, sound asleep in the foreground, and the moonlit tent opening. Dobbs gets his boots on, and with pistol in hand, heads off to see what Howard is up to.

Ever since the men agreed to split the goods (gold) gathered each day into thirds, and thus be responsible for their own cut, tensions have been on the increase.

Howard's return to the tent wakens Curtin who, spotting Dobbs' empty "bed," heads out to see what he's up to. When Dobbs returns and sees that Curtin is now "missing," he is just about to head out again, when Curtin, seen approaching through the tent opening, makes his way back to bed. It is worth noting that this scene might play as an over-the-top Fado or Marx Brothers' comedy, but for the *atmosphere* established by the suspenseful score and dangers of night.

THE BRIDGE ON THE RIVER KWAI

Chapter 28, "Bathing with the Enemy" @ 1:53:29 Major Warden and Lieutenant Joyce give chase when a single Japanese soldier escapes into the jungle. Here is an obstacle "quick on the heels" of but a few moments prior when the team faced a Japanese platoon. This new "snag" must be done away with or the entire mission will be compromised.

> MAJOR WARDEN
> Use your knife man, or we'll be shooting each other.

The two commandos finally confront the Japanese soldier. At the decisive moment Lieutenant Joyce hesitates and Warden receives a comparatively minor injury. However, under the circumstances of the story, the wound establishes a new and crucial obstacle.

Let's have a look at a variety of obstacles.

RIFIFI

Chapter 10, "Casing the Joint" @ 0:35:34, concludes with a Close-Up of a *SURALARM* control box. The Close-Up is a point of view (POV) as located by Cesar — pretending to be a wastrel customer — in the prestigious Paris jewelry store, Mappin & Webb.

The alarm is the "overriding" obstacle to the thieves' enterprising heist plans, and with a brilliantly lucid dissolve we get to **Chapter 11, "Suralarm"** **@ 0:35:38**. The alarm control box on Mappin & Webb's wall dissolves to an identical model carried away from the camera by Cesar and Mario. The box is mounted — in a Long-Shot composed by the men continuing away from the lens — on a drain pipe in their cellar workshop, and plugged in and turned on for study. As Mario reports, "It's no pushover. It's the latest model... It's getting harder to make a living."

A series of engaging tests is conducted: Cutting the electrical cord instantly activates the alarm, and it rings loudly. Tony disconnects the power source to the box, "blowing" the cellar lights; the alarm is activated again. Jo lights a match, "The bastards thought of everything." Mario now demonstrates how the jewelry store's small sensors will trigger the alarm in response to moderate sounds and vibrations.

Take special note of the character composition, motion, and object engagement, beginning @ **0:37:50** with Mario's mallet strike which sounds the alarm. Mario, with a nearly "eaten" cigar butt in his mouth, then in his right hand, reads from the *SURALARM* manual — loudly above the ongoing clang — which describes the "foolproof" back-up systems that guarantee the thieves a challenging obstacle. Cesar, on a ladder, is amused by their inscrutable quandary. Watch how engagingly enjoyable it is to see people at work on an intricately demanding task!

THE SHOP ON MAIN STREET

Chapter 32, "Our Laws are Kind" @1:45:53

As the Jews of the village are gathered and identified in the town square, Tono and Mrs. Lautmann remain safe in the button shop. Tono has assured her that he will not let her be harmed, though she remains unaware of the outside events.

Tono returns to the street side of the shop declaring, to his inebriated self, "Everything will be all right." He offers himself a salute into a wall mirror, "Damn the fascist guards."

Tono moves forward, toward the shop door, so that what was a Master-Shot brings him into Close-Up. A cut to the outside, in POV with a Zoom-In, recognizes Tono's brother-in-law at a podium: "Jews, listen to me!" He assures them that they will not be harmed, only sent to labor camps to work. But, as we see Tono in a Medium-Shot slowly opening the shop door slightly, we hear his brother-in-law announce, "We shall punish everyone who dares to oppose the law! Jew or not."

Here is a clear and present danger — an obstacle to surviving — but at the outset Tono's obstacle is his own tormenting ambivalence. While much of the final scenes in the shop are handled in the complex difficulties of continuous action, here the structure loosens as Tono labors under threat of outside (world) events, and conscience:

At **1:46:38** Tono, in a Medium Long-Shot from over his right shoulder, closes the door, the outside bright, and clearly visible through the glass panes of the shop's doorway. The next cut is dark, and holds no action "match" to the last few beats on Tono as his head nearly comes to rest against one of the glass panes. In a Medium-Shot, Tono steps down from the doorway, turning to face inside the shop. He sits on the single wooden step, bringing his face into Close-Up: "Bastard! You wanted to trap me? Now I know."

Tono's eyes search inside the shop — and inside his soul. A cut to a wide-angle Long-Shot, in an above angle, lets us see Tono seated in the upper half of the frame, his bottle sits on the counter; all "feels" gray. Tono buries his head in his hands. A striking cut in both image and audio occurs @ **1:47:04**: Tono stares into the mirror, the camera looking up at the downward tilt of the mirror's frame. Haunting musical notes in drawn-out strings enter the shop. Another cut takes us to a Medium-Shot of Tono already behind the counter. He winds a round, giant-bell alarm clock. His vodka bottle, to his left (screen right), draws his attention.

A cut to an Extreme Long-Shot — there is no more music — shows us Mrs. Lautmann opening the door at the back of the shop which separates the store from her living area. She is upset that the shop is still not shut for the Sabbath. A beautiful move brings the camera to meet her; Mrs. Lautmann passes to screen left, now becoming aware of the outside occurrences. The moving camera pans right, as it reaches the end of the counter it finds Tono with vodka bottle in hand, sitting in Mrs. Lautmann's shop chair. He watches her, and in a POV Long-Shot we watch, from behind Mrs. Lautmann, as she slowly approaches the shop's doors, and the somewhat more evident announcements being "broadcast" across the village square. Tono's obstacle might be determined to be cosmic events that threaten the entire world, but to the immediacy in time and place it is his brother-in-law. This obstacle can be easily "conquered" by betraying the "real" one: Mrs. Lautmann.

Chapter 12, "Without Help" @ 0:46:10 thru Chapter 13, "Preparing Documents" @ 0:51:48 The documentary director, Zana Briski, who is teacher and guardian to a small group of Calcutta children, takes us along on her exasperating night-mare dealing with the ineffectual and overwhelmed local bureaucracy. She is determined to obtain legal identification and health certification for all of "her" children, so as to give them a chance to be free of a dreadful existence with little more than ill-fated prospects. Via sequences of frustration and fatigue contrasted by perseverance and delight, the filmmakers prove that a path burdened by obstacles is indispensable to storytelling drama in every form.

performance

Film's association with theatre fosters the belief that *performance* can be attrib-uted to the actor communicating the writer's words. A single simple premise argues that in film, the actor (alone) is not *performance*.

While it is very possible — film history records its frequency — to "induce" a great film performance by a non-actor, it is far from likely, if even possible, live on stage. This is so because a film performance is, to a far greater extent than theatre, determined by a complex integration of disciplines: screenwriting, casting, production design, costume design, make-up, acting, cinematography, directing, editing, composing, sound design and recording, re-recording, mixing, and so many others, in a *non-linear* work environment, which produces *start and stop fragments*, later to be arranged into a linear construction.

Alexander MacKendrick brings up one intriguingly nurturing factor in the collaboration of performance:

> One of the best editors I ever worked with was a former actor. I used to watch him as he sat at the editing bench, running the unedited footage over and over again. While he did this you could see on his face that he was absorbing the actions and words of the actors, instinctively acting

along with their performances until he found the precise frame where the actor was, essentially, telling him to make a cut. A good editor will even rediscover magical elements of the footage that the writer, actor and director didn't know they had put there.

While I will include illustrations of distinguished *performances* by experienced professionals, they will nonetheless demonstrate the all-encompassing labors of many artists and craftsmen. First let's begin with the alluring magic of an inexpert child.

BURNT BY THE SUN

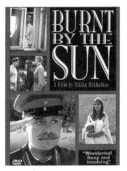

Chapter 22, "Small Talk" @ 1:46:37
The sleek black sedan has arrived at "Dacha Number Nine." It will be taking "Uncle" Mitya — of Stalin's secret police — and Nadya's dear father Sergei Kotov to Moscow and ruin.

Nadya is fascinated by the shining beauty of a car, admiring it through the diagonal slats of the Dacha's gate. The opening Long Shot of the car and Nadya's Close-Up are joined by the visual logic of point of view (POV). Take time to admire — as the child does the car — Nadya's tilted head resting parallel within the gate's diagonal lines.

Nadya's marvel at the black sedan is indeed ironic, but it is touched with several interesting points of dramatic irony. She is going to be allowed to "drive" the vehicle a short distance down the road (a bit of double irony given her father's destiny) and her checking and re-checking that no one in the house can see, together with her effort to unlatch the gate in covert silence, are an essential reinforcement of the child's warning not to leave the safety of the family's dacha. This gathering of situations is a key player in the child's "acting." Nadya's performance results from an overall context, the immediacy of every fresh moment that is linked to the overall effect: the integration of ongoing actions and re-actions in beats and pauses produced in variously composed set-ups. The child's gestures can be obtained in directed imitation, and mimicked words; the post-production fabricates an artificially constructed time, "deceptive" emotions derived via juxtaposed images and sound.

The tranquility of the scene, but for an occasional shrill bird or insect, and the ever-so-light creaking gate hinge, delivers impressions in dreamy magic. Nadya's secret meeting with the inhabitants of Stalin's secret police car produces contrasts which add to the overall performance.

The child's hushed grooming — note her glowing back-lit blonde hair with ribbons — in the mirror-like reflections of the polished car's headlamp is disparate to the perspiring, food-dipping, lip-smacking thugs seated inside.

Nadya's slow stroll past the camera, dragging her hand squeaking across the auto's black shine, is easy and enthralling. Her knock on the windshield begins a brief dialogue with one of the hoodlums — a contrast between Nadya's cheerfully inquisitive tone and thug-like chewing, mumbling grunts — and an almost annoying dog bark-yelp in the background.

It is well worth mentioning that the director and cinematographer have chosen an unusual composition: Nadya does not go to the passenger side window, but rather stands at the passenger corner of the windshield. This arrangement provides an aesthetic contrast between Nadya's luminous face and the darker interior of the auto, and, in the set-up over Nadya's right shoulder, a thug in the back is visible atop the right shoulder of the grunting one in the front seat.

One sign of a genuine professional is in his ability to handle Dramatic Transitions: inflection and/or topic changes, often boldly sweeping from one line — or moment/beat — to the next.

SERPICO

Chapter 2, "We'll Take the Collar" @ 0:13:30.
A line of suspects facing indictment exit the station house. Frank Serpico follows the last of them — the rape suspect he nabbed last night — to a police van. The suspect is bruised and swollen following a harsh beating by a detective. Serpico addresses a fellow officer.

> SERPICO
>
> Hey Charlie, let me have five minutes with him?

> CHARLIE
>
> Sure.

> SERPICO
>
> Thanks.

Serpico unlocks the rape suspect's cuff, freeing him from the line of prisoners.

> SERPICO (cont)
>
> Thank you, Charlie.

Serpico and the suspect move away and to the side of the van. Serpico "examines" how awful the suspect looks.

> SERPICO
>
> That prick really worked you over. How do you feel?

> SUSPECT
>
> How come you didn't stay for the fun?

> SERPICO
>
> That's not my kind of fun.

> SUSPECT (in a whisper)
>
> Shit!

> SERPICO
>
> I want to talk to you. I want to take you across the street, get you a cup of coffee... without cuffs.

I have underlined two of Serpico's lines. From the first to the second is a dramatic transition. Here is a case of a clear and *observable* inflection change. You'll notice that Pacino handles the transition on his own. There is no adjustment by an editor making use of a cut to alter the rhythm or beat construction to provide believability to the inflection shift. The entire scene plays in Master-Shot. Pacino drops his left arm, which has been bracing him to the side of the police van, pauses and looks "across the street." His body turns back toward the suspect as he begins, "I want to talk to you." Serpico's eyes look to the ground until he finishes that phrase. These several beats permit a smooth shift. Pacino does not use, "Listen!" or "Anyway!" or "Speaking of" or any number of other unnecessary declarations as a "lever" to aid in the inflection shift.

How smart the instinct to look "across the street" in the progression from "That's not my kind of fun," so as to "find" the transition to the new inflection, "I want to talk to you."

The camera moves left following Serpico and the Suspect to a "private area." This exterior scene is joined to the next — an interior — scene with incoming dialogue that precedes a cut to a local food shop, creating a physically distinct transition. The shop provides Serpico a "diplomatic" setting to convince the suspect to reveal the identities of his cohorts. At **0:14:45** of the Police Van scene, Serpico taps the suspect high on the left arm saying, "Come on." Serpico then turns away and walks ahead as the suspect follows. Serpico pauses, taking the suspect with a gentle touch of his arm.

SERPICO
It's a goddamn shame you gotta take this whole rap yourself.

The word "yourself" overlaps the cut @ **0:14:52**; and we see Serpico lean back, and left, from behind the suspect, with a cup of coffee. Frank removes the paper cup's lid and hands the coffee to the suspect. This transition uses a line of dialogue from the food shop scene to precede the scene's first shot. The dialogue is, in this case, well integrated with the action of the Police Van scene.

Getting a cup of coffee for the suspect takes the audience through another transition: The plausibility of convincing and encouraging the suspect to talk.

This is a splendid example of how choices in *objects* and *motion* inspire *performance*, and contribute to the effortless accessibility of *dialogue*.

Actor Donald Sutherland, in an interview, told of his insistent request that any film he appears in must begin with a middle scene. Sutherland's vast experience taught him that he needs at least a few days at work for his, and his character's, comfort and security: "An audience will ignore or forgive mistakes made later in the film that they would not forgive earlier in the film."

Here is a perfect illustration of both Donald Sutherland's performance concerns and the function of film's remarkable ability to conceal its fragmented production schedule.

LITTLE BIG MAN

Chapter 17, "A Custer Decision" @ 1:47:03
Jack Crabb, respecting his friend Wild Bill Hickok's "last wish," delivers money to Wild Bill's favorite "widow," Lulu Kane. Jack enters a local "house of ill fame" and recognizes Lulu as Mrs. Pendrake, the wife of the Reverend Silas Pendrake, and early care-taker of Jack.

Listen to the markedly puckered intonation in Dustin Hoffman's performance. Quite peculiar on two counts: It is not so exaggeratedly employed in any other scene, though there are many modifications. And no one ever takes "hearing" exception or seems perturbed. Could this have been an early scene in the course of production? Did Dustin Hoffman and/or director Arthur Penn decide to discontinue this heavily "accented" inflection, knowing they would not have to re-shoot?

More than a couple of decades ago I came across an article in a film anthology. It sat on a table of magazines in my doctor's waiting room. By chance I opened to a page which talked about **The Shop on Main Street**. I was fortunate to have seen the film at its opening in New York City. The anthology's entry about this Academy Award winner — Best Foreign Film (1965) — referenced Ida Kaminská, whose performance as Mrs. Lautmann won her an Academy Award. What fixed my attention was a comment, as best I can recall it, that "Josef Kroner's portrayal of Tono Brtko may be the finest performance by an actor in the entire history of cinema." This is quite the praise, even if off by two or three... or a few dozen.

Chapter 32, "Our Laws are Kind" @ 1:43:11

A nearly drunk Tono is confined to Mrs. Lautmann's button shop. Outside, in the Czechoslovakian village square, the Jews have been ordered to assemble for removal. A public address system echoes with the called out names — in alphabetical order — as the local Nazi officials verify attendance. Tono stares into a wall mirror and recalls the words of his brother-in-law, announcing the order that made him Aryan controller of the Jewish widow's shop: "according to paragraph one I appoint Anthony Brtko". The camera pans right, and away from the mirror, bringing Tono into a Close-Up as he turns away from the mirror, looking toward the outside. Another recall: "manager of the Jewish shop. *Na Stráz!*" Tono turns quickly in response toward the shop's wall of samples. The camera now searches out Mrs. Lautmann's chair, and the "inventory" on shelves and drawers. Tono hears his brother-in-law's voice: "Yes. You'll be a rich man by tomorrow." A Long-Shot in wide angle shows Tono at the far end of the shop's counter, the wall of samples behind him. His brother-in-law's voice continues: "You can throw your carpenter's tools out the window."

Tono brings the vodka bottle to his lips for a fast swallow. He walks along the inside aisle of the counter as he engages the voice, "A rich man." The camera follows right as Tono stops with bottle in hand, his back to us, and the background now the wall of buttons. He laughs, sarcastically petting a stack of button boxes, and takes another swig. He puts the bottle on the counter and exits frame right, announcing, "Fool!"

A Medium-Close up brings us — in a cut — to Tono, now at the shop's window, facing out to the square. Tono turns toward the camera moving into a Close-Up and continues his turn along the counter toward the back of the shop as the camera pans left with him and dollies, keeping Tono in a Medium-Shot, his back staying to the camera. As he moves he engages the outside broadcast, responding to the announced names: "He still owes for the ladder!" Another name echoes from the square: "The baker too!" Tono pauses at hearing the next name; a contemplative look in his eyes, he turns facing screen left: "Who? I don't know him..." He completes the turn, toward the camera and brings the vodka bottle up for another strong gulp. Tono returns the bottle to the counter. The camera follows his action and holds on the centered bottle. The announcements continue and Tono enters from the left. Now behind the counter, he grips the bottle, sounding agitated murmurs and grunts — rejoinders to the continuing list of village residents. The camera tilts upward framing him in Medium Close-Up as he drinks from the bottle in full pours. His grunts continue as the camera moves with him around the counter and toward the back of the shop. He grunts louder and quicker, he desperately covers his ears — his right hand clenches the bottle against that ear. He takes but a few steps and spins around to face the shop's door: "You bastards!... You bastards." He drinks more and seems to calm himself. He stumbles, clearly less steady on his feet, toward the back of the shop. The camera has held its position and Tono is in Long-Shot. Another name rings aloud, and Tono swings about to face the front: "Katz? What has Katz done to you? For shaving your ungrateful face?" Tono now marches back to the shop's doorway with his vodka bottle as a ready weapon: "You scoundrels! Dirty stinking Fascist guards!" A cut allows us, and Tono, to see into the crowded square through the glass panes in the closed doors. We are behind Tono as he waves his bottle, and continues his curses!

A cut takes us outside the shop. In Medium-Shot, with the people in the square reflected in the door's glass, we see Tono inside the shop. Outside crowd noises and address system speakers, still broadcasting the names of Jewish residents, make it all but impossible to hear Tono's enraged outburst inside. He turns away and disappears into the darkness of the shop.

Mr. Kroner's Tono Brtko is beyond amazing, but truth be told, we must credit all who participated in this remarkable work of context, light, place, sound, motion, and form! Distinguished respect must, of course, go to Mr. Joseph Kroner for giving us Tono, but far more for the brilliance, and esteem, his work furnished *all* the cast and crew through his collaboration.

A simple scene, featuring a lone actor, confined in a single room designed of commanding despair, grabs our full concentration; the outcome of *all* the information and details distributed in word and deed, image and sound, structure and rhythm: Performance!

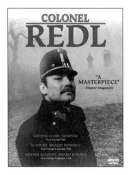

Chapter 26, "Lonely Farewell" @ 2:12:00

Alfred Redl has been arrested, and confronts accusations of treason. To avoid the public scrutiny of a trial likely to embarrass Emperor Franz Joseph, Archduke Ferdinand orders Kristofer Kubinyi to deliver a service revolver to the hotel room in which Redl has been quartered, and a message, "to be brief."

This is another example of a gripping performance made possible by the fullness in collaboration: The design and furnishings provide a parlor of elegant living, contemporaneous with one for funerals; the glowing light of the desktop lamp, reflected in the bureau's mirror — the sorrow in the single chair framed in the mirror's central panel — prompts a scattering of reflected illumination to the sparsely lit space, aided by the soft near-bleeding light owing to a lacey scrim of a curtain in the hotel window. There is a purity of silence within the room — not the slightest lilt trails the preceding cut beyond the walls. A fixed "flash," as in a freeze frame, of photographic art opens Redl's last moments!

Redl comes alive, shoving back the seating stool upon which his foot had rested and placing the glass pitcher onto the desk. He stands in seeming slow-motion, for a moment his face silhouetted in the back light of the window. He walks toward the camera, buttoning his dress tunic — oblivious to his pressing against and sliding the stool — and the camera moves to him, bringing Redl into a Close-Up as the last bright button, along the collar, is fastened.

Redl turns — seeming to hold his breath — to screen right, as the camera pans with him to a mirrored commode. He picks up his heavy military overcoat. He emits gasps and gagging sounds followed by a deep, but faint, cough. The camera follows Redl back to screen left, this time staying close behind him until he reaches the desk, framed in the whitish-blue light of the window. His right hand reaches and covers the pistol. He does not look down to it, but slides the weapon until he holds its handle; he turns to face the camera and, still not looking at the pistol, his left hand click-slides the mechanism, which brings a bullet into its chamber.

He holds the pistol aimed ahead, and at the ready, walking toward the camera, nearly tip-toeing. At **2:13:41** the first cut, in one hundred seconds, brings the viewer into a reverse Long-Shot. We are behind Redl as he approaches and stops at the door. He brings the pistol ever so slightly upward. Is he considering an escape attempt?

Two Master-Shots occur next:

1. Guards are in the hallway; one patrols back and forth, just the other side of the door.

2. A pan left past the hotel's elaborate lobby staircase; guards on waiting alert. One sits in a stuffed chair exhaling a puff from his cigarette.

A cut returns to Redl in his room: The Close-Up positioned in his stop at the door. Redl aims the gun upward, and the camera pans with him to screen right. This time the camera holds its position. Redl walks away and to the back of the room creating a Master-Shot. Now clutching the pistol in both hands, he stops past the soft-edge glow of the desk lamp. He looks back toward the door. He leans into the walls that create one corner in the room.

Three Extreme Long-Shots reveal guards on the cobblestoned street outside the hotel. All is calm but for the click-shuffle of boots on the street's stones. During the third shot, a policeman approaches the corner and a guard orders him to, "get out of here quickly."

A cut back to Redl is disquieting. We are on the left side of the room in Medium-Shot. At the very moment of the cut Redl bolts from the corner, knocking over the desk chair. Gasping in agonizing groans he skips toward the door, but angles right, into a Long-Shot, and flicks on the chandelier's three glowing lights. A new Close-Up of Redl brings us to the door side of the room. The pistol is pointed up, and Redl nearly smiles before hurrying to screen right. The camera holds its position, only panning with him. Redl coughs and groans as he circles the room.

The voyeuristic horror is setting upon us.

After a pause in Medium Long-Shot, Redl erupts into the room-circling action. This time a cut, as his back is to us, brings him from the background into a Close-Up. His gasping is worse: Hack-heaving coughs carry him away from us, only to have a cut from the door side of the room bring him to us again. Now he patrols back and forth from the door to the window, hitting furniture in his path. He increases the pace of his scramble, hitting the door on the last two back-and-forth rushes.

Now, in a tighter Close-Up, Redl catches his breath in audible exhales. The camera moves in with gentleness. A tear touches the lower lid of his right eye, and clings to his cheek. Adrenaline and a rapid pulse bid calm, but as the pistol slowly arrives at Redl's right temple, facial tremors are visible.

The shot is heard a few frames after an above-angle Long-Shot looks onto the street. Three soldiers on a field of cobblestones look-up to the camera, salute each other — heels click — and exit the frame, two to the right and the other left. The scene ends in a Master-Shot of Redl on the Persian-carpeted floor.

We could say that the scene depicts the suicide of Alfred Redl, carried out with a single shot to the head. We would be correct. We would also be very wrong.

I have made a point to describe each of Redl's actions: the rhythms in static beats, the choreographed motion in and outside of the room, across dozens of set-ups. To be sure, Klaus Maria Brandauer's work is superb, but it is the creation of many disciplined hours of pre-production, production, and post-production teamwork. A brilliant alliance bestows brilliance in performance. The irony is that the entire crew disappears for the *Character* and the *Place*, a large, dedicated yet "vanished" team shaped the *Story*.

a conclusion

Enduring Memories, Lifelong Dreams

Gathering the interviews and movie selections for this book established a re-flexive addendum to the film registry already in my brain. A billion visions have combined in the storehouse of memory, colliding one — or two or three — with another, attempting to uncover connections in form, emotions, and notions and significance.

My half-century affection, devotion, and attention to film, with more than four decades as an editor and teacher, have meant an abundant accumulation of images in my mind, many amazingly accurate after so many years between view-ings, and some unexpectedly false in varying degrees.

Butch Cassidy and the Sundance Kid chimed a wonderful collision in my brain's time machine. In **Chapter 23, "Again on the Outlaw Trail" @ 1:37:45**, Butch and Sundance ride into San Vincente, Bolivia. A boy escorts their horses, and the rustled white mule to a tie-up post. He recognizes the animal's branded emblem — an "A" with a horizontal line at its peak — and runs to report Butch and Sundance to the police.

I grabbed another of the selected DVDs! In **Chapter 34, "Marked for Execution" @ 1:54:38** of the John Huston classic, bandits ride into a Mexican village. A boy follows them and soon spots a branded emblem on one of the pack animals that was taken from the murdered Dobbs. This emblem too is an "A," with a horizontal line across its peak; the line atop this "A" curls upward at both ends.

I last saw *Treasure of the Sierra Madre* in its entirety in 1954, and so, though not a "picture-perfect" match, it was so commanding in memory, I'd say, "Close and a cigar!"

I was not yet twenty when I saw Truffaut's *The 400 Blows*. What struck me, and apparently will be affixed forever, are Antoine's endless efforts to break free from adult world duplicity, enmity, and disaffection. He escapes from a juvenile detention center (**Chapter 6, "Behind Bars" @ 1:35:00**), fleeing under a fence, after tossing a soccer ball into the field of play; one "officer" gives chase blowing whistle bursts into the countryside.

In the end Antoine settles into a ceaselessly slowing run to the sea. A harp in single string-tugs keeps pace with his steps across the sand and small splashes around and over Antoine's shoes, the sound becoming clock-like in its count down to an evocative freeze frame — discussed with friends for many months, and inspiring movie endings for years — at the water's edge which brings at least momentary tranquility.

Is it any wonder then that Truffaut's film was inspiringly projected in my brain when I viewed *Born into Brothels* (**Chapter 10, "Photos by Avijit"** @ **0:39:33**)? Photographer (director) Zana Briski buses her young Indian photography students to the beach. The event — the ocean as muse — and its significance in the lives of these camera-enthused children is expressed in the first spirited words as the bus comes to a stop: "Look at the water!"

Still photos (freeze frames) of the day's adventure are inter-cut with the glorious live action footage of smiles, giggles, and splashes. Briski's kids are — for the moment — free of Calcutta's grisly red-light district.

My stumbled-upon surprises enforced a "view" of great movies as a supplemental subconscious, an assembly of fragmented imagery which engages the mind, in an effort to grasp a bit of meaning in the chance and chaos of life.

I first had to dismiss — delete from my head — the frequently awful celebratory movie history montages presented at the Academy Awards, where, in a matter of seconds, the entire work of an actor, director, or nation flashes or sputters before our eyes. They are as much a visual and aural attack, as they are like an anxiety dream!

But, in my failed efforts to delete such nonsense, a fresh "look" occurred to me.

Walter Murch's book, *In the Blink of an Eye: A Persepective on Film Editing*, contains a chapter called "Don't Worry, It's Only a Movie." The chapter title expresses the common adult reassurance to a child frightened by a movie and, as Murch points out, its similarity to the assurance, "Don't worry, darling, it's only a dream."

I do not intend to challenge Webster's, American Heritage's or Oxford's standard definition of "dream": *A series of thoughts, images or emotions occurring while asleep*. There is also an acceptance of non-sleep dreaming: *A dream-like vision; daydream or reverie: The state of being lost in thought*. So, as I continue with my investigation, please don't consider that I'm "off the wall," or *too* off the wall!

Murch's writing takes us back to the fragmented nature of film production, and links the juxtaposition of these fragments through the "brutality of the process of cutting" to the possibility that the full spirit of cinema — from its production to presentation in a darkened hall — provokes our subconscious, arousing notions of diverse and symbolic realities. This holds true throughout the history of moviemaking's post-production processes: The splicer, with razor-sharp blades striking film strips with guillotine-like action, most suitable, one might imagine, to the editing of horror movies alone. The old-time mechanics of a cut — the sprocketed Mylar (splicing tape) used to join the selected pieces — have disappeared, replaced by a virtual cutting. Computer wares in the service of fleeting responses to mouse and keyboard: still dream-like moviemaking.

"Aha!" I thought; maybe that's why I find "dream sequences" to be (most often) so ineffectual! It has seemed to me for a very long while, that a dream scene in a film is conceptually redundant: Cinema is an outwardly stimulated presentation that is not merely like a dream. It is absolutely in the ambit of dreams.

We are still and quiet, we are in the "dark," gazing at a beam of light "reflecting" decipherable pictures: light that can stir flashes of comprehension.

David Mamet suggests that film students read Sigmund Freud's *The Interpretation of Dreams*. I agree, but please don't use the reading to permit a more accurate design of dream sequences. Not at all! Read Freud (and Jung, Ernest Becker, and others) in an attempt to comprehend our species, our motives, our treacherous propensities, insights, and our art.

In an atmosphere both tranquil and blunt, Federico Fellini's *8½* parades the subconscious, the fantastical, the unrestrained dreams and impulses which deliver originality, creation, and shame.

Chapter I, "Come Into the Light" @ 0:00:24 drives the audience — in the backseat of Guido's automobile — from probable reality into nightmarish irascibility, through intolerable panic and resurrection.

Is Atom Egoyan's *The Sweet Hereafter*, **Chapter 2, "Fathers and Daughters"** @ 0:03:36, any less a dream-stimulated terror? Attorney Mitchell Stephens also takes us on a ride from the backseat of his auto — into a carwash. In the midst of a storm of water and rubber scrubbers he gets a collect call on his cell phone. It is his estranged daughter Zoe, angry and a junky. Is Zoe in the telephone booth less than a bad dream? Are her friends and cars, and the scene's desolate place, *not* a dream?

Is there a single moment in *Burnt by the Sun* that mirrors confirmed reality? In **Chapter 27, "Wrong Place, Wrong Time"** @ 1:59:37, the sleek black sedan transporting Colonel Kotov to Moscow clatters along a grain lined lane. It is obstructed by a jalopy of a truck, stacked with furniture destined for Zagorianka, or is it Zagorienka? The driver, "that shit blocking the road" has, "used up all of [his] gasoline driving around all day." His wife washed his shirt with the address in it, and he's followed faulty directions, "No one knows anything. They're all mongoloids. They send you one way and then another." Kotov attempts to show him how to get to Nagorié. He is stopped, as he is about to exit the car, and brutally beaten. The truck driver flees into the shoulder-high grain, tripping and falling in his escape. Mitya orders him to "Halt! About face." The driver obeys, returning to his truck with desperate pleadings for compassion, "The address faded away... I don't make much money... My papers are in order." Mitya commands, "Hands behind your head!" Mitya strolls into the field as his henchman handcuffs Kotov; the sedan, in Extreme Long Shot, sways in gasps and bloodied noses.

A cut-away carries us to a glimmering silver cigarette case. Mitya — looking handsomely groomed — prepares a smoking break for himself, accompanied by lasting truck driver supplications, "the customer... the boss is waiting for me... he's been waiting all day... comrade... comrade."

Suddenly, on the horizon we see the spherical tip of a puff of a ball. It is metallic gray and rises over the grain. We hear Mitya's match strike; his eyes locate the floating ball and he does not light the cigarette in his mouth. The large balloon moves higher, revealing webs of rope attached to a red banner portrait of Joseph Stalin. The hue is so luminous that the red vibrates. Mitya instantly — as if a magic trick — flips his tongue, and his cigarette, in its holder, darts across his lips. With the burnt match held between fingers, Mitya opens his cupped hand; and in an agonizingly slow lift, his hand contacts his brow in a salute, his face in a teeth-clenched, fiendish grin.

A lashing orchestration — pipe-banging-like in tempo — joins the climbing balloon, notes shatter as blasts of wind shake Stalin. The truck driver, hands still atop his head, moves to the right — the camera pans with him — staring in astonishment. His face suffers small red wounds from grain stalk pokes, his mouth drops open, "Comrade Stalin."

Does director Mikhalkov's work "really" reflect a world recognizable as in our everyday consciousness? Is this not the true value and meaning of Neo-Realism?

This brings to mind the Mackendrick student who expressed gratitude to his teacher. "The highest praise I can give him is that he showed us how superficially we looked at cinema."

Sometime long ago I attended several programs under the title "Reel Pieces" at the 92nd Street Y in New York City. The program's moderator was Annette Insdorf, chair of the Cinema Studies Graduate Program at Columbia

University. Her guests were prominent filmmakers from every discipline. I best recall the evening with Sven Nykvist, a cinematographer of enormous talent, whose contributions on behalf of such directors as Louis Malle, Woody Allen, and most especially Ingmar Bergman are, without a doubt, legendary.

Nykvist gave an account of his 'brief' experience as a director. "One day I asked for another take, and an actor asked if I'd thought the last take was not good. I said, 'It was good,' and the actor asked, 'Then why do another take?' I had no answer! So I realized I should not be a director."

He told how he and Bergman would tour museums and art and photo galleries during pre-production planning. They would discuss color, light, value, contrast, lens, and composition choices for their new project, utilizing the array of images they viewed as reference. This helped assure intelligibility in their choices.

"A great collaborative idea", I thought. Then Nykvist proceeded to reveal just how collaborative was Ingmar Bergman's work:

> "Weeks before production, Ingmar would provide each and every crew member a copy of the screenplay. This included production assistants. Then, several days before shooting began, everyone would meet together in Ingmar's house to discuss the script; to offer suggestions, raise concerns, express confusions; to honestly and candidly speak their mind."

Bergman's gathering not only accomplished a list of good ideas, it also "inspired a dedication to work and craft that money alone would not."

One spectacular day in June of 2005, my friend and colleague, Everett Aison — co-founder of the School of Visual Arts Film Department — and I sat in Central Park. With sandwiches and fruit juices, we chatted about Everett's philosophy and approach to teaching Screenwriting and Storytelling.

Everett believes strongly that the screenplay form must be taught early, and that "students should be encouraged to describe what the audience sees, rather than using a prose form." Every so often Everett would pause, to explain that he was aware of the fact that he might have "strayed" into areas of Production Design, or Cinematography, or Directing, or Editing. "The longer I teach, and the added experience that comes from writing, and seeing more and more films, the clearer it becomes that the many disciplines which make up pre-production, production, and post-production, are better taught when not strictly separated. All the years have convinced me that it is mandatory to stress filmmaking's collaboration."

With nominal expense, students of film — take note that I did not say film students — can screen great works over and over again on DVDs; and listen to the "lectures" of screenwriter, director, cinematographer, production designer, actor, composer, sound specialist, or editor provided in the commentary. Film teachers share their favorite scenes, sequences, and entire films via in-class DVD projections. The showings are used to illustrate all of the basic and subsidiary elements crucial to the highest quality of work across all of cinema's disciplines. Most especially and admirably, they demonstrate filmmaking's grand, *mutual* adventure.

"Do stuff. Be clenched, curious; not waiting for inspiration's shove or society's kiss on your forehead. Pay attention. It's all about paying attention. Attention is vitality. It connects you with others. It makes you eager. Stay eager."

— Susan Sontag's advice to her Vassar College students

bibliography

American Film Institute and NHK Japan Broadcasting Corp. *Visions of Light: The Art of Cinematography*. Directed by Arnold Glassman, Todd McCarthy, and Stuart Samuels. 20th Century Fox Home and Image Entertainment, 1992 (2000).

Bergman, Ingmar. *Images: My Life in Film*. Translated by Marianne Ruuth. New York: Arcade Publishing, 1990.

Boggs, Joseph M. *The Art of Watching Films*. 2nd Edition. Palo Alto, CA: Mayfield Publishing, 1985.

Cotter, Holland. "On Sontag: Essayist As Metaphor and Muse." *New York Times* Weekend Arts, August 18, 2006

Dancyger, Ken. *The Technique of Film & Video Editing*. Boston: Focal Press, 1993.

Dmytryk, Edward. *On Film Editing: An Introduction to the Art of Film Construction*. Boston: Focal Press, 1984.

Dmytryk, Edward. *On Screen Directing*. Boston: Focal Press, 1984.

Egri, Lajos. *The Art of Dramatic Writing: Its Basis in the Creative Interpretation of Human Motives*. New York: Touchstone, 1942 (1988).

Eisenstein, Sergei. *Film Form: Essays in Film Theory and the Film Sense*. Cleveland & New York: Meridian Books, 1957.

Fairservice, Don. *Film Editing: History, Theory, and Practice*. Manchester: Manchester University Press, 2001.

Guare, John. *Collaborations: Writers on Directors:* "John Guare on Louis Malle." *New Yorker* Vol. LXX, March 21, 1994.

Gibson, William. *The Miracle Worker*. New York: Pocket Books, 2002.

Gorchakov, Nikolai M. *Stanislavsky Directs*. New York: Grosset & Dunlap, 1954.

Haase, Cathy. *Acting for Film*. New York: Allworth Press, 2003.

Hollyn, Norman. *The Editing Room Handbook: How to Manage the Near Chaos of the Cutting Room*. 3rd Edition. Hollywood, CA. Lone Eagle Publishing, 1984 (1999).

IMAGO: The Federation of European Cinematographers. *Making Pictures: A Century of European Cinematography*. New York: Abrams, 2003.

James, Clive. "How to Write About Film: A Century of Movies through the Eyes of America's Best Critics." Review of *American Movie Critics: From the Silents Until Now* by Philip Lopate. *New York Times* Book Review, June 4, 2006.

Katz, Steven D. *Film Directing. Shot by Shot: Visualizing from Concept to Screen*. Studio City, CA: Michael Wiese Productions: 1991.

LoBrutto, Vincent. *Selected Takes: Film Editors on Editing*. New York: Praeger, 1991.

LoBrutto, Vincent. *By Design: Interviews with Production Designers*. New York: Praeger, 1992.

LoBrutto, Vincent. *Principal Photography*. New York: Praeger, 1999.

Lumet, Sidney. *Making Movies*. New York: Alfred Knopf, 1995.

Mamet, David. *On Directing Film*. New York: Viking Penguin, 1991.

Mackendrick, Alexander. *On Film-Making: An Introduction to the Craft of Directing*. New York: Faber and Faber, 2004.

Mascelli, Joseph V. *The Five C's of Cinematography: Motion Picture Filming Techniques*. Los Angeles: Silman-James Press, 1965.

McKee, Robert. *Story: Substance, Structure, Style, and the Principles of Screenwriting*. New York: Regan Books/HarperCollins, 1997.

Murch, Walter. *In the Blink of an Eye: A Perspective on Film Editing.* 2nd Edition. Los Angeles: Silman-James Press, 1995 (2001).

Osborne, John. T*om Jones: A Film Script*. New York: Grove Press, 1964.

O'Steen, Sam. *Cut to the Chase: Forty-Five Years of Editing America's Favorite Movies*. Studio City, CA: Michael Wiese Productions, 2001.

Pepperman, Richard D. *The Eye is Quicker. Film Editing: Making a Good Film Better*. Studio City, CA: Michael Wiese Productions, 2004.

Pepperman, Richard D. *Setting Up Your Scenes: The Inner Workings of Great Films*. Studio City, CA: Michael Wiese Productions, 2005.

Proulx, Annie. *Brokeback Mountain. New York: Scribner, 1997.*

Purdy, Jedediah. *For Common Things: Irony, Trust and Commitment in America Today*. New York: Vintage Press, 2000.

Reisz, Karel & Millar, Gavin. *The Technique of Film Editing*. 2nd Edition. London: Focal Press, 1968.

Rosenblum, Ralph & Robert Karen. *When the Shooting Stops. . . the Cutting Begins. A Film Editor's Story*. New York: Da Capo Press, 1979.

Samuels, Charles Thomas. *Encountering Directors*. New York: Da Capo Press, 1972.

Shaffer, Peter. *Amadeus*. New York: Harper & Row, 1980 (1981).

Sillitoe, Alan. *New and Collected Stories*. New York: Carol & Graf Publishers, 2003 (2005).

Sharff, Stefan. *The Elements of Cinema; Toward a Theory of Cinesthetic Impact*. New York, Columbia University Press, 1982.

Starz Encore Entertainment; TCEP, Inc. & The American Cinema Editors (ACE). *The Cutting Edge: The Magic of Movie Editing*. Warner Home Video, 2005.

Tarkovsky, Andrei. *Sculpting in Time*. Austin: University of Texas Press, 1989.

Van Sijll, Jennifer. *Cinematic Storytelling: The 100 Most Powerful Film Conventions Every Filmmaker Must Know*. Studio City, CA: Michael Wiese Productions, 2005.

Weston, Judith. *Directing Actors: Creating Memorable Performances for Film and Television*. Studio City, CA: Michael Wiese Productions, 1996.

Alexander Nevsky • 1938 • B&W • 108 minutes • Image Entertainment.

Amadeus • 1984 • Color • 160 minutes • Warner Home Video.

Atlantic City • 1981 • Color • 103 minutes • Paramount/Viacom.

Ballad of a Soldier • 1959 • B&W • Criterion Collection.

Bonnie and Clyde • 1967 • Color • Warner Home Video.

Born into Brothels • 2004 • Color • Approx. 123 minutes • Thinkfilm.

Breaker Morant • 1980 • Color • Approx. 107 minutes • Fox Lorber Home Video.

Breathless • 1959 • B&W • 90 minutes • Wellspring.

The Bridge on the River Kwai • 1957 • Color • Approx. 162 minutes • Columbia/Tristar.

Burnt by the Sun • 1994 • Color • Approx 135 minutes • Columbia /Tristar.

Butch Cassidy and the Sundance Kid • 1969 • Color • Approx. 110 minutes • 20th Century Fox.

Casablanca • 1942 • B&W • 103 minutes • Warner Home Video.

Catch-22 • 1970 • Color • 121 minutes • Paramount Home Video.

Central Station • 1998 • Color • Approx 106 minutes • Columbia/Tristar.

Colonel Redl • 1984 • Color • 142 minutes • Anchor Bay Entertainment.

The Day of the Jackal • 1973 • Color • 143 minutes • Universal.

Dr. Strangelove • 1964 • B&W • 102 minutes • Columbia/Tristar.

Dog Day Afternoon • 1975 • Color • 124 minutes • Warner Home Video.

8½ • 1963 • B&W • 139 minutes • Image Entertainment.

The Exorcist • 1973 • Color • 132 minutes • Warner Home Video.

The 400 Blows • 1959 • B&W • 99 minutes • Fox Lorber Home Video.

The French Connection • 1971 • Color • Approx. 104 minutes • 20th Century Fox.

The Godfather • 1972 • Color • 175 minutes • Paramount Home Entertainment.

High Noon • 1952 • B&W • 85 minutes • Artisan Home Entertainment.

Hiroshima mon amour • 1959 • B&W • 90 minutes • Criterion Collection.

Jean de Florette • 1986 • Color • 122 minutes • Renn/RAI-TV/D.D. A2.

Ju Dou • 1990 • Color • 94 minutes • Razor Digital.

Kolya • 1996 • Color • 105 minutes • Miramax Home Entertainment.

The Ladykillers • 1955 • Color • 91 minutes • Anchor Bay.

Little Big Man • 1970 • Color • 139 minutes • CBS DVD.

The Loneliness of the Long Distance Runner • 1962 • B&W • 100 minutes
• Nostalgia Family Video.

The Miracle Worker • 1962 • B&W • 106 minutes • MGM Home
Entertainment.

Osama • 2003 • Color • Approx. 83 minutes • MGM Home Entertainment.

Plenty • 1985 • Color • 129 minutes • Anchor Bay.

Psycho • 1960 • B&W • 109 minutes • Universal.

Rosemary's Baby • 1968 • Color • 136 minutes • Paramount Home Video.

Rififi • 1955 • B&W • 118 minutes • Criterion Collection.

Serpico • 1973 • Color • 130 minutes • Paramount Home Video.

The Shop on Main Street • 1965 • B&W • 125 minutes • Criterion Collection.

The Steamroller and the Violin • 1960 • Color • 43 minutes • Facets Video.

The Sweet Hereafter • 1997 • Color • Approx. 116 minutes • New Line
Home Video.

Talk to Her • 2002 • Color • Approx 114 minutes • Columbia/TriStar.

Tom Jones • 1963 • Color • 129 minutes • MGM DVD.

Touch of Evil • 1958 • B&W • 108 minutes • Universal.

The Treasure of the Sierra Madre • 1947 • B&W • 126 minutes • Warner
Home Video.

The Verdict • 1982 • Color • Approx. 129 minutes • 20th Century Fox.

The Virgin Spring • 1960 • B&W • 89 minutes • Criterion Collection.

Viridiana • 1961 • B&W • 91 minutes • Criterion Collection.

Witness • 1985 • Color • 112 minutes • Paramount Home Video.

Z • 1969 • Color • 127 minutes • Wellspring.

index

RICHARD D. PEPPERMAN has worked in film for more than forty years. His credits include work as an editor, post-production supervisor, and consultant on features, documentaries, industrials, and commercials.

Richard's film collaborations have been official selections to many international festivals, including Aspen, Berlin, Cannes, the Hamptons, Karlovy Vary (Czech Republic), London, Montreal, Munich, Rotterdam, Sitges (Barcelona), Tel Aviv, and Toronto.

His collaborations have been honored with the Outstanding Documentary Award by the Academy of Motion Picture Arts & Sciences, an Andy Award, and a Clio Award. Other honors have included serving as Screenwriting Judge for the Nicholl Fellowships, Academy of Motion Picture Arts & Sciences and a Distinguished Artist-Teacher Award from the School of Visual Arts, New York City.

Richard has designed and taught editing workshops, seminars, and lectures at Film/Video Arts, Pratt Institute, and The New School University. He currently teaches the "Art of Editing" at the School of Visual Arts in New York City where he is completing his thirty-fifth year.

Richard is the author of *The Eye Is Quicker. Film Editing: Making a Good Film Better* and *Setting Up Your Scenes: The Inner Workings of Great Films.* He lives with his wife Betsy, big dog Ollie, and small parrot Holly in Monmouth County, New Jersey and Mount Holly, Vermont.

SETTING UP YOUR SCENES
THE INNER WORKINGS
OF GREAT FILMS

RICHARD D. PEPPERMAN

Every great filmmaker has films which inspired him or her to greater and greater heights. Here, for the first time, is an awe-inspiring guide that takes you into the inner workings of classic scenes, revealing the aspects that make them great and the reasons they have served as inspirations.

An invaluable resource for screenwriter, cinematographer, actor, director, and editor, Pepperman's book uses examples from six decades of international films to illustrate what happens when story, character, dialogue, text, subtext, and set-ups come together to create cinematic magic.

With over 400 photos of selected movie clips laid out beautifully in a widescreen format, this book shows you how to emulate the masters and achieve your dreams.

"Setting Up Your Scenes *is both visually stunning and very useful for students of cinema. Its design, layout, and content make the book unique and irresistible.*"
> – Amresh Sinha, New York University/The School of Visual Arts

"*Pepperman has written a book which should form the basis for an intelligent discussion about the basic building blocks of great scenes across a wide variety of films. Armed with the information in this book, teachers, students, filmmakers, and film lovers can begin to understand how good editing and scene construction can bring out the best storytelling to create a better film.*"
> – Norman Hollyn, Associate Professor and Editing Track Head,
> School of Cinema-Television at the University of Southern California

"*Pepperman dissects some very infamous scenes from some very famous movies — providing us with the most breathtaking black and white stills — in order to highlight the importance of the interplay between dialogue, subtext, and shot selection in great filmmaking.*"
> – Lily Sadri, Writer, Screenwriter, *Fixing Fairchild*,
> Contributor to *www.absolutewrite.com*

RICHARD D. PEPPERMAN has been a film editor for more than 40 years and a teacher for more than 30. He is the author of *The Eye Is Quicker*.

$24.95 · 245 PAGES · ORDER NUMBER 42RLS · ISBN: 1932907084

THE EYE IS QUICKER
FILM EDITING: MAKING A GOOD FILM BETTER

RICHARD D. PEPPERMAN

Did you ever want to know how to apply simple and practical work techniques to all that film editing theory? Here is an authentic "how-to" guide — adaptable to all tools and technologies — to make you a better editor of film or video. This is the most comprehensive book on the principles, methods, and strategies vital to the creative art of film editing.

Pepperman's vibrant approach uses dozens of terrific sequences from a wide array of films to teach you how editing can make a good film better. He defines what is constant in all great work and gives you all the tips you need to achieve your own greatness.

The Eye is Quicker is indispensable for screenwriters, directors, and, of course, film and video editors.

"The qualities that have made Richard so inspiring and beloved a teacher — passion, curiosity, humor, and humility — make this book as alive and enticing as a class or conversation with him. The Eye Is Quicker *will benefit future generations of film editors. It is a very good read for film lovers, and a rich mine for practitioners in the other arts."*
— Jennifer Dunning, *New York Times*

"Pepperman brings decades of experience as an editor and teacher to lessons supported by example and illustration. Here is a voice that is caring and supportive. To read The Eye Is Quicker *is to attend a master class."*
— Vincent LoBrutto, Author, *Stanley Kubrick: A Biography*

"Pepperman not only shares his knowledge of editing's art and craft, he gives wholly of himself — insights, philosophies, humor, and risks of being fully alive to seeing and feeling. To study with Richard is a privilege; to read this book is to receive a profound gift."
— Louis Phillips, Playwright,
Author, *The Last of the Marx Brothers' Writers*

"A highly informative book — stimulating material."
— Chris Newman, Three-time Academy Award®-Winning
Production Sound Mixer

RICHARD D. PEPPERMAN is a teacher and thesis advisor at The School Of Visual Arts in New York City. He is the author of *Setting Up Your Scenes*.

$27.95 · 268 PAGES · ORDER NUMBER 116RLS · ISBN: 0941188841

SAVE THE CAT!™ GOES TO THE MOVIES
THE SCREENWRITER'S GUIDE
TO EVERY STORY EVER TOLD

BLAKE SNYDER

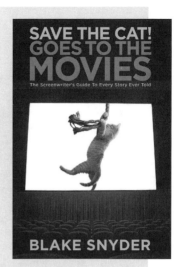

In the long-awaited sequel to his surprise bestseller, *Save the Cat!*, author and screenwriter Blake Snyder returns to form in a fast-paced follow-up that proves why his is the most talked-about approach to screenwriting in years. In the perfect companion piece to his first book, Snyder delivers even more insider's information gleaned from a 20-year track record as "one of Hollywood's most successful spec screenwriters," giving you the clues to write *your* movie.

Designed for screenwriters, novelists, and movie fans, this book gives readers the key breakdowns of the 50 most instructional movies from the past 30 years. From *M*A*S*H* to *Crash*, from *Alien* to *Saw*, from *10* to *Eternal Sunshine of the Spotless Mind*, Snyder reveals how screenwriters who came before you tackled the same challenges you are facing with the film you want to write – or the one you are currently working on.

Writing a "rom-com"? Check out the "Buddy Love" chapter for a "beat for beat" dissection of *When Harry Met Sally…* plus references to 10 other great romantic comedies that will make your story sing.

Want to execute a great mystery? Go to the "Whydunit" section and learn about the "dark turn" that's essential to the heroes of *All the President's Men*, *Blade Runner*, *Fargo* and hip noir *Brick* – and see why ALL good stories, whether a Hollywood blockbuster or a Sundance award winner, follow the same rules of structure outlined in Snyder's breakthrough method.

If you want to sell your script and create a movie that pleases most audiences most of the time, the odds increase if you reference Snyder's checklists and see what makes 50 films tick. After all, both executives and audiences respond to the same elements good writers seek to master. They want to know the type of story they signed on for, and whether it's structured in a way that satisfies everyone. It's what they're looking for. And now, it's what you can deliver.

BLAKE SNYDER, besides selling million-dollar scripts to both Disney and Spielberg, is still "one of Hollywood's most successful spec screenwriters," having made another spec sale in 2006. An in-demand scriptcoach and seminar and workshop leader, Snyder provides information for writers through his website, *www.blakesnyder.com*.

$24.95 · 270 PAGES · ORDER NUMBER 75RLS · ISBN: 9781932907353

FILM & VIDEO BOOKS

Archetypes for Writers: *Using the Power of Your Subconscious*
Jennifer Van Bergen / $22.95

Art of Film Funding, The: *Alternate Financing Concepts*
Carole lee Dean / $26.95

Cinematic Storytelling: *The 100 Most Powerful Film Conventions Every Filmmaker Must Know* / Jennifer Van Sijll / $24.95

Complete Independent Movie Marketing Handbook, The: *Promote, Distribute & Sell Your Film or Video* / Mark Steven Bosko / $39.95

Creating Characters: *Let Them Whisper Their Secrets*
Marisa D'Vari / $26.95

Crime Writer's Reference Guide, The: *1001 Tips for Writing the Perfect Crime*
Martin Roth / $20.95

Cut by Cut: *Editing Your Film or Video*
Gael Chandler / $35.95

Digital Filmmaking 101, 2nd Edition: *An Essential Guide to Producing Low-Budget Movies* / Dale Newton and John Gaspard / $26.95

Directing Actors: *Creating Memorable Performances for Film and Television*
Judith Weston / $26.95

Directing Feature Films: *The Creative Collaboration Between Directors, Writers, and Actors* / Mark Travis / $26.95

Elephant Bucks: *An Insider's Guide to Writing for TV Sitcoms*
Sheldon Bull / $24.95

Eye is Quicker, The: *Film Editing; Making a Good Film Better*
Richard D. Pepperman / $27.95

Fast, Cheap & Under Control: *Lessons Learned from the Greatest Low-Budget Movies of All Time* / John Gaspard / $26.95

Fast, Cheap & Written That Way: *Top Screenwriters on Writing for Low-Budget Movies*
John Gaspard / $26.95

Film & Video Budgets, *4th Updated Edition*
Deke Simon and Michael Wiese / $26.95

Film Directing: *Cinematic Motion, 2nd Edition*
Steven D. Katz / $27.95

Film Directing: *Shot by Shot, Visualizing from Concept to Screen*
Steven D. Katz / $27.95

Film Director's Intuition, The: *Script Analysis and Rehearsal Techniques*
Judith Weston / $26.95

Film Production Management 101: *The Ultimate Guide for Film and Television Production Management and Coordination* / Deborah S. Patz / $39.95

Filmmaking for Teens: *Pulling Off Your Shorts*
Troy Lanier and Clay Nichols / $18.95

First Time Director: *How to Make Your Breakthrough Movie*
Gil Bettman / $27.95

From Word to Image: *Storyboarding and the Filmmaking Process*
Marcie Begleiter / $26.95

Hollywood Standard, The: *The Complete and Authoritative Guide to Script Format and Style* / Christopher Riley / $18.95

Independent Film Distribution: *How to Make a Successful End Run Around the Big Guys* / Phil Hall / $26.95

Independent Film and Videomakers Guide – 2nd Edition, The: *Expanded and Updated*
Michael Wiese / $29.95

Inner Drives: *How to Write and Create Characters Using the Eight Classic Centers of Motivation* / Pamela Jaye Smith / $26.95

I'll Be in My Trailer!: *The Creative Wars Between Directors & Actors*
John Badham and Craig Modderno / $26.95

Moral Premise, The: *Harnessing Virtue & Vice for Box Office Success*
Stanley D. Williams, Ph.D. / $24.95

Myth and the Movies: *Discovering the Mythic Structure of 50 Unforgettable Films*
Stuart Voytilla / $26.95

On the Edge of a Dream: *Magic and Madness in Bali*
Michael Wiese / $16.95

Perfect Pitch, The: *How to Sell Yourself and Your Movie Idea to Hollywood*
Ken Rotcop / $16.95

Power of Film, The
Howard Suber / $27.95

Psychology for Screenwriters: *Building Conflict in your Script*
William Indick, Ph.D. / $26.95

Save the Cat!: *The Last Book on Screenwriting You'll Ever Need*
Blake Snyder / $19.95

Save the Cat! Goes to the Movies: *The Screenwriter's Guide to Every Story Ever Told*
Blake Snyder / $24.95

Screenwriting 101: *The Essential Craft of Feature Film Writing*
Neill D. Hicks / $16.95

Screenwriting for Teens: *The 100 Principles of Screenwriting Every Budding Writer Must Know* / Christina Hamlett / $18.95

Script-Selling Game, The: *A Hollywood Insider's Look at Getting Your Script Sold and Produced* / Kathie Fong Yoneda / $16.95

Selling Your Story in 60 Seconds: *The Guaranteed Way to get Your Screenplay or Novel Read* / Michael Hauge / $12.95

Setting Up Your Scenes: *The Inner Workings of Great Films*
Richard D. Pepperman / $24.95

Setting Up Your Shots: *Great Camera Moves Every Filmmaker Should Know*
Jeremy Vineyard / $19.95

Shaking the Money Tree, 2nd Edition: *The Art of Getting Grants and Donations for Film and Video Projects* / Morrie Warshawski / $26.95

Sound Design: *The Expressive Power of Music, Voice, and Sound Effects in Cinema*
David Sonnenschein / $19.95

Special Effects: *How to Create a Hollywood Film Look on a Home Studio Budget* /
Michael Slone / $31.95

Stealing Fire From the Gods, 2nd Edition: *The Complete Guide to Story for Writers & Filmmakers* / James Bonnet / $26.95

Ultimate Filmmaker's Guide to Short Films, The: *Making It Big in Shorts*
Kim Adelman / $16.95

Way of Story, The: *The Craft & Soul of Writing*
Catherine Anne Jones / $22.95

Working Director, The: *How to Arrive, Thrive & Survive in the Director's Chair*
Charles Wilkinson / $22.95

Writer's Journey, – 3rd Edition, The: *Mythic Structure for Writers*
Christopher Vogler / $26.95

Writing the Action Adventure: *The Moment of Truth*
Neill D. Hicks / $14.95

Writing the Comedy Film: *Make 'Em Laugh*
Stuart Voytilla and Scott Petri / $14.95

Writing the Killer Treatment: *Selling Your Story Without a Script*
Michael Halperin / $14.95

Writing the Second Act: *Building Conflict and Tension in Your Film Script*
Michael Halperin / $19.95

Writing the Thriller Film: *The Terror Within*
Neill D. Hicks / $14.95

Writing the TV Drama Series – 2nd Edition: *How to Succeed as a Professional Writer in TV* / Pamela Douglas / $26.95

DVD & VIDEOS

Field of Fish: *VHS Video*
Directed by Steve Tanner and Michael Wiese, Written by Annamaria Murphy / $9.95

Hardware Wars: DVD / Written and Directed by Ernie Fosselius / $14.95

Sacred Sites of the Dalai Lamas– DVD, The: *A Pilgrimage to Oracle Lake*
A Documentary by Michael Wiese / $24.95

To Order go to *www.mwp.com* or Call 1-800-833-5738